# Lecture Notes in Computer Science 6186

# Lecture Notes in Computer Science 6188

Commenced Publication in 1973
Founding and Former Series Editors:
Gerhard Goos, Juris Hartmanis, and Jan van Leeuwen

## Editorial Board

Alessandro Armando Gavin Lowe (Eds.)

# Automated Reasoning for Security Protocol Analysis and Issues in the Theory of Security

Joint Workshop, ARSPA-WITS 2010
Paphos, Cyprus, March 27-28, 2010
Revised Selected Papers

Springer

Volume Editors

Alessandro Armando
Università di Genova
DIST Dipartimento di Informatica, Sistematica e Telematica
Viale Causa 13, 16145 Genova, Italy
E-mail: armando@dist.unige.it

Gavin Lowe
Oxford University Computing Laboratory
Wolfson Building, Parks Road, Oxford, OX1 3QD, UK
E-mail: gavin.lowe@comlab.ox.ac.uk

Library of Congress Control Number: 2010936301

CR Subject Classification (1998): D.4.6, K.6.5, C.2, E.3, D.2, D.3

LNCS Sublibrary: SL 4 – Security and Cryptology

ISSN 0302-9743
ISBN-10 3-642-16073-5 Springer Berlin Heidelberg New York
ISBN-13 978-3-642-16073-8 Springer Berlin Heidelberg New York



springer.com


Printed in Germany

Typesetting: Camera-ready by author, data conversion by Scientific Publishing Services, Chennai, India
Printed on acid-free paper 06/3180

# Preface

This volume contains the workshop proceedings of ARSPA-WITS 2010, the Joint Workshop on Automated Reasoning for Security Protocol Analysis and Issues in the Theory of Security, held during March 27–28, 2010 in Paphos (Cyprus). ARSPA-WITS 2010 offered a forum for discussing new results in theories of computer security, open questions and fundamental concerns about existing theories, and issues related to the development and application of automated reasoning techniques and tools for the formal specification and analysis of security protocols.

There were 28 submissions. All the submissions were thoroughly evaluated on the basis of at least three referee reports, and an electronic Program Committee meeting was held by using the EasyChair on-line conference system. The committee decided to accept the 11 papers included in this volume. The authors were given the opportunity to revise their paper in light of the feedback received during the workshop. The workshop program was enriched by two invited talks by Flemming Nielson and Catuscia Palamidessi, whose titles and abstracts are also included in this volume.

April 2010

Alessandro Armando
Gavin Lowe

# Conference Organization

## Program Chairs

| | |
|---|---|
| Alessandro Armando | Università di Genova, Italy (Co-chair) |
| Gavin Lowe | Oxford University, UK (Co-chair) |

## Program Committee

| | |
|---|---|
| Lujo Bauer | CMU, USA |
| Yannick Chevalier | Université Toulouse III, France |
| Luca Compagna | SAP Research, France |
| Cas Cremers | ETHZ, Switzerland |
| Jorge Cuellar | Siemens, Germany |
| Pierpaolo Degano | Università di Pisa, Italy |
| Sandro Etalle | Technical University of Eindhoven and University of Twente, The Netherlands |
| Riccardo Focardi | Università di Venezia, Italy |
| Dieter Gollman | Technische Universität Hamburg-Harburg, Germany |
| Joshua Guttman | MITRE, USA |
| Jan Jürjens | TU Dortmund and Fraunhofer ISST, Germany |
| Gavin Lowe | Oxford University, UK (Co-chair) |
| Catherine Meadows | Naval Research Laboratory, USA |
| John Mitchell | Stanford University, USA |
| Sebastian Mödersheim | IBM Zurich Research Lab, Switzerland |
| Michael Rusinowitch | INRIA-Lorraine, France |
| Mark Ryan | University of Birmingham, UK |
| Graham Steel | INRIA, France |
| Luca Viganò | Università di Verona, Italy |
| Bogdan Warinschi | University of Bristol, UK |

## External Reviewers

Aizatulin, Mihhail
Arapinis, Myrto
Bartoletti, Massimo
Bauer, Andreas
Bodei, Chiara
Bugliesi, Michele
Bursuc, Sergiu
Centenaro, Matteo
Colon, Michael
Delaune, Stephanie
Dupressoir, Francois
Ferrari, Gian-Luigi
Hevia, Alejandro
Hirsch, Martin

Koleini, Masoud
Meier, Simon
Pellegrino, Giancarlo
Perreira, Olivier
Pontes Soares Rocha, Bruno
Portokalidis, Georgios
Qunoo, Hasan
Schoenmakers, Berry
Sgandurra, Daniele

# Table of Contents

# The CaPiTo Approach to Protocol Validation
## (Invited Talk)

Flemming Nielson, Han Gao, and Hanne Riis Nielson

DTU Informatics
The Technical University of Denmark

**Abstract.** We show how to model service-oriented applications using the process algebra CaPiTo so that, on the one hand, we can achieve an abstract specification without being overwhelmed by the underlying implementation details and, on the other hand, we can obtain a concrete specification respecting the industrial standards used for ensuring security. We consider this development important in order to get a good agreement between the protocols analysed by formal tools and the applications developed by practitioners.

We then show how to transform the concrete specification into the LySa analysis framework, used in the SENSORIA EU project and originally developed in the DEGAS EU project, for analysing cryptographic protocols under a Dolev-Yao attacker. This allows us to perform a control flow analysis for ensuring the authenticity (as well as confidentiality) of messages exchanged between services. The LySa analysis framework is implemented in polynomial time in the size of the protocol specification using the Succinct Solver, that can solve a superset of Datalog clauses.

A. Armando and G. Lowe (Eds.): ARSPA-WITS 2010, LNCS 6186, p. 1, 2010.

# Reasoning about Probabilistic Security Using Task-PIOAs*

Aaron D. Jaggard[1,**], Catherine Meadows[2,***], Michael Mislove[3,***], and Roberto Segala[4,†]

[1] Rutgers University, New Brunswick, NJ
adj@dimacs.rutgers.edu
[2] Naval Research Lab, Washington, DC
catherine.meadows@nrl.navy.mil
[3] Tulane University, New Orleans, LA
mwm@math.tulane.edu
[4] University of Verona, Italy
roberto.segala@univr.it

**Abstract.** Task-structured probabilistic input/output automata (Task-PIOAs) are concurrent probabilistic automata that, among other things, have been used to provide a formal framework for the universal composability paradigms of protocol security. One of their advantages is that that they allow one to distinguish high-level nondeterminism that can affect the outcome of the protocol, from low-level choices, which can't. We present an alternative approach to analyzing the structure of Task-PIOAs that relies on ordered sets. We focus on two of the components that are required to define and apply Task-PIOAs: discrete probability theory and automata theory. We believe our development gives insight into the structure of Task-PIOAs and how they can be utilized to model crypto-protocols. We illustrate our approach with an example from anonymity, an area that has not previously been addressed using Task-PIOAs. We model Chaum's Dining Cryptographers Protocol at a level that does not require cryptographic primitives in the analysis. We show via this example how our approach can leverage a proof of security in the case a principal behaves deterministically to prove security when that principal behaves probabilistically.

## 1 Introduction

Process algebras and other models of concurrent computation have become a staple for reasoning about security (cf. [1, 20], to name two examples). Originally,

* The authors wish to thank the Center for Discrete Mathematics and Theoretical Computer Science and the DIMACS Special Focus on Communication Security and Information Privacy for their support that allowed us to gather at Rutgers to work on this project for a week in May/June, 2008.

** The author wishes to acknowledge the support of NSF grant 0751674 and of the ONR during this research.

*** These authors wish to acknowledge the support of the ONR during this research.

† The author acknowledges the support of the MIUR PRIN project "SOFT" and FP7 grant INFSO-ICT-223844.L.

A. Armando and G. Lowe (Eds.): ARSPA-WITS 2010, LNCS 6186, pp. 2–22, 2010.

this work concentrated on the "Dolev-Yao" model in which cryptographic algorithms were modeled as black boxes. However, there is a growing body of research aimed at marrying concurrency theory with cryptographic reasoning. Prominent among these approaches is the work of Canetti, Lynch, Segala, et al. [6], which uses *Task-PIOAs* to provide a formalization of Canetti's Universal Composability model [5]. Task-PIOAs are probabilistic input/output automata equipped with *tasks*, which define their execution sequences. The approach is highlighted by two aspects: First, this approach encodes the basic constituents of cryptography – one-way functions, hardcore predicates, etc., into the model and reasons about them in proving security properties.

The second distinguishing aspect of [6] is that it divides the nondeterminism in a concurrent system into high-level choices that can affect the outcome of the protocol, and low-level nondeterminism that does not affect the outcome. By allowing the adversary to see the outcomes only of the low-level choices, the model overcomes the problem that concurrency models generally afford the adversary too much power by allowing it to see the outcomes of all the choices made during the execution of a protocol.

Because of all this, the Task-PIOA work is often cited as a promising approach to modeling crypto-protocols. At the same time, the Task-PIOA analysis of oblivious transfer [6], for example, is daunting. Indeed, there are three components that must be mastered to appreciate the subtleties of Task-PIOAs: the theory of discrete probability that is applied to Task-PIOAs, the theory of probabilistic automata that underlies Task-PIOAs, and the incorporation of cryptographic primitives that requires detailed and often-tedious reasoning. We note that this rather formidable array of components is inherent in all approaches to marrying formal methods with cryptographic reasoning, and is not specific to Task-PIOAs; all approaches to marrying these aspects suffer from the same complexity. Our approach is to separate the cryptographic primitives in the model from the other aspects, and to treat these other facets first, reserving a similar analysis of the cryptographic components for future work.

Thus, the purpose of the current paper is to present the first two components – discrete probability theory applied to Task-PIOAs, and the theory of probabilistic automata needed to analyze Task-PIOAs – from a different perspective, one we hope will make the technology more easily digested. Our approach relies on ordered sets as an underlying theme for both discrete probability and for the automata theory needed to describe Task-PIOAs.

The universal composability approach to proving security employs the notion of a simulator as part of a mechanism to compare "real-world" processes with "ideal processes" that are secure by design. Task-PIOAs use simulation relations common to cryptographic proofs to carry out such comparisons. These relations validate security properties by showing the trace distributions on visible events of the real-world process are contained in those of the simulating process. As a result, an unbiased observer cannot tell if it is interacting with the real-world process or with the simulator, and the security of the real-world process follows.

We illustrate our results with an example in which cryptographic primitives don't play a role. This allows us to demonstrate the techniques developed in this paper to model a security protocol, avoiding cryptographic details that are independent of our approach to combining discrete probability theory with the theory of probabilistic automata. The example comes from anonymity: it is the canonical example of Chaum's Dining Cryptographers Protocol [9]. Our approach also has the advantage that it explicitly models a method by which the choice of who pays is made, a detail left unspecified in Chaum's original paper, and one that is also left unspecified in other approaches such as [4].

Task-PIOAs use task schedules to resolve nondeterminism, and a Task-PIOA simulation relation typically shows that each task schedule for a real-world process has a corresponding schedule for its simulating process. In this paper we introduce a somewhat simpler notion of simulation we call *Task-PIOA maps.* The main difference is that, while Task-PIOA simulations utilize maps between task schedules, Task-PIOA maps map states to states, actions to actions, and tasks to tasks. This makes defining a Task-PIOA map somewhat simpler, and their use is well-suited for indistinguishability proofs in which the only difference between the two processes is the choice of a secret. This is the case for our proof of anonymity of Dining Cryptographers. Anticipating some details, the protocol is secure if the probability distributions on the announcements of the cryptographers doesn't vary depending on which one is paying. Our analysis shows that the distributions in the case of a probabilistic choice of who pays can be calculated compositionally from the distributions that arise from its deterministic subprocesses. Our argument relies on Chaum's original use of conditional probability [9] to prove anonymity, an approach also applied in [4,7].

The rest of the paper is organized as follows. In the next section, we give a comparison with other work. The following sections give some results about discrete probability theory based on order-theoretic arguments, and the basic definitions and results used by Task-PIOAs. Following that, we give the main results of the paper which define Task-PIOA maps and show they preserve trace distributions of task-based probabilistic input/output automata. This is followed by a brief description of the Dining Cryptographers Protocol and how to encode it using process algebra. We next encode the Dining Cryptographers Protocol using a task-based probabilistic input/output automata and then show that the protocol is secure if the choice of who pays is either deterministic or probabilistic. In the final section we summarize our results and discuss possible future work.

## 2 Comparison with Other Work

As we already commented, the use of process algebras and of models of concurrency is now commonplace in analyzing crypto-protocols, as well as other areas of security. What is novel about the Task-PIOA approach as presented in [6] is the level of detail at which processes are treated. Most security models operate under the traditional Dolev-Yao assumption and assume perfect encryption. However, these assumptions have been shown to be unrealistic in some contexts [17], which is one of the impetuses for the universal composability approach [5] to modeling security. This need for more realism has been accompanied by a myriad of details that make analyses much more intricate. In particular, in what is probably the most closely-related work to the Task-PIOA approach, [17, 20], Probabilistic Polynomial-time Turing Machines are used as the basis for a model. This approach also involves myriad details about computations, details we seek to abstract away in our approach to understanding parts of the PIOA approach.

Part of the problem with these more realistic models is the level of detail, but an added problem with [6] is the presentation of the model. Indeed, the Task-PIOA approach is composed of two parts: (i) the presentation of task-structured probabilistic input/output automata (Task-PIOAs), and (ii) the application of these automata to model cryptographic primitives in the analysis of the oblivious transfer protocol. Here, we give an alternative presentation of Task-PIOAs, using techniques from order theory. While our approach requires familiarity with ordered sets, the results needed are not especially deep, and the ordered sets approach carries with it computational intuitions that are not so clear in [6].

The Dining Cryptographers Protocol originated in the work of Chaum [9], and it quickly became a prototypical test example for modeling anonymity. For example, Schneider and Sidiropoulos [21] use CSP to analyze the protocol, after first replacing probabilistic choice by nondeterministic choice. While CSP is limited to nondeterministic choice, there are models of concurrency that support both nondeterminism and probabilistic choice, and these require a mechanism to account for how the nondeterminism in the system is resolved. The most commonly used approach is to include a *scheduler* that resolves the nondeterministic choices. In security analyses, the scheduler is often seen as an adversary that can control the occurrence of events in order to maximize the chances of compromising the security of the system. Garcia et al. [11] introduce *admissible schedulers* that limit the power of the adversary so that it is "realistic" and cannot see the outcomes of choices that should be hidden from it.

Probably the most exhaustive treatment of the Dining Cryptographers using concurrency appears in the papers [4,7,8]. In [4], an analysis shows the limitations of substituting nondeterminism for probabilistic choice, as was done in [21], and analyses are presented of the Dining Cryptographers with users that are nondeterministic or probabilistic in their choices, under some added hypotheses. In [7], the pi-calculus is augmented with labels guarding choices, so that the scheduler can enable a choice, but not control or see its outcome. In [8], a new notion of *conditional capacity* of a channel is introduced, and this is used to analyse the degree of anonymity of a system in which some information is leaked on purpose. Finally, [14] applies simulation relations based on coalgebras to analyze the Dining Cryptographers. As is typical of other treatments, the presentation is at an abstract level, concentrating solely on the case in which the choice of who pays is deterministic, and in which the implementation of the choice is left unspecified. Moreover, this model does not support nondeterminism, and presents everything in a purely probabilistic framework.

There is a growing body of literature on modeling probabilistic processes, including models of concurrency that support both nondeterminism and probabilistic choice (see, e.g., [18]), as is the case here. A major theme along this line stems from the seminal work of Larsen and Skou [16] on labeled Markov processes (see also [10, 19]). A major difference between Task-PIOAs and that work is the nature of the transition relation that defines the evolution of the processes. We comment in more detail on this point in Section 9. Nevertheless, it should be noted that the Task-PIOA maps we introduce are a form of functional simulation.

In summary, our main results are as follows:

- The use of order theory to analyze Task-PIOAs, and in particular, the Apply operator that applies a task to a probabilistic input/output automaton, which make clear how processes evolve under the application of task schedules.
- The notion of a *Task-PIOA map* and the proof that, under a given task schedule, these maps take the trace distributions of a domain Task-PIOA into the trace distributions of the target Task-PIOA.
- An analysis of the Dining Cryptographers Protocol using Task-PIOAs. Our version of Dining Cryptographers includes a Master that chooses who pays (either one of the cryptographers or the Master itself), a concept introduced in [4]. We prove the anonymity of the protocol from the point of view of the cryptographers when the Master is deterministic, and then use that result to show that anonymity also holds in the case of a probabilistic Master.

## 3 Ordered Structures and Domain-Theoretic Arguments

In this section we present the results on ordered sets and their application to models of computation we need to analyze probabilistic input/output automata. We emphasize at the outset that our results are valid in the case of directed complete partial orders (e.g., *domains*) but we restrict the presentation to the case of ordered sets, since that's all that is needed in the current setting.

**Definition 1.** *An* ordered set *is a non-empty set together with a partial order, i.e., a reflexive, antisymmetric and transitive relation. If $P$ and $Q$ are ordered sets, and if $f\colon P \to Q$ is a mapping between them, then*

- $f$ *is* monotone *if $x \leq_P y$ implies $f(x) \leq_Q f(y)$.*
- $f$ *is* progressive *if $P = Q$ and $x \leq_P f(x)$ for all $x \in P$.*

*We use* Ord *to denote the category of ordered sets and monotone maps.*

The prototypical example of an ordered set is the family $A^*$ of finite words over an alphabet $A$ in the *prefix order:* $s \leq t \Leftrightarrow (\exists u \in A^*)\ t = su$.

If $X$ is a set, then a *discrete probability measure over* $X$ has the form $\sum_{i \in I} r_i \delta_{x_i}$, where $I$ is a countable set, $\delta_{x_i}$ denotes the point mass at $x_i \in X$ and

$\sum_i r_i = 1$, where $0 < r_i$ for each $i$. If $I$ is finite, then the measure is said to be *simple*. For $\mu = \sum_{i \in I} r_i \delta_{x_i}$, then the *support of* $\mu$ is defined by $\mathsf{supp}\,\mu = \{x_i \mid i \in I\}$.

If $P$ is an ordered set, the order on $P$ lifts to the family $\mathsf{Disc}(P)$ of discrete probability measures on $P$: $\sum_i r_i \delta_{x_i} \leq \sum_j s_j \delta_{y_j}$ iff $\sum\{r_i \mid x_i \in A\} \leq \sum\{s_j \mid y_j \in A\}$ for each *upper set* $A$.[1] Thus, $\mu \leq \nu$ iff $\mu(A) \leq \nu(A)$ for every upper set $A$. For simple measures $\sum_{i=1}^m r_i \delta_{x_i} \leq \sum_{j=1}^n s_j \delta_{y_j}$ iff there is a family $t_{ij} \geq 0$, $1 \leq i \leq m$ and $1 \leq j \leq n$ satisfying:

$$\text{(a) } (\forall i)\ r_i = \textstyle\sum_j t_{ij}, \quad \text{(b) } (\forall j)\ \sum_i t_{ij} = s_j, \text{ and} \quad \text{(c) } t_{ij} > 0 \Rightarrow x_i \leq_P y_j.$$

(Cf. Theorem 4.10 of [15] for details.) There is a monad $\mathsf{Disc}\colon \mathsf{Ord} \to \mathsf{Ord}$ that associates to each ordered set $P$ the family $\mathsf{Disc}(P)$ of discrete probability measures on $P$ and that sends each monotone mapping $f\colon P \to Q$ to the mapping $\mathsf{Disc}(f)\colon \mathsf{Disc}(P) \to \mathsf{Disc}(Q)$ by $\mathsf{Disc}(f)(\sum_i r_i \delta_{x_i}) = \sum_i r_i \delta_{f(x_i)}$. The unit of the monad is the mapping $x \mapsto \delta_x$ and the multiplication $m\colon \mathsf{Disc}(\mathsf{Disc}(P)) \to \mathsf{Disc}(P)$ is just integration: $\sum_i r_i \delta_{\sum_j s_{ij} \delta_{x_{ij}}} = \sum_{ij} r_i s_{ij} \delta_{x_{ij}}$. This monad multiplication is used implicitly in the definition of the function $\mathsf{Apply}(-,-)$ – cf. Remark 1.

## 4 Probabilistic Input/Output Automata

We use task-structured probabilistic input/output automata as our basic model of computation. This notion is due to Canetti, Lynch, et al. [6]. In this section, we summarize the main ideas from [6] that are necessary to understand this paper.

**Definition 2.** *A* Probabilistic Input/Output Automaton $\mathcal{A} = (Q, \overline{q}, I, O, H, D)$ *is a 6-tuple where:*

1. *$Q$ is a countable set of* states *containing $\overline{q} \in Q$ as the* start state*;*
2. *$I$, $O$ and $H$ are pairwise disjoint, countable sets of* actions*, referred to as* input, output *and* internal actions*, respectively. The set $\mathsf{Act} ::= I \cup O \cup H$ is called the set of* actions *of $\mathcal{A}$. The set of* external *actions of $\mathcal{A}$ is $E ::= I \cup O$ and the set of* locally controlled *actions is $L ::= O \cup H$.*
3. *$D \subseteq Q \times \mathsf{Act} \times \mathsf{Disc}(Q)$ is a* transition relation*. An action $a$ is* enabled *in state $q$ if $(q, a, \mu) \in D$ for some $\mu \in \mathsf{Disc}(Q)$, which we denote by $\mu_{q,a}$.*
   *We also assume $D$ satisfies:*
   Input enabling: *For every $q \in Q$ and $a \in I$, $a$ is enabled in $q$.*
   Transition determinism: *For every $q \in Q$ and $a \in \mathsf{Act}$, there is at most one $\mu \in \mathsf{Disc}(Q)$ such that $(q, a, \mu) \in D$.*

*Probabilistic input/output automata also admit a* hiding operator*: If $S \subseteq O_{\mathcal{A}}$ is a set of output actions of $\mathcal{A}$, then $\mathcal{A} \setminus S$ denotes the process where $O = O_{\mathcal{A}} \setminus S$ and $H = H_{\mathcal{A}} \cup S$. The result is that the output of actions in $S$ are visible only to the process executing them, and to the recipient processes of the actions.*

---

[1] $A$ is an *upper set* if $A = \uparrow A = \{x \in P \mid (\exists a \in A)\ a \leq_P x\}$.

A probabilistic input/output automaton can be viewed as a labelled transition system where the transition relation is a partial function $\Delta\colon Q \times \mathsf{Act} \rightharpoonup \mathsf{Disc}(Q)$ defined by $\Delta(q, a) = \mu_{q,a}$, if such a measure exists. Input enabling implies the restriction $\Delta|_{Q\times I}\colon Q \times I \to \mathsf{Disc}(Q)$ is a total function.

We also need a method for composing PIOAs.

**Definition 3.** *Let $\mathcal{A}_i = (Q_i, \overline{q}_i, I_i, O_i, H_i, D_i)$, $i = 1, 2$ be PIOAs. We say $\mathcal{A}_1$ and $\mathcal{A}_2$ are* compatible *if $\mathsf{Act}_1 \cap H_2 = \mathsf{Act}_2 \cap H_1 = \emptyset = O_1 \cap O_2$. If this is the case, then we define $\mathcal{A}_1 \| \mathcal{A}_2 = (Q_{\mathcal{A}_1\|\mathcal{A}_2}, \overline{q}_{\mathcal{A}_1\|\mathcal{A}_2}, I_{\mathcal{A}_1\|\mathcal{A}_2}, O_{\mathcal{A}_1\|\mathcal{A}_2}, H_{\mathcal{A}_|\|\mathcal{A}_2}, D_{\mathcal{A}_1\|\mathcal{A}_2})$ where:*

- $Q_{\mathcal{A}_1\|\mathcal{A}_2} = Q_1 \times Q_2$, $\overline{q}_{\mathcal{A}_1\|\mathcal{A}_2} = \langle \overline{q}_1, \overline{q}_2 \rangle$,
- $I_{\mathcal{A}_1\|\mathcal{A}_2} = (I_1 \cup I_2) \setminus (O_1 \cup O_2)$, $O_{\mathcal{A}_1\|\mathcal{A}_2} = O_1 \cup O_2$, *and* $H_{\mathcal{A}_1\|\mathcal{A}_2} = H_1 \cup H_2$,
- $D_{\mathcal{A}_1\|\mathcal{A}_2} = \{(\langle q_1, q_2 \rangle, a, \mu_1 \times \mu_2) \mid (a \in \mathsf{Act}_i \Rightarrow (q_i, a, \mu_i) \in D_i),$ $\text{and } (a \notin \mathsf{Act}_j \Rightarrow \mu_j = \delta_{q_j})\}$.

The main points to note of the composition are that (1) each output action and each hidden action is confined to exactly one component, (2) the inputs of either component can be provided by outputs of the other component, so the composition of processes can be *closed* – its set of inputs can be empty, and (3) if an action is in the alphabet of only one component, then the other component "idles" in its current state while the enabled component executes the action. However, even though one component may be able to perform an action in a given state, the other component can block the action if the action is in its alphabet, but it cannot execute the action in its current state.

### 4.1 Tasks

Tasks provide a mechanism for resolving nondeterminism – the choice of which action to execute in a given state, in the execution of a PIOA.

**Definition 4.** *A* Task-structured Probabilistic Input/Output Automaton *(Task-PIOA) is a pair $\mathcal{T} = (\mathcal{A}, \mathcal{R})$ where*

- *$\mathcal{A} = (Q, \overline{q}, I, O, H, D)$ is a probabilistic I/O automaton, and*
- *$\mathcal{R} \subseteq (O \times O) \cup (H \times H)$ is an equivalence relation on the locally controlled actions. The equivalence classes of $\mathcal{R}$ are called* tasks.

*A Task-PIOA $\mathcal{T}$ is said to be* action deterministic *if for each state $q \in \mathcal{A}$ and each task $T \in \mathcal{R}$, there is at most one action $a \in T$ that is enabled in $q$.*

A task schedule *for a Task-PIOA $\mathcal{T}$ is a finite sequence $\rho = T_1 T_2 \cdots T_n$ of tasks in $\mathcal{R}$.*[2]

[2] Our results in general include a treatment of the case of infinite task schedules (in which case the utility of domain theory comes to the fore), but since we only need finite task schedules in the present setting, we limit our presentation to that case. Nonetheless, the order-theoretic approach pays a dividend by giving a clear and concise definition of the application of a task to a process.

### 4.2 Applying Task Schedules

Since we have no final states in $Q$, there is a question of what constitutes a computation of a Task-PIOA. We use task schedules to specify the sequences of actions a process should execute. The probability distribution generated by the process as it executes that sequence of tasks then defines a computational behavior of the process.

Our interest is in the trace distributions over finite sequences of observable events of the automaton $\mathcal{A}$. For an automaton $\mathcal{A} = (Q, \overline{q}, I, O, H, D)$, we let

$$\mathsf{Exec}^*\mathcal{A} = \{\overline{q}a_0 \dots q_{n-1}a_{n-1}q_n \mid q_i \in Q, a_i \in \mathsf{Act}, q_{i+1} \in \mathsf{supp}\, \mu_{q_i,a_i}\ (\forall i < n)\}.$$ [3]

Note that $\mathsf{Exec}^*\mathcal{A}$ is ordered by the prefix ordering as a subset of $Q \times (\mathsf{Act} \times Q)^*$. If $a \in \mathsf{Act}$, then we define the set of finite execution fragments whose last state enables the action $a$:

$$A_a = \{\alpha \in \mathsf{Exec}^*\mathcal{A} \mid a \text{ enabled in } \mathsf{lstate}(\alpha)\},$$

where $\mathsf{lstate}(\alpha) = q_n$ is the final state of $\alpha = \overline{q}a_0 \cdots a_{n-1}q_n$. Likewise, for a task $T$, let $A_T$ be the set of finite execution fragments whose last state enables the task $T$:

$$A_T = \{\alpha \in \mathsf{Exec}^*\mathcal{A} \mid (\exists a \in T)\ a \text{ enabled in } \mathsf{lstate}(\alpha)\}.$$

For each finite execution fragment $\alpha \in A_T$, if the action $a \in T$ is enabled in $\mathsf{lstate}(\alpha)$, we let $\mu_{\mathsf{lstate}(\alpha),a}$ be the target measure of the unique transition $(\mathsf{lstate}(\alpha), a, \mu_{\mathsf{lstate}(\alpha),a}) \in D$. Then we define

$$\mathsf{Apply}(-,-)\colon \mathsf{Disc}(\mathsf{Exec}^*\mathcal{A}) \times \mathcal{T} \to \mathsf{Disc}(\mathsf{Exec}^*\mathcal{A})$$

by

$$\mathsf{Apply}(\mu, T) = \sum_{\alpha \notin A_T} \mu(\alpha)\delta_\alpha + \sum_{\alpha \in A_T} \mu(\alpha) \left( \sum_s \mu_{\mathsf{lstate}(\alpha),a_T}(s)\delta_{\alpha a_T s} \right). \quad (1)$$

*Remark 1.* There are some points to note about this definition.

1. Since each task $T$ allows only one action $a_T \in T$ to be enabled in $\mathsf{lstate}(\alpha)$ for each $\alpha \in \mathsf{supp}\,\mu$, there is no sum over actions in the second summand on the right. This implicitly uses the monad $\mathsf{Disc}$: the restriction on tasks implies there is a partial map $(q,T) \mapsto \sum_{q'} \mu_{q,a_q}(q')\delta_{q'} : Q \times \mathcal{T} \rightharpoonup \mathsf{Disc}(Q)$, where $a_q \in T$ is enabled in $q$, which $\mathsf{Disc}$ extends to define the second summand of the map $\mathsf{Apply}$.
2. The execution sequences in whose last state $T$ is *not* enabled still appear as the first summand on the right in the definition of $\mathsf{Apply}(\mu, T)$. This ensures that the result of applying $T$ to $\mu$ is a probability distribution (without the first summand, the result would have a total mass of $1 - \mu(A_T)$).

[3] Note that all such sequences begin at $\overline{q}$. Recall $x \in \mathsf{supp}\,\mu$ iff $\mu(x) > 0$.

Thus, $\mathsf{Apply}(\mu, T)$ applies the task $T$ to each execution fragment $\alpha \in \mathsf{supp}\,\mu$, thus resolving the nondeterminism of which action should occur after $\alpha$ has been executed. For a finite task schedule $\rho = T_1 \cdots T_n$, we define

$$\mathsf{Apply}(\mu, \rho) = \mathsf{Apply}(\mathsf{Apply}(\mu, T_1 \cdots T_{n-1}), T_n).$$

**Proposition 1.** *Let* $\mu = \sum_\alpha \mu(\alpha)\delta_\alpha \in \mathit{Disc}(\mathit{Exec}^*(\mathcal{A}))$, *then*

$$\mu \leq \mathit{Apply}(\sum_\alpha \mu(\alpha)\delta_\alpha, \rho) = \sum_\alpha \mu(\alpha)\mathit{Apply}(\delta_\alpha, \rho).$$

*In particular,* $\mathit{Apply}(\mu, \rho)$ *is well-defined for any task sequence* $\rho = T_1 \cdots T_n$.

*Proof.* By induction on the length of $\rho$ – see Appendix.

**Corollary 1.** *If* $\mu = \sum_i p_i\mu_i$, *then* $\mu \leq \mathit{Apply}(\sum_i p_i\mu_i, \rho) = \sum_i p_i \mathit{Apply}(\mu_i, \rho)$.

*Proof.* By the Proposition, we know that $\mu_i \leq \mathsf{Apply}(\mu_i, \rho)$ for each index $i$, so

$$\mu = \sum_i p_i\mu_i \leq \sum_i p_i \mathsf{Apply}(\mu_i, \rho) = \mathsf{Apply}(\sum_i p_i\mu_i, \rho),$$

the last equality following by expanding each $\mu_i$ as a convex sum of point masses and then applying the Proposition once again.

## 5 Comparing PIOAs

An important component of any modeling paradigm is the ability to compare models of distinct processes, in order to analyze the differences between them. In the development of Task-PIOAs in [6], this is done via *simulation relations*, which are used to show that the probability distributions over observable behaviors of one Task-PIOA are a subset of those of another Task-PIOA. This is useful for simplifying a process by devising a simpler, *simulating process*, and then deductions about the behavior of the simpler process can be used to prove properties about the more complicated one. This approach is based on matching a task schedule for the first process to one for the simulating process, but in our setting, the security specification requires we use *the same task schedule* for both processes. Rather than use the Task-PIOA simulation relations from [6], we present a simpler approach to simulation that meets this requirement. The setting is as follows:

If $\mathcal{T} = (\mathcal{A}, \mathcal{R})$ is a Task-PIOA, and $A \subseteq (I \cup O)$ is a set of *observable actions*, then $\mathsf{trace}_A \colon \mathsf{Exec}^*\mathcal{A} \to A^*$ is the function that extracts the sequence of $A$-actions (i.e., the sequences from $A^*$) from an execution sequence of $\mathcal{A}$. Since we are using only discrete measures, all sets are measurable, and so $\mathsf{trace}_A$ is a measurable map. Then $\mathsf{Disc}(\mathsf{trace}_A)(\mu) = \mu \circ \mathsf{trace}_A^{-1}$ is a measure on $A^*$ for each measure $\mu \in \mathsf{Disc}(\mathsf{Exec}^*\mathcal{A})$. In fact, if $\mu = \sum_i r_i\delta_{\alpha_i}$, then $\mathsf{Disc}(\mathsf{trace}_A)(\mu)$

$= \sum_i r_i \delta_{\mathsf{trace}_A(\alpha_i)}$. We let $\mathcal{S}_\mathcal{A}$ denote the family of task schedules on $\mathcal{A}$, and for $\rho \in \mathcal{S}_\mathcal{A}$, let $\mathsf{Apply}(\delta_{\overline{q}}, \rho) = \sum_{\alpha \in \mathsf{supp}\, \mathsf{Apply}(\delta_{\overline{q}}, \rho)} r_\alpha \delta_\alpha$. Then we define

$$\mathsf{tdist}^\rho_A(\mathcal{A}) = \mathsf{Disc}(\mathsf{trace}_A)(\mathsf{Apply}(\delta_{\overline{q}}, \rho)) = \sum_{\alpha \in \mathsf{supp}\, \mathsf{Apply}(\delta_{\overline{q}}, \rho)} r_\alpha \delta_{\mathsf{trace}_A(\alpha)}$$

be the measure on $A^*$ induced by $\mathsf{trace}_A$ from the measure $\mathsf{Apply}(\delta_{\overline{q}}, \rho)$. We also call

$$\mathsf{tdists}_A(\mathcal{A}) = \{\mathsf{tdist}^\rho_A(\mathcal{A}) \mid \rho \in \mathcal{S}_\mathcal{A}\}$$

the *A-trace distributions* of $\mathcal{A}$. We elide the subscript if $A = I \cup O$.

**Definition 5.** *Let $\mathcal{A}_i = (Q_i, \overline{q}_i, I_i, O_i, H_i, D_i), i = 1, 2$ be two Task-PIOAs, with task sets $\mathcal{T}_i, i = 1, 2$, respectively. We define a* Task-PIOA map $\phi\colon \mathcal{A}_1 \to \mathcal{A}_2$ *to consist of*

- *A mapping $\phi\colon Q_1 \to Q_2$ of the states of $\mathcal{A}_1$ to the states of $\mathcal{A}_2$ satisfying $\phi(\overline{q}_1) = \overline{q}_2$. We call this the* state component *of $\phi$.*
- *A mapping $\phi\colon \mathsf{Act}_1 \to \mathsf{Act}_2$ of actions of $\mathcal{A}_1$ to actions of $\mathcal{A}_2$. We call this the* action component *of $\phi$.*

*We also require the mapping $\phi\colon \mathcal{A}_1 \to \mathcal{A}_2$ to satisfy the* compatibility conditions:

*(i) $\langle q, a, \mu\rangle \in D_1 \Rightarrow \langle \phi(q), \phi(a), \mathsf{Disc}(\phi)(\mu)\rangle \in D_2$; i.e., if $q \in Q_1$ and $a \in \mathsf{Act}_1$ is enabled in state $q$, then $\phi(a)$ is enabled in state $\phi(q)$ and $\mathsf{Disc}(\phi)(\mu_{q,a}) = \mu_{\phi(q),\phi(a)}$.*
*(ii) For each $T \in \mathcal{T}_1$, $\phi(T) \in \mathcal{T}_2$.*

*Remark 2.* Note that if $\phi$ does not rename states or actions, then this coincides with the notion of *refinement* in process algebra.

The map $\phi$ induces $\mathsf{Exec}^*\phi\colon \mathsf{Exec}^*\mathcal{A}_1 \to \mathsf{Exec}^*\mathcal{A}_2$ by

$$\mathsf{Exec}^*\phi(\overline{q}a_0 \cdots a_{n-1}q_n) = \phi(\overline{q})\phi(a_0)\cdots\phi(a_{n-1})\phi(q_n),$$

which in turn gives $\mathsf{Disc}(\mathsf{Exec}^*\phi)\colon \mathsf{Disc}(\mathsf{Exec}^*\mathcal{A}_1) \to \mathsf{Disc}(\mathsf{Exec}^*\mathcal{A}_2)$ by

$$\mathsf{Disc}(\mathsf{Exec}^*\phi)(\sum_i r_i \delta_{\alpha_i}) = \sum_i r_i \delta_{\mathsf{Exec}^*\phi(\alpha_i)}.$$

Our main result is:

**Theorem 1.** *Let $\phi\colon \mathcal{A}_1 \to \mathcal{A}_2$ be a Task-PIOA map of Task-PIOAs satisfying $\phi(A_T) = A_{\phi(T)}$ for each task $T \in \mathcal{T}_1$. If $A \subseteq \mathsf{Act}_1$ is the set of observable actions, then $\mathsf{Disc}(\phi|^*_A)(\mathsf{tdist}(\mathcal{A}_1)) \subseteq \mathsf{tdist}(\mathcal{A}_2)$.*

*Proof.* We give an outline of the proof here, and provide full details in the Appendix. First, if $\mu \in \mathsf{Disc}(\mathsf{Exec}^*\mathcal{A}_1)$, then $\mu = \sum_{\alpha \in \mathsf{supp}\, \mu} r_\alpha \delta_\alpha$. So, for $T \in \mathcal{T}_1$, we can apply our definition of Apply from Equation 1 and of $\mathsf{Disc}(\mathsf{Exec}^*\phi)$ above to show $\mathsf{Disc}(\mathsf{Exec}^*\phi)(\mathsf{Apply}(\mu, T)) = \mathsf{Apply}(\mathsf{Disc}(\mathsf{Exec}^*\phi)(\mu), \phi(T))$. An induction on $n$ then shows the analogous result holds with any task schedule $\rho = T_1 \cdots T_n$ in place of $T$. The next step is to use this equation to show

$$\mathsf{Disc}(\phi|^*_A)(\mathsf{Disc}(\mathsf{trace})(\mathsf{Apply}(\mu, \rho))) = (\mathsf{Disc}(\mathsf{trace}) \circ \mathsf{Disc}(\mathsf{Exec}^*\phi))(\mathsf{Apply}(\mu, \rho)),$$

which implies the result.

## 6 Dining Cryptographers

The Dining Cryptographers Protocol is originally due to Chaum [9]. It postulates several cryptographers who are dining together. They are trying to determine whether one of them paid for dinner or NSA paid, without revealing to each other which cryptographer paid. In [9] the implementation of the decision of who pays is left unspecified; we use the solution of Bhargava and Palamadessi [4] in which a Master (that is, NSA) chooses who pays. The cryptographers use the following protocol to accomplish this. Each cryptographer has a coin that he flips, and he reports the outcome of that flip to the cryptographer to his right. The cryptographers then report the outcomes of the two coin flips they know – theirs and the one to their left – by announcing either *Agree* or *Disagree.* A cryptographer reports the outcome correctly if she is not paying, but if she is paying for dinner, then she reverses the announcement and lies about the outcome of the coin tosses she has witnessed. A simple argument based on parity shows that the Master is paying if the number of *Disagree* announcements is even, while one of the cryptographers is paying if there are an odd number of *Disagree* announcements. Moreover, if the cryptographers are honest and if the coins they use are fair, this protocol protects the identity of the paying cryptographer from the other cryptographers, as long as there are at least three cryptographers.

We will use probabilistic input/output automata [6] to model the Dining Cryptographers. The formal model will be introduced below, but first we give a process algebraic description of the component processes. We focus on the least number of cryptographers that makes the analysis meaningful, which is three. The processes are:[4]

$$\begin{aligned} \mathit{Master} &::= \mathit{choose\_payer} \circ \mathit{tell\_pay}_0 \circ \mathit{tell\_pay}_1 \circ \mathit{tell\_pay}_2 \\ \mathit{Crypto}_i &::= \mathit{rec\_pay}_i \circ \mathit{flip\_coin}_i \circ \mathit{learn\_coin}_{i-1} \circ \mathit{tell\_coin}_i \circ \\ &\qquad \mathit{compare\_coins} \circ \mathit{announce}_i \circ \mathit{receive\_announcements} \end{aligned}$$

The composition operator $\circ$ in this syntax is a meant to allow the actions to occur in any order specified by the environment. The action $\mathit{tell\_pay}_i$ sends the message to cryptographer $i$, $i = 0, 1, 2$ indicating whether or not she is paying. We believe the meaning of the components of the processes listed here is clear, so they require no further explanation. But some names will change when we encode the processes as probabilistic input/output automata, in order make the communications synchronous. The process representing our protocol is then the composition

$$\mathit{Master} \parallel \mathit{Crypto}_0 \parallel \mathit{Crypto}_1 \parallel \mathit{Crypto}_2,$$

where $\parallel$ denotes parallel composition.

## 7 A Model of Dining Cryptographers

We now show how to model the Dining Cryptographers using task-based probabilistic input/output automata. Figure 1 describes the Master process and its

[4] We us indices $i = 0, 1, 2$ modulo 3, so $0 - 1 = 2$, $2 + 1 = 0$, etc.

transition relation. This includes the set of actions for the process, labeled according to whether they are input, output or internal actions; it also gives the state space of the process and the list of tasks. The Master has an internally defined distribution $r \cdot \delta_{\langle master, \perp_{Q_0} \rangle} + \sum_i r_i \delta_{\langle crypto_i, \perp_{Q_0} \rangle}$ that gives the probability of choosing the payer – i.e., $r + \sum_i r_i = 1$. Also, the transition relation encodes the Master's actions of sending messages to each of the cryptographers indicating which one, if any, is paying, and the state space records the fact that the message to each cryptographer has been sent. The Master also observes the announcements of the cryptographers. Actions determine tasks: e.g., one of the Master's tasks is $pay_i = \{pay_i(T), pay_i(F)\}$.

*Master*

**Actions:**

Input:

Output:

$pay_j(c), c \in \{T, F\}, j \in \{0, 1, 2\}$

Internal:

*choose_payer*

**State:**

$Payer \times Q_0$, where $Q_0 = \prod_{i=0}^{2} \{\perp, T\}$,

$Payer = \{\perp, Master, Crypto_i \mid i = 0, 1, 2\}$,

all initially $\perp$

**Tasks:**

$\{choose\_payer\}$,

$\{pay_j(c) \mid c \in \{T, F\}\}_{j=0,1,2}$

**Transitions:**

$$\begin{aligned} D = \{ & \langle \langle \perp, \perp_{Q_0} \rangle, choose\_payer, r \cdot \delta_{\langle Master, \perp_{Q_0} \rangle} + \textstyle\sum_i r_i \delta_{\langle Crypto_i, \perp_{Q_0} \rangle} \rangle \} \\ & \cup \{ \langle \langle Master, q \rangle, pay_j(F), \delta_{\langle Master, q' \rangle} \mid q_j = \perp, q'_j = T,\ j = 0, 1, 2 \} \\ & \cup \{ \langle \langle Crypto_i, q \rangle, pay_i(T), \delta_{\langle Crypto_i, q' \rangle} \rangle \mid q_i = \perp \;\&\; q'_i = T \} \\ & \cup \{ \langle \langle Crypto_i, q \rangle, pay_j(F), \delta_{\langle Crypto_j, q' \rangle} \rangle \mid q_j = \perp \;\&\; q'_j = T,\ j \neq i \} \end{aligned}$$

**Fig. 1.** The Master automaton chooses the payer

*Crypto*$_i$

**Actions:**

Input:

$pay_i(c), c \in \{T, F\}$

$coin_{i-1}(c), c \in \{H, T\}$

(We again use subtraction mod 3.)

$announce_{i-1}(c), c \in \{Agree, Disagree\}$

$announce_{i+1}(c), c \in \{Agree, Disagree\}$

Output:

$coin_i(c), c \in \{H, T\}$

$announce_i(c), c \in \{Agree, Disagree\}$

Internal:

$flip_i$

$compare_i$

**State:**

$Q_i = Pay_i \times Coin_{i-1} \times Coin_i \times Coin\_sent_i \times Compare_i \times Announce_{i-1} \times Announce_{i+1}$

$Pay_i = \{pay_i(c) \mid c \in \{\perp, T, F\}\}$ initially $\perp$

$Coin_{i-1} = \{coin_{i-1}(c) \mid c \in \{\perp, H, T\}\}$ initially $\perp$

$Coin_{i-1} = \{coin_{i-1}(c) \mid c \in \{\perp, H, T\}\}$ initially $\perp$

$Coin\_sent_i = \{coin\_sent_i(x) \mid x \in \{F, T\}\}$ initially $F$

$Compare_i = \{\perp, T, F\}$, initially $\perp$

$Announce_j = \{announce_j(c)\}, j = i-1, i+1$ $c \in \{\perp, Agree, Disagree\}$, initially $\perp$

**Tasks:**

$\{flip_i\}, \{coin_i(c)\}, \{compare_i\}$, $\{announce_i(c)\}$

**Fig. 2.** The actions, tasks and state set of *Cryptographer i*

$Crypto_i$
**Transitions:**
$Q_i = Pay_i \times Coin_{i-1} \times Coin_i \times Coin\_sent_i \times Compare_i \times Announce_i$
$Pay_i = Compare_i = \{\bot, T, F\}$; $Coin_{i-1} = Coin_i = \{\bot, H, T\}$;
$Announce_i = \{\bot, Agree, Disagree\}$

$$
\begin{aligned}
D = &\{\langle q, pay_i(c), \delta_{q'}\rangle \mid q_1 = \bot, q_1' = c, j \neq 1 \Rightarrow q_i = q_i'\}\\
&\cup\{\langle q, coin_{i-1}(c), \delta_{q'}\rangle \mid q_2 = \bot, q_2' = c, j \neq 2 \Rightarrow q_i = q_i''\}\\
&\cup\{\langle q, flip_i, \tfrac{1}{2}\delta_{q'} + \tfrac{1}{2}\delta_{q''}\rangle \mid q_3 = \bot, q_3' = H, q_3'' = T, j \neq 3 \Rightarrow q_i = q_i' = q_i''\}\\
&\cup\{\langle q, coin_i(c), \delta_{q'}\rangle \mid q_3 = c \neq \bot, q_4 = F, q_4 = T, j \neq 3, 4 \Rightarrow q_i = q_i'\}\\
&\cup\{\langle q, compare_i, \delta_{q'}\rangle \mid q_2 = q_3 \neq \bot, q_5 = \bot, q_5' = T, j \neq 5 \Rightarrow q_j = q_j'\}\\
&\cup\{\langle q, compare_i, \delta_{q'}\rangle \mid \bot \neq q_2 \neq q_3 \neq \bot, q_5 = \bot, q_5' = F, j \neq 5 \Rightarrow q_j = q_j'\}\\
&\cup\{\langle q, announce_i(c), \delta_{q'}\rangle \mid q_1 = F, q_5 = T, q_6' = \bot, c = q_6' = Agree, j \neq 6 \Rightarrow q_j = q_j'\}\\
&\cup\{\langle q, announce_i(c), \delta_{q'}\rangle \mid q_1 = T, q_5 = T, q_6' = \bot, c = q_6' = Disagree, j \neq 6 \Rightarrow q_j = q_j'\}\\
&\cup\{\langle q, announce_i(c), \delta_{q'}\rangle \mid q_1 = F, q_5 = F, q_6' = \bot, c = q_6' = Disagree, j \neq 6 \Rightarrow q_j = q_j'\}\\
&\cup\{\langle q, announce_i(c), \delta_{q'}\rangle \mid q_1 = T, q_5 = F, q_6' = \bot, c = q_6' = Agree, j \neq 6 \Rightarrow q_j = q_j'\}
\end{aligned}
$$

**Fig. 3.** The transition relation for *Cryptographer i*

Figure 2 gives the actions, state set and tasks of the cryptographers, while the transition relation is given in Figure 3. Together, these model the cryptographers as task-based probabilistic input/output automata. These are the most complicated Task-PIOAs we use, having several states and actions to perform. In essence, each cryptographer receives a message from the Master indicating whether she is paying, and then uses this information in determining whether to honestly announce the outcome of the coin flips seen, or to lie. Each cryptographer also has an unbiased coin: this is specified by the output of $flip_i$ that is $\frac{1}{2}\delta_H + \frac{1}{2}\delta_T$. $Crypto_i$ reports the outcome of her coin flip to $Crypto_{i+1}$, compares her flip with the one from $Crypto_{i-1}$ and announces the outcome as described.[5] The component names have changed from the syntax in Section 6; for example, $rec\_pay_i$ is now the input action $pay_i$ for $Crypto_i$, while $learn\_coin_{i-1}$ is shortened to the input action $coin_{i-1}$; this synchronizes the outputs of one process with the inputs of another.

Our model of the Dining Cryptographers is then the composition

$$DC = Master \parallel Crypto_0 \parallel Crypto_1 \parallel Crypto_2,$$

of the Master with the cryptographers. Note that all actions except the announcements are hidden. Indeed, by definition, the outputs of one component that are inputs of another become hidden in the composition of the two: the Master has no input actions, its outputs are the inputs to the cryptographers, while each cryptographer provides the input for the "next" cryptographer (the

[5] Here again, we are using arithmetic modulo 3.

one to the right, numbering in the counterclockwise direction). Since all input actions are from other components, $DC$ is a closed Task-PIOA.

A prototypical task schedule for this combined process is:

$$choose\_payer, pay_0, pay_1, pay_2, flip_0, flip_1, flip_2, coin_0, coin_1, coin_2, compare_0, compare_1, compare_2, announce_0, announce_1, announce_2$$

# 8 Proving the Protocol Secure

To say $DC$ is secure, we mean that if one of the cryptographers is paying, then none of the non-paying cryptographers can tell which of the other cryptographers is paying. In [9] this is expressed by the fact that the *a priori* probability that a particular cryptographer is paying before the protocol is run is the same as the *a posteriori* probability that cryptographer is paying after it is run.

Our proof is broken down into two cases. We first consider the case that the Master is deterministic, in which case we show the anonymity of the paying cryptographer from the perspective of the other cryptographers. We then use this result to prove the anonymity of the paying cryptographer in the case of a probabilistic Master who randomly chooses a cryptographer (or himself) to pay.

## 8.1 A Deterministic Master

The anonymity guarantee of the Dining Cryptographers – if one of the cryptographers is paying for dinner, then neither of the two non-payers can distinguish the behaviors of the remaining cryptographers – can be proved by showing that neither non-paying cryptographer can see a difference in the distributions on the announcements of the other two cryptographers. To accomplish this, we define a deterministic Master using the distribution $r \cdot \delta_{\langle Master, \perp_{Q_0}\rangle} + \sum_i r_i \delta_{\langle Crypto_i, \perp_{Q_0}\rangle}$ satisfying $r_i = 1$ and $r = 0 = r_j$ for $j \neq i$, that specifies a Master $\mathcal{M}_i$ that selects $Crypto_i$, $i = 0, 1$ or 2 as the payer. Let

$$\mathcal{A}_i = \mathcal{M}_i \parallel C_0 \parallel C_1 \parallel C_2 \tag{1}$$

denote the process with Master $\mathcal{M}_i$, $i = 0, 1, 2$. We also let $\mathcal{S}$ denote the set of task schedules.

**Proposition 2.** *If all cryptographers use fair coins, then*

$$(\forall \rho \in \mathcal{S})\ \mathsf{tdist}^{\rho}_{A_i}(\mathcal{A}_{i+1}) = \mathsf{tdist}^{\rho}_{A_i}(\mathcal{A}_{i-1})\ (\forall i = 0, 1, 2),^{6}$$

*where $A_i$ is the set of actions observable by cryptographer $i$.*

*Proof.* Without loss of generality, we also assume $i = 0$ (so $Crypto_0$ is not paying). The proof proceeds by defining a mapping from $\phi\colon \mathcal{A}_1 \to \mathcal{A}_2$ that simply reverses the roles of $Crypto_1$ and $Crypto_2$ and reverses the values of the received messages, $pay_1(c)$ and $pay_2(c)$.

[6] We are again counting mod 3, since there are three cryptographers.

More formally, we wish to apply Theorem 1. Let $\mathcal{T}$ denote the set of tasks of $DC$, and let $Q_{\mathcal{A}_i} = Q_M \times \prod_{i=0}^{2} Q_i$ denote the state space of $\mathcal{A}_i$, $i = 1, 2$, where $Q_M = \{Master, Crypto_i \mid i = 0, 1, 2\} \times \prod_{j=0}^{2} \{\bot, T\}$ is the state space of the Master and $Q_j$ is the state space of the $j^{th}$ cryptographer.

Define $\phi \colon Q_{\mathcal{A}_1} \to Q_{\mathcal{A}_2}$ by $\phi(Crypto_1) = Crypto_2$, $\phi(Crypto_2) = Crypto_1$, and $\phi$ is the identity on all other states. Next, define $\phi \colon \mathsf{Act}_1 \to \mathsf{Act}_2$ by $\phi(pay_1(c)) = pay_2(c)$, and $\phi(pay_2(c)) = pay_1(c)$. On all other actions, $\phi$ is the identity. We show $\phi \colon \mathcal{A}_1 \to \mathcal{A}_2$ is a Task-PIOA map satisfying the hypothesis of Theorem 1.

We begin by checking conditions (i) and (ii) of Definition 5. For (i), the crucial points are first, what happens to $pay_1(T)$, which is enabled in $\langle Crypto_1, \bot \rangle$. But $\phi(pay_1(T)) = pay_2(T)$, which is enabled in $\langle Crypto_2, \bot \rangle$ in $\mathcal{A}_2$. Likewise, $pay_2(F)$ is enabled in $\langle Crypto_1, \bot \rangle$ in $\mathcal{A}_1$, while $\phi(pay_2(F)) = pay_1(F)$, which is enabled in $\langle Crypto_2, \bot \rangle$ in $\mathcal{A}_2$. Next, we have that $\phi(\delta_{Crypto_1}) = \delta_{\phi(Crypto_1)}$, which is the output distribution of the action *choose_payer*; this follows because $\phi(Crypto_1) = Crypto_2$.

The second point is to check that $\phi(\delta_{\langle Crypto_1, T \rangle}) = \delta_{\langle \phi(Crypto_1), \phi(T) \rangle}$, but this holds because $\phi(Crypto_1) = Crypto_2$ and $\phi(T) = T$. Lastly, the fact that all coins are fair implies that $\mathsf{Disc}(\phi)(\langle \bot, \mathit{flip}_1, \frac{1}{2}\delta_H + \frac{1}{2}\delta_T \rangle) = \langle \bot, \mathit{flip}_2, \frac{1}{2}\delta_H + \frac{1}{2}\delta_T \rangle$, which is the only case in which $\mu_{q,a}$ is not a point mass; for point masses the result follows from the definition of $\phi$ and from $\mathsf{Disc}(\phi)(\delta_x) = \delta_{\phi(x)}$. This validates the remaining requirement in condition (i) of Definition 5.

Finally, $\mathcal{A}_1$ and $\mathcal{A}_2$ have the same tasks, and $\phi$ permutes the two actions listed and their corresponding enabling states, so $\phi(T)$ is a task and $\phi(A_T) = A_{\phi(T)}$ for each task $T$. Thus $\phi$ is a Task-PIOA map satisfying the hypothesis of Theorem 1, so $\mathsf{tdist}(\mathcal{A}_1) \subseteq \mathsf{tdist}(\mathcal{A}_2)$, but since $\phi$ is its own inverse, the reverse is also true.

**Corollary 2.** *The Dining Cryptographers is deterministically secure: i.e., in the case that one of the cryptographers is paying, a non-paying cryptographer cannot tell which one of the other cryptographers is paying.*

*Proof.* We first calculate the probability distributions on the announcements: For a non-paying cryptographer, the coins are fair, so the outcome of his own coin is $\frac{1}{2}\delta_H + \frac{1}{2}\delta_T$. The same is true of the coin he sees from his neighbor on the left, so the probability of announcing *Agree* is $\frac{1}{4}\delta_{HH} + \frac{1}{4}\delta_{TT}$, which is $\frac{1}{2}$. Obviously the probability of announcing *Disagree* is also $\frac{1}{2}$. The payer has just been shown to have the same probability distribution on announcements, so the probability is $\frac{1}{2}$*Agree* and $\frac{1}{2}$*Disagree* as well.

Now, a non-paying cryptographer sees the same distribution on the announcements of each of the other cryptographers regardless of which one is paying, so a non-paying cryptographer cannot tell which one is paying on the basis of the probability distributions on announcements they make.

### 8.2 The Probabilistic Case

In this section we consider the case of a probabilistic Master – i.e., one that chooses the payer probabilistically. This uses the rest of the definition of the

Master as given in Figure 1. Thus, the Master process begins with the probabilistic choice $\mathcal{M}_{pr} = r \cdot \delta_{master} + \sum_{i=0}^{2} r_i \delta c_i$ which denotes choosing the Master with probability $r$ and choosing cryptographer $i$ with probability $r_i$. We call this Master $\mathcal{M}_{pr}$, so our system now is

$$\mathcal{A}_{pr} := \mathcal{M}_{pr} \parallel C_0 \parallel C_1 \parallel C_2.$$

Even though the Master paying is one possibility, the notion of anonymity remains clear: *if* a cryptographer pays, then the identity of the payer should remain unknown to the other cryptographers. Indeed, anonymity is now a *conditional probability*: for a given sample space $X$ and probability measure $P$, the *conditional probability of $A$ given that $B$ has occurred* is $P(A|B) = \frac{P(A \cap B)}{P(B)}$, provided $P(B) \neq 0$.

The set $\mathcal{E}$ of observable events consists of possible sequences of announcements by the cryptographers. We denote the probability of a sequence $O \in \mathcal{E}$ under the probability measure induced by applying the task sequence $\rho$ to the process $\mathcal{A}_{pr}$ as $\mathsf{Apply}(\delta_{\overline{q}}^{\mathcal{A}_{pr}}, \rho)(O)$, and if $O$ is conditioned on the event $O'$, we denote the probability by $\mathsf{Apply}(\mathcal{A}_{pr}, \rho)(O|O')$.

**Theorem 2.** *If all cryptographers use unbiased coins, then the Dining Cryptographers is* probabilistically secure, *by which we mean* $(\forall \rho \in \mathcal{S})$ $(\forall O \in \mathcal{E})$

$$\mathsf{Apply}(\delta_{\overline{q}}^{\mathcal{A}_{pr}}, \rho)(O|\mathcal{M}_0) = \mathsf{Apply}(\delta_{\overline{q}}^{\mathcal{A}_{pr}}, \rho)(O|\mathcal{M}_1) = \mathsf{Apply}(\delta_{\overline{q}}^{\mathcal{A}_{pr}}, \rho)(O|\mathcal{M}_2).$$

*I.e., the probability distributions on announcements are the same whether the probabilistic Master chooses cryptographer 0, 1 or 2 as the payer.*

*Proof.* There are eight possible announcement sequences under any $\rho$. If the Master has chosen to pay, any of the four with an even number of *Disagree* announcements occurs, but if one of the cryptographers is paying, then one of the four with an odd number of *Disagree* announcements occurs. We divide $\mathcal{E}$ into the set $\mathcal{E}_E$ of sequences with an even number of *Disagree* announcements, and $\mathcal{E}_O$ of sequences with an odd number of *Disagree* announcements.

For any $\rho$, Corollary 1 implies $\mathsf{Apply}(\delta_{\overline{q}}^{\mathcal{A}_{pr}}, \rho) = r \cdot \mathsf{Apply}(\delta_{\overline{q}}^{\mathcal{A}_m}, \rho) + \sum_i r_i \cdot \mathsf{Apply}(\delta_{\overline{q}}^{\mathcal{A}_i}, \rho)$, where $\mathcal{A}_i$ is as in Equation 1 and $\mathcal{A}_m$ denotes the case of a deterministic Master choosing himself to pay. We assume $r \neq 0 \neq r_j$ for $j = 0, 1, 2$.

Proposition 2 shows the probability distributions $\mathsf{Apply}(\delta_{\overline{q}}^{\mathcal{A}_i}, \rho)$ all agree on the observable events, and Corollary 2 notes the probability that any of the cryptographers announces *Agree* is $\frac{1}{2}$, as is the probability that any of them announces *Disagree*; it's easy to show the same in case the Master is paying. Hence, for any sequence $O$ of announcements and each master $\mathcal{M}_j, j = 0, 1, 2$,

$$\begin{aligned}\mathsf{Apply}(\delta_{\overline{q}}^{\mathcal{A}_{pr}}, \rho)(O \cap \mathcal{M}_j) &= \mathsf{Apply}(\delta_{\overline{q}}^{\mathcal{A}_{pr}}, \rho)((O \in \mathcal{E}_E) \cap \mathcal{M}_j) \\ &\quad + \mathsf{Apply}(\delta_{\overline{q}}^{\mathcal{A}_{pr}}, \rho)((O \in \mathcal{E}_O) \cap \mathcal{M}_j).\end{aligned}$$

In case $O \in \mathcal{E}_E$, then the Master is paying, and the only event that can occur is $\mathcal{M}_m$, in which case the probability of any of the possible announcement sequences is $\frac{1}{4}$, since they are equally likely.

The other possibility is that a cryptographer is paying, i.e., $O \in \mathcal{E}_O$. Then

$$\begin{aligned}\mathsf{Apply}(\delta_{\overline{q}}^{\mathcal{A}_{pr}}, \rho)((O \in \mathcal{E}_O) \cap \mathcal{M}_j) &= \left(\sum_i r_i \mathsf{Apply}(\delta_{\overline{q}}^{\mathcal{A}_i}, \rho)\right)((O \in \mathcal{E}_O) \cap \mathcal{M}_j) \\ &= \sum_i r_i \mathsf{Apply}(\delta_{\overline{q}}^{\mathcal{A}_i}, \rho)((O \in \mathcal{E}_O) \cap \mathcal{M}_j) = \frac{r_j}{4}.\end{aligned}$$

Since $\mathsf{Apply}(\delta_{\overline{q}}^{\mathcal{A}_{pr}}, \rho)(\mathcal{M}_j) = r_j \neq 0$, we have $\mathsf{Apply}(\delta_{\overline{q}}^{\mathcal{A}_{pr}}, \rho)(O|\mathcal{M}_j) = 1/4$. This holds for each $j = 0, 1, 2$ for which $r_j \neq 0$. This proves that the paying cryptographer is unknown to the other two.

## 9 Summary and Future Work

We have presented an alternative derivation of the Task-PIOA framework of Canetti, et al. [6] based on order theory. The presentation focuses on two of the components needed for Task-PIOAs, discrete probability and probabilistic automata theory. Our main result is a proof that Task-PIOA maps preserve trace distributions on observable events. We applied our approach by analyzing the Dining Cryptographers Protocol. Our model has much more detail than traditional analyses of the protocol using concurrency, but the point has been to illustrate the use of the Task-PIOAs. Of particular note is the modularity of our proof that the protocol meets its security specification – the anonymity of a paying cryptographer from the other cryptographers. We first show this for the case of a deterministic Master, and then use this result to prove the result also holds in the case of a probabilistic Master.

We purposely have avoided the use of cryptographic primitives, and our presentation has been restricted to an example where these aspects are not needed. The addition of encryption would allow an interesting extension of the Dining Cryptographers. Namely, it would support adding a component process one might call *Anonymizer* that provides the service of making the paying cryptographer anonymous even to the Master, one of the original goals of the protocol [9]. This could be accomplished by having the Master's messages to the cryptographers first sent to the *Anonymizer*, which then reroutes the messages using a randomized permutation of the recipients.

We commented in Section 2 that the PIOA approach differs significantly from the approach utilizing labeled Markov processes, as in [10,16,19]. The difference concerns the transition relation $D \subseteq Q \times \mathsf{Act} \times \mathsf{Disc}(Q)$ that defines the evolution of processes. For labeled Markov processes, this relation (or the closely related $D \subseteq Q \times \mathsf{Disc}(\mathsf{Act} \times Q)$), assume $D$ generates a function $\Delta\colon Q \times \mathsf{Act} \to \mathsf{Disc}(Q)$ (resp., $\Delta\colon Q \to \mathsf{Disc}(\mathsf{Act} \times Q)$), but in the PIOA approach, $\Delta$ is a partial function (cf. comments following Definition 2). The usual method for transforming partial functions into total functions – adjoining a deadlock state and mapping elements of the domain where $\Delta$ is not defined to that deadlock state (or, more precisely, point mass at deadlock in the present situation) won't work for PIOAs, because of how the executions of PIOAs are defined (see the footnote to Equation 1).

In future work, we plan to apply our approach to other settings where they are appropriate. Among the areas being scrutinized is the Goldreich-Micali-Wigderson [13] secure multiparty computation protocol, where we also anticipate using the universal composability result for oblivious transfer from [6]. The GMW Protocol works by composing a number of simpler protocols, including oblivious transfer and communication mechanisms similar to those among the Dining Cryptographers. The work presented in this paper is thus the first step in that path.

## Acknowledgment

We wish to thank the referees for their helpful comments on the first draft of this paper.

## References


1. Abadi, M., Gordon, A.: A calculus for cryptographic protocols: The spi calculus. Information and Computation 148, 1–70 (1999)
2. Abramsky, S., Jung, A.: Domain theory. In: Abramsky, S., Gabbay, D.M., Maibaum, T.S.E. (eds.) Handbook of Logic in Computer Science, vol. 3, pp. 1–168. Clarendon Press, Oxford (1994)
3. de Alfaro, L., Henzinger, T., Jhala, R.: Compositional methods for probabilistic systems. In: Larsen, K.G., Nielsen, M. (eds.) CONCUR 2001. LNCS, vol. 2154, pp. 351–365. Springer, Heidelberg (2001)
4. Bhargava, M., Palamidessi, C.: Probabilistic anonymity. In: Abadi, M., de Alfaro, L. (eds.) CONCUR 2005. LNCS, vol. 3653, pp. 171–185. Springer, Heidelberg (2005)
5. Canetti, R.: Universally Composable Security: A New Paradigm for Cryptographic Protocols, `http://eprint.iacr.org/2000/067`
6. Canetti, R., Lynch, N., et al.: Using Probabilistic I/O Automata to Analyze an Oblivious Transfer Protocol (preprint), `http://hdl.handle.net/1721.1/33154`
7. Chatzikokolakis, K., Palamidessi, C.: Making Random Choices Invisible to the Scheduler. In: Caires, L., Vasconcelos, V.T. (eds.) CONCUR 2007. LNCS, vol. 4703, pp. 42–58. Springer, Heidelberg (2007)
8. Chatzikokalakis, K., Palamidessi, C., Panangaden, P.: Anonymity protocols as noisy channels. Information and Computation 206, 378–401 (2008)
9. Chaum, D.: The dining cryptographers problem: Unconditional sender and recipient untraceability. Journal of Cryptology 1, 65–75 (1988)
10. Desharnais, J., Gupta, V., Jagadeesan, R., Panangaden, P.: Approximating Labeled Markov Processes. Information and Computation 184(1), 160–200 (2003)
11. Garcia, F., van Rossum, P., Sokolova, A.: Probabilistic anonymity and admissible schedulers, June 2 (2007) arXiv:0706.1019, `http://eprintweb.org/S/authors/All/so/Sokolova`
12. Goldreich, O.: Secure Multi-party Computation, `http://www.wisdom.weizmann.ac.il/~oded/pp.html`
13. Goldreich, O., Micali, S., Wigderson, A.: Proofs that yield nothing but their validity, or All languages in NP have Zero-knowledge proofs. JACM 38, 691–729 (1991)

14. Hasuo, I., Kawabe, Y.: Probabilistic anonymity via coalgebraic simulations. In: De Nicola, R. (ed.) ESOP 2007. LNCS, vol. 4421, pp. 379–394. Springer, Heidelberg (2007)
15. Jones, C.: Probabilistic non-determinism. University of Edinburgh, Edinburgh (1992)
16. Larsen, K.G., Skou, A.: Bisimulation through Probabilistic Testing. Information and Computation 94(1), 1–28 (1991)
17. Lincoln, P., Mitchell, J.C., Mitchell, M., Scedrov, A.: A Probabilistic Poly-Time Framework for Protocol Analysis. In: ACM Conference on Computer and Communications Security, pp. 112–121 (1998)
18. Mislove, M.: Nondeterminism and probabilistic choice: obeying the laws. In: Palamidessi, C. (ed.) CONCUR 2000. LNCS, vol. 1877, pp. 350–364. Springer, Heidelberg (2000)
19. Mislove, M., Pavlovic, D., Worrell, J.: Labelled Markov Processes as Generalized Stochastic Relations. Electronic Notes Theoretical Computer Science 172, 459–478 (2007)
20. Mitchell, J., Ramanathan, A., Scedrov, A., Teague, V.: A probabilistic polynomial-time process calculus for the analysis of cryptographic protocols. Theoretical Computer Science 353, 118–164 (2006)
21. Schneider, S., Sidiropoulos, A.: CSP and anonymity. In: Martella, G., Kurth, H., Montolivo, E., Bertino, E. (eds.) ESORICS 1996. LNCS, vol. 1146, pp. 198–218. Springer, Heidelberg (1996), `http://dx.doi.org/10.1007/3-540-61770-1_38`
22. Segala, R.: Modeling and Verification of Randomized Distributed Real-time Systems, PhD Thesis, MIT Technical Report MIT/LCS/TR-676 (1995)
23. Segala, R., Lynch, N.: Probabilistic simulations for probabilistic processes. Nordic Journal of Computing 2, 250–273 (1995)

# A Appendix - Proofs

We present the proofs of selected results not proved in the body of the paper.

**Proposition 1.** Let $\mu = \sum_\alpha \mu(\alpha)\delta_\alpha \in \mathsf{Disc}(\mathsf{Frags}^*(\mathcal{A}))$, then

$$\mu \leq \mathsf{Apply}(\sum_\alpha \mu(\alpha)\delta_\alpha, \rho) = \sum_\alpha \mu(\alpha)\mathsf{Apply}(\delta_\alpha, \rho).$$

In particular, $\mathsf{Apply}(\mu, \rho)$ is well-defined for any task sequence $\rho = T_1 \cdots T_n$.

*Proof.* If $\rho = \lambda$ the empty sequence, then $\mathsf{Apply}(\mu, \rho) = \mu$, so the result is trivial, while if $\rho = T$ is a single task, then

$$\begin{aligned} \mathsf{Apply}(\mu, T) &= \sum_{\alpha \notin A_T} \mu(\alpha)\delta_\alpha + \sum_{\alpha \in A_T} \mu(\alpha) \left( \sum_s \mu_{\mathsf{lstate}(\alpha),a}(s)\delta_{\alpha a s} \right) \qquad (2) \\ &= \sum_{\alpha \notin A_T} \mu(\alpha)\mathsf{Apply}(\delta_\alpha, T) + \sum_{\alpha \in A_T} \mu(\alpha)\mathsf{Apply}(\delta_\alpha, T) \\ &= \sum_\alpha \mu(\alpha)\mathsf{Apply}(\delta_\alpha, T). \end{aligned}$$

The fact that $\mu \leq \mathsf{Apply}(\mu, T)$ is obvious from Equation 2.

Next, if $\rho = \rho' T$ is finite, then

$$\begin{aligned}\mathsf{Apply}(\mu,\rho) &= \mathsf{Apply}(\mathsf{Apply}(\mu,\rho'),T) = \mathsf{Apply}(\sum_\alpha \mu(\alpha)\mathsf{Apply}(\delta_\alpha,\rho'),T)\\ &= \sum_\alpha \mu(\alpha)\mathsf{Apply}(\mathsf{Apply}(\delta_\alpha,\rho'),T)\end{aligned}$$

Assuming by induction that $\mu \leq \mathsf{Apply}(\mu,\rho')$, then $\mu \leq \mathsf{Apply}(\mu,\rho)$ follows from the basis step.

**Theorem 1.** *Let $\phi\colon \mathcal{A}_1 \to \mathcal{A}_2$ be a Task PIOA map of task PIOAs satisfying $\phi(A_T) = A_{\phi(T)}$ for each task $T \in \mathcal{T}_1$. If $A \subseteq \mathsf{Act}_1$ is the set of observable actions, then $\mathsf{Disc}(\phi|^*_A))(\mathsf{tdist}(\mathcal{A})) \subseteq \mathsf{tdist}(\mathcal{A}_2)$.*

*Proof.* We first show that if $A_i \subseteq \mathsf{Act}_i, i = 1,2$ are the sets of *observable events* and if $\phi(A_1) \subseteq A_2$, then the following diagram commutes:

$$\begin{array}{ccccc}
\mathsf{Disc}(\mathsf{Exec}^*\mathcal{A}_1)\times\mathcal{T} & \xrightarrow{\mathsf{Apply}} & \mathsf{Disc}(\mathsf{Exec}^*\mathcal{A}_1) & \xrightarrow{\mathsf{Disc}(\mathsf{trace})} & \mathsf{Disc}(A_1^*)\\
\downarrow{\scriptstyle \mathsf{Disc}(\mathsf{Exec}^*\phi)\times\phi} & & \downarrow{\scriptstyle \mathsf{Disc}(\mathsf{Exec}^*\phi)} & & \downarrow{\scriptstyle \mathsf{Disc}(\phi|^*_{A_1})}\\
\mathsf{Disc}(\mathsf{Exec}^*\mathcal{A}_2)\times\mathcal{T} & \xrightarrow[\mathsf{Apply}]{} & \mathsf{Disc}(\mathsf{Exec}^*\mathcal{A}_2) & \xrightarrow[\mathsf{Disc}(\mathsf{trace})]{} & \mathsf{Disc}(A_2^*),
\end{array}$$

where $\phi^*\colon A_1^* \to A_2^*$ is given by $\phi^*(a_0\cdots a_n) = \phi(a_0)\cdots\phi(a_n)$. Indeed, the commutativity of the left square is a diagram chase, with one twist: we need $\phi(T) \in \mathcal{T}_2$ for each $T \in \mathcal{T}_1$: Indeed, if $\sum_i r_i\delta_{\alpha_i} \in \mathsf{Disc}(\mathsf{Exec}^*\mathcal{A}_1)$ and $T \in \mathcal{T}_1$, then

$$\begin{aligned}
&\mathsf{Disc}(\mathsf{Exec}^*\phi)(\mathsf{Apply}(\sum_i r_i\delta_{\alpha_i},T)) =\\
&= \mathsf{Disc}(\mathsf{Exec}^*\phi)\left(\sum_{\alpha_i\notin A_T} r_i\delta_{\alpha_i} + \sum_{\alpha_i\in A_T} r_i \sum_{q\in Q_1}\mu_{\mathsf{lstate}(\alpha_i),a_T}(q)\delta_{\alpha_i a_T q}\right)\\
&\stackrel{1}{=} \sum_{\alpha_i\notin A_T} r_i\delta_{\mathsf{Exec}^*\phi(\alpha_i)} + \sum_{\alpha_i\in A_T} r_i\sum_{q\in Q_1}\mu_{\mathsf{lstate}(\mathsf{Exec}^*\phi(\alpha_i)),\phi(a_T)}(\phi(q))\delta_{\mathsf{Exec}^*\phi(\alpha_i a_T q)}\\
&\stackrel{2}{=} \sum_{\mathsf{Exec}^*\phi(\alpha_i)\notin A_{\phi(T)}} r_i\delta_{\mathsf{Exec}^*\phi(\alpha_i)} +\\
&\qquad \sum_{\mathsf{Exec}^*\phi(\alpha_i)\in A_{\phi(T)}} r_i\sum_{\phi(q)\in Q_2}\mu_{\mathsf{lstate}(\mathsf{Exec}^*\phi(\alpha_i)),\phi(a_T)}(\phi(q))\delta_{\mathsf{Exec}^*\phi(\alpha_i a_T q)}\\
&= \mathsf{Apply}\left(\mathsf{Disc}(\mathsf{Exec}^*\phi)(\sum_i r_i\delta_{\alpha_i}),\phi(T)\right),
\end{aligned}$$

where $\stackrel{1}{=}$ follows from the definition of $\mathsf{Disc}(\mathsf{Exec}^*\phi)$, while $\stackrel{2}{=}$ follows from the assumptions (i) that $\phi(T) \in \mathcal{T}_2$ is a task in $\mathcal{A}_2$ and (ii) that $\phi(A_T) = A_{\phi(T)}$ (to preserve the first summand in each case), and from the calculation that $\mathsf{Exec}^*\phi(\mathsf{lstate}(\alpha_i)) = \mathsf{lstate}(\mathsf{Exec}^*\phi(\alpha_i))$. The right square is then a simple diagram chase.

Now the result follows: Let $\rho = T_1 \cdots T_n \in \mathcal{T}_1^*$ be a task schedule. Then for $\sum_i r_i\delta_{\alpha_i} \in \mathsf{Disc}(\mathsf{Exec}^*\mathcal{A}_1)$, we have

$$\mathsf{Disc}(\mathsf{Exec}^*\phi)(\mathsf{Apply}(\sum_i r_i\delta_{\alpha_i}, \rho)) = \mathsf{Disc}(\phi^*)(\mathsf{Apply}(\mathsf{Apply}(\sum_i r_i\delta_{\alpha_i}, T_1 \cdots T_{n-1}), T_n)))$$

$$= \mathsf{Apply}\left(\mathsf{Disc}(\mathsf{Exec}^*\phi)(\mathsf{Apply}(\sum_i r_i\delta_{\alpha_i}, T_1 \cdots T_{n-1})), \phi(T_n))\right)$$

by 2). It then follows by induction on $n$ that

$$\mathsf{Disc}(\mathsf{Exec}^*\phi)(\mathsf{Apply}(\sum_i r_i\delta_{\alpha_i}, \rho)) = \mathsf{Apply}\left(\mathsf{Disc}(\mathsf{Exec}^*\phi)(\sum_i r_i\delta_{\alpha_i}), \phi(T_1) \cdots \phi(T_n)\right).$$

Thus,

$$\mathsf{Disc}(\mathsf{trace}) \circ \mathsf{Disc}(\mathsf{Exec}^*\phi)(\mathsf{Apply}(\sum_i r_i\delta_{\alpha_i}, \rho)) =$$

$$\mathsf{Disc}(\mathsf{trace})\left(\mathsf{Apply}\left(\mathsf{Disc}(\mathsf{Exec}^*\phi)(\sum_i r_i\delta_{\alpha_i}), \phi(T_1) \cdots \phi(T_n)\right)\right).$$

But the left square in 2) implies

$$\mathsf{Disc}(\mathsf{trace}) \circ \mathsf{Disc}(\mathsf{Exec}^*\phi)(\mathsf{Apply}(\sum_i r_i\delta_{\alpha_i}, \rho)) = \mathsf{Disc}(\phi|_{A_1}^*)\left(\mathsf{Disc}(\mathsf{trace})(\mathsf{Apply}(\sum_i r_i\delta_{\alpha_i}, \rho))\right),$$

which implies the claim.

# Secrecy and Authenticity Types for Secure Distributed Messaging*

Michele Bugliesi, Stefano Calzavara, and Damiano Macedonio

Università Ca' Foscari Venezia, Dipartimento di Informatica
{michele,scalzava,mace}@dsi.unive.it

**Abstract.** We introduce a calculus with mobile names, distributed principals and primitives for secure remote communication, without any reference to explicit cryptography. The calculus is equipped with a system of types and effects providing static guarantees of secrecy and authenticity in the presence of a Dolev-Yao intruder. The novelty with respect to existing type systems for security is in the structure of our secrecy and authenticity types, which are inspired by the formulas of BAN Logic, and retain much of the simplicity and intuitive reading of such formulas. Drawing on these types, the type system makes it possible to characterize authenticity directly as a property of the data exchanged during a protocol rather than indirectly by extracting and interpreting the effects the protocol has on that data.

## 1 Introduction

Distributed protocols draw on cryptographic constructs to protect the secrecy and integrity of sensitive data against any potential attack. When designing distributed applications, however, it is often convenient to rely on more abstract, structured primitives for secure remote messaging and let a compiler automatically build defensive implementations on top of the underlying cryptographic infrastructure.

Following an increasingly popular approach in the specification of distributed systems, in [7,6] the first author and Focardi isolated a core set of security abstractions for programming distributed protocols, and showed them effective both for high-level protocol design and for security analysis in adversarial settings. In the present paper, we further investigate the effectiveness of that approach by developing a typed version of the abstractions.

We introduce a variant of the calculus in [6], that features mobile names, distributed principals and primitives for secure remote communication, without any reference to explicit cryptography. The calculus is equipped with a system of types and effects which disciplines the use of the messaging abstractions to provide static guarantees of strong secrecy and strong authenticity in the presence of a Dolev-Yao intruder. Strong secrecy is formalized in terms of behavioral

* Work partially supported by MIUR Projects SOFT "*Security Oriented Formal Techniques*" and IPODS "*Interacting Processes in Open-ended Distributed Systems*".

A. Armando and G. Lowe (Eds.): ARSPA-WITS 2010, LNCS 6186, pp. 23–40, 2010.

equivalence in the style of Abadi's seminal work [1]. Authenticity, in turn, is proved by establishing a form of injective agreement between statements and expectations in the style of [13].

The novelty with respect to existing security type systems is in the choice of our secrecy and authenticity types. Specifically, the type system makes it possible to characterize authenticity directly as a property of the data exchanged during a protocol rather than indirectly by extracting and interpreting the effects the protocol has on that data. Our types are inspired by the formulas of BAN Logic [8], and retain much of the simplicity and intuitive reading of such formulas; their use for type-checking similarly inherits the declarative style of BAN Logic's deductive system. The simple structure of the types, and the relative ease of type-checking also derive from the high-level nature of the underlying process calculus and its messaging primitives, that encapsulate and abstract away all cryptographic details. To illustrate, we may write a principal specification of the form[1]:

$$\mathsf{receive}\ (\mathsf{x} : \mathsf{From}(\mathsf{p}))\ \mathsf{on}\ \mathsf{a}.P$$

to mean that we expect a piece of data on channel $\mathsf{a}$ from principal $\mathsf{p}$, and be guaranteed statically that, in all protocol runs to which this principal participates, any piece of data received on $\mathsf{a}$ at this step does indeed come from $\mathsf{p}$.

In spite of their simplicity, the calculus and the type system are rather expressive and support a wide range of distributed protocol idioms. We exemplify the practical effectiveness of our approach by showing the type system at work on the security analysis of a variant of the 2KP e-payment protocol [5].

**Plan.** §2 presents the calculus, §3 the system of types and effects. §4 details the secrecy and authenticity properties enforced by the system. §5 presents the e-payment protocol case study, and §6 concludes the presentation. We omit proofs for lack of space (see [9] for details).

## 2 The Calculus

**Syntax.** We presuppose three countable sets of disjoint symbols, for principal identities $p, q, r$, (channel) names $a, b, c$ and variables $w, x, y, z$. We let $m, n$ range over all names and $u, v$ over names or variables when the distinctions are immaterial. Tuples are indicated by a tilde, as in $\tilde{n}, \tilde{x}, \tilde{v}$.

The calculus is a variant of the calculus from [7], where we structure the syntax in two layers, for networks and processes, and introduce the explicit network form $p[\![P]\!]$ to note the process $P$ running on behalf of the principal identity $p$.

$$\begin{array}{llll} \textit{Networks} & M, N, O ::= & p[\![P]\!] & \text{(Principal)} \\ & \mid & M|N & \text{(Parallel)} \\ & \mid & (\nu a : \tau)M & \text{(Restriction)} \\ & \mid & \mathbf{0} & \text{(Empty)} \end{array}$$

[1] The actual syntax of our calculus is different from the one used in this illustrative example.

| | | | |
|---|---|---|---|
| *Processes* | $P, Q, R$ ::= | $\overline{u}@v\langle\underline{*} : \tilde{u}\rangle^{\circ}$ | (Output) |
| | \| | $a(\underline{u} : \tilde{x})^{\circ}.P$ | (Input) |
| | \| | $0$ | (Inaction) |
| | \| | $P \mid Q$ | (Parallel) |
| | \| | $\text{test}(u = v)$ then $P$ else $Q$ | (Choice, test $\in$ {if,check}) |
| | \| | rec $X.P$ | (Recursion) |
| | \| | $X$ | (Recursion Var) |
| | \| | $(\nu a : \tau)P$ | (Restriction) |

The null, parallel composition, and recursive forms are just as in the pi-calculus. Conditionals are also like pi-calculus matching: for typing purposes, however, we use a special syntax to express the matching that corresponds to nonce-checks. The restriction operators (both for processes and networks) have the familiar pi-calculus syntax, but weaker scoping rules (see below); they are annotated with tagged types to be described in § 3. As to input/output, we have various messaging forms, depending on the instantiation of $\underline{*}$, $\underline{u}$ and $\circ$. The notation $\underline{*}$ stands for $*$ or '$-$' ($\underline{u}$ similarly abbreviates $u$ or '$-$'), where '$-$' can be interpreted as an *anonymous* identity; instead, $\circ$ is short for $\bullet$ or the empty string $\varepsilon$. The intuitive reading is as follows: $\overline{u}@v\langle\underline{*} : \tilde{u}\rangle^{\circ}$ denotes an output on channel $u$ directed to principal $v$ with payload $\tilde{u}$; the payload is certified as originating from the sender if $\underline{*}$ is $*$, and it is secret for the receiver $v$ if $\circ$ is $\bullet$. Dually, $a(\underline{u} : \tilde{x})^{\circ}.P$ denotes an input on $a$ from principal $\underline{u}$ of the payload $\tilde{x}$. As we detail below, input and output must agree on the secrecy and authenticity tags to synchronize. Note, finally, that the subject of an input must be a channel (not a variable): like in the *local* pi-calculus [18], we thus disallow the transmission of the input capability on any channel. The notions of free and bound names and variables arise as expected.

**Semantics.** We formalize the semantics of networks via a *labelled transition system*. Following [2] (and the MIM semantics of [6]) in our transition system two principals can never synchronize directly; rather, every interaction requires the mediation of the intruder, which intercepts each message exchanged and then delivers it to the recipient when the recipient is ready to consume it. To formalize the dynamics of message interception, we extend the syntax of networks with an additional, run-time process form to represent the copies of the messages stored (or cached) upon interception:

$$M, N ::= \ldots \text{as above} \ldots \mid \overline{c}@q\langle\underline{p} : \tilde{m} \| \tilde{n}\rangle_i^{\circ}$$

Each intercepted output is cached at a fresh index $i$ which is generated upon interception and remains available as a reference to the cached output. The cached output exhibits two views of the message content: the actual payload $\tilde{m}$, and the view of the payload $\tilde{n}$ as available to an external observer. As we discuss below, the two views differ when the intercepted output bears the secrecy tag $\circ = \bullet$.

**Table 1.** Labelled Transition System

(Input)
$$\frac{\sigma = \{\tilde{m}/\tilde{x}\}}{p[\![c(\underline{q} : \tilde{x})^\circ.P]\!] \xrightarrow{c@p(\underline{q}:\tilde{m})^\circ} p[\![P\sigma]\!]}$$

(Plain Output)
$$\frac{p \neq q, \quad \underline{p} = p \text{ iff } \underline{*} = *, \quad i \text{ fresh}}{p[\![\overline{c}@q\langle \underline{*} : \tilde{m}\rangle]\!] \xrightarrow{(i)\overline{c}@q\langle \underline{p}:\tilde{m}\rangle_i} \overline{c}@q\langle \underline{p} : \tilde{m} \| \tilde{m}\rangle_i}$$

(Secret Output)
$$\frac{p \neq q, \quad \underline{p} = p \text{ iff } \underline{*} = *, \quad |\tilde{n}| = |\tilde{m}|, \quad i, \tilde{n} \text{ fresh}}{p[\![\overline{c}@q\langle \underline{*} : \tilde{m}\rangle^\bullet]\!] \xrightarrow{(i,\tilde{n}:Public)\overline{c}@q\langle \underline{p}:\tilde{n}\rangle_i^\bullet} \overline{c}@q\langle \underline{p} : \tilde{m} \| \tilde{n}\rangle_i^\bullet}$$

(Open Process)
$$\frac{(\nu a : \tau)p[\![P]\!] \xrightarrow{\alpha} N}{p[\![(\nu a : \tau)P]\!] \xrightarrow{\alpha} N}$$

(Open Network)
$$\frac{N \xrightarrow{(i,\tilde{b}:\tilde{\tau})\overline{c}@q\langle \underline{p}:\tilde{m}\rangle_i^\circ} N', \ a \in \{\tilde{m}, c\} \setminus \{\tilde{b}, i\}}{(\nu a : \tau)N \xrightarrow{(i,\tilde{b}:\tilde{\tau},a:\tau)\overline{c}@q\langle \underline{p}:\tilde{m}\rangle_i^\circ} N'}$$

(Forward)
$$\frac{N \equiv (\nu\tilde{a} : \tilde{\tau})(\hat{N}|\overline{c}@q\langle p : \tilde{m} \| \tilde{n}\rangle_i^\circ), \quad \hat{N} \xrightarrow{c@q(p:\tilde{m})^\circ} N'}{N \xrightarrow{(i)} (\nu\tilde{a} : \tilde{\tau})N'}$$

(Replay)
$$\frac{N \equiv (\nu\tilde{a} : \tilde{\tau})(\hat{N}|\overline{c}@q\langle - : \tilde{m} \| \tilde{n}\rangle_i^\circ), \quad \hat{N} \xrightarrow{c@q(-:\tilde{m})^\circ} N'}{N \xrightarrow{(i)} (\nu\tilde{a} : \tilde{\tau})(N'|\overline{c}@q\langle - : \tilde{m} \| \tilde{n}\rangle_i^\circ)}$$

(Test True)
$$\frac{p[\![P]\!] \xrightarrow{\alpha} p[\![R]\!]}{p[\![\text{test } (m = m) \text{ then } P \text{ else } Q]\!] \xrightarrow{\alpha} p[\![R]\!]}$$

(Test False)
$$\frac{p[\![Q]\!] \xrightarrow{\alpha} p[\![R]\!], \quad m \neq n}{p[\![\text{test } (m = n) \text{ then } P \text{ else } Q]\!] \xrightarrow{\alpha} p[\![R]\!]}$$

(Recursion)
$$\frac{p[\![P\{\text{rec } X.P/X\}]\!] \xrightarrow{\alpha} p[\![P']\!]}{p[\![\text{rec } X.P]\!] \xrightarrow{\alpha} p[\![P']\!]}$$

(New)
$$\frac{N \xrightarrow{\alpha} N', \quad a \notin n(\alpha)}{(\nu a : \tau)N \xrightarrow{\alpha} (\nu a : \tau)N'}$$

(Parallel Process)
$$\frac{p[\![P]\!]|p[\![Q]\!] \xrightarrow{\alpha} N}{p[\![P|Q]\!] \xrightarrow{\alpha} N}$$

(Parallel Network)
$$\frac{M \xrightarrow{\alpha} M', \quad bn(\alpha) \cap fn(N) = \emptyset}{M|N, N|M \xrightarrow{\alpha} M'|N, N|M'}$$

The labelled transitions are collected in Table 1. We comment on the input/output and replay/forward rules, the remaining rules are standard. The (Input) rule allows a principal to input values from the network and proceed after propagating the bindings for the input variables to the continuation process. The (Output) rules formalize the interplay between output and interception. An output generates a label and caches a copy of the intercepted message at a fresh index. The label shows the view of the output available to an observer, while the cached copy holds both the internal and the external view of the payload. If the output is plain, the two views coincide; if it is secret, the external view is a tuple $\tilde{n}$ of fresh names: as discussed in [7], this corresponds to assume an implementation of a secret output in terms of randomized encryption. The (Open) rules implement the scope extrusion mechanisms: notice that channel names are always extruded in an output. All bound names (bar the intercept indexes) in the output labels come with associated type annotations: these bear no computational/observational meaning, and are only convenient when we formalize the properties of the type system. The (Replay) and (Forward) rules allow two principal to synchronize via the intruder by transmitting the cached outputs to their intended receivers. If the original output was certified, the cached copy gets consumed when used; non-certified outputs, instead, may be replayed back to an input-ready principal any number of times. It is worth noticing that private (restricted) names exchanged via a secret output are never exposed to an observer, unless of course the receiver leaks them. To see that, notice that the exchange arises as a result of a (Secret Output) transition, which does not expose the private names of its payload, followed by a (Replay)/(Forward) transition, which only exhibits the index of the intercepted message. The secret exchange of restricted names is still possible, and achieved in (Forward) and (Reply), relying on structural congruence for scope extrusion. The definition of structural congruence is standard, and omitted for brevity.

## 3 The Type System

**Types, effects and type environments.** The type system is built around types $(T, U, V)$ and effects $(E, F)$, both assigned to values and variables. The structure and intuitive reading of types is as follows:

- *Public*: values that are known or can be leaked publicly;
- $Secret(\tilde{u})$: values that must be kept secret among the principals in $\tilde{u}$;
- *Any*: values with unknown status, might be either *Public* or *Secret*;
- $Chan\langle\tilde{T};\tilde{U}\rangle$: channels with payload a tuple of type $\tilde{T},\tilde{U}$;
- *Prin*: principal identities.

When occurring in a type (and later in an effect), the notation $\tilde{u}$ indicates a set rather than a tuple. In a channel type $Chan\langle\tilde{T};\tilde{U}\rangle$, we assume that each $U \in \tilde{U}$ is a *Secret* type, while each $T \in \tilde{T}$ is a type other than *Secret*. *Secret* types allow us to define *groups of secrecy* (much in the spirit of the work in [10]) and these, in turn, will be instrumental in deriving authenticity judgements. *Any* plays the

**Table 2.** Types and environments formation

(Good Type)
$$\frac{\Gamma; \Delta \vdash \diamond, \quad \tau \ consistent, \quad fn(\tau) \cup fv(\tau) \subseteq dom(\Gamma) \cup dom(\Delta)}{\Gamma; \Delta \vdash \tau}$$

(Empty) $$\frac{}{\emptyset; \emptyset \vdash \diamond}$$

(Type) $$\frac{\Gamma; \Delta \vdash T, \quad u \notin dom(\Gamma)}{\Gamma, u : T; \Delta \vdash \diamond}$$

(Effect) $$\frac{\Gamma; \Delta \vdash \tilde{E}, \quad u \notin dom(\Delta)}{\Gamma; \Delta, u : \tilde{E} \vdash \diamond}$$

same role as in [1]: values with this type must be protected as secrets, but cannot be used as secrets, because they might in fact be public.

As to effects, their purpose is to encode time-dependent information about values: as such, unlike types, they are not invariant through reduction. Their syntax and intuitive reading is as follows:

- $From^p(\tilde{u})$: values received by $p$ coming from any of the principals $\tilde{u}$;
- $Fresh^p(\tilde{u})$: fresh values received by $p$ coming from any of the principals $\tilde{u}$;
- $With^p(\tilde{u})$: values received by $p$ in a message with payload $\tilde{u}$;
- $Nonce(p)$ and $Checked(p)$: nonces created/checked[2] by $p$.

The effects *From*, *Fresh* and *With* are only associated with variables (not names or identities), as they express properties that pertain to the transmission of a name (hence to the variable where the name gets received) rather than to the name itself. The effects *Nonce* and *Checked*, in turn, help to single out the steps of nonce verification.

A type $T$ and a set of effects $\tilde{E}$ can be composed to form what we call a *tagged type*, noted $T/\tilde{E}$. We let $\tau$ range over tagged types, and use $T$ and $T/\emptyset$ interchangeably, as we do for $\tilde{E}$ and $Any/\tilde{E}$. Also, we let $\tau.T$ and $\tau.E$ denote the type and effect components of a tagged type, respectively. Throughout, we assume that the effect sets in a tagged type are *consistent*, that is they do not contain more that one $Nonce$ and/or $Checked$ element. Further, we introduce the following notion of *generative* types, i.e., of types that may legally be associated with fresh names: $T/\tilde{E}$ is generative for a principal $p$ iff $T \in \{Public, Secret(\tilde{u}), Chan\langle \tilde{U}; \tilde{V}\rangle\}$ and $\tilde{E} \subseteq \{Nonce(p)\}$; $\tau$ is generative for a network $M$ iff $M \equiv (\nu \tilde{a} : \tilde{\tau})(p[\![P]\!] \mid M')$ and $\tau$ is generative for $p$.

The type system derives various forms of typing and subtyping judgements. The type environments for these judgements consist of two components, $\Gamma$ and $\Delta$, mapping names and variables to types and (sets of) effects, respectively. All environments occurring in a typing judgement must be well-formed, according to the rules in Table 2. We make the implicit assumption that the effects associated with a variable do not include $Nonce$ elements, and dually, that the effects given

[2] Although, strictly speaking, *Nonce* and *Checked* are not time-dependent, it is technically convenient to treat them as effects.

**Table 3.** Ordering on types and effects

(IdPublic)
$$\frac{}{\mathit{Prin} \le \mathit{Public}}$$

(ChanPublic)
$$\frac{}{\mathit{Chan}\langle \tilde{T}; \tilde{U}\rangle \le \mathit{Public}}$$

(FreshFrom)
$$\frac{}{\mathit{Fresh}^{p}(\tilde{v}) \le \mathit{From}^{p}(\tilde{v})}$$

(NonceChecked)
$$\frac{}{\mathit{Nonce}(p) \le \mathit{Checked}(p)}$$

(ContraWith)
$$\frac{\tilde{u} \subseteq \tilde{v}}{\mathit{With}^{p}(\tilde{v}) \le \mathit{With}^{p}(\tilde{u})}$$

(CoFresh)
$$\frac{\tilde{v} \subseteq \tilde{u}}{\mathit{Fresh}^{p}(\tilde{v}) \le \mathit{Fresh}^{p}(\tilde{u})}$$

(CoFrom)
$$\frac{\tilde{v} \subseteq \tilde{u}}{\mathit{From}^{p}(\tilde{v}) \le \mathit{From}^{p}(\tilde{u})}$$

(EffectSet)
$$\frac{\forall F \in \tilde{F}.\ \exists E \in \tilde{E}.\ E \le F}{\tilde{E} \le \tilde{F}}$$

to names only include *Nonce* and *Checked* elements. We use the notation $\tilde{v} : \tilde{\tau}$ for $v_1 : \tau_1, \ldots, v_n : \tau_n$ and $\tilde{v} : \tau$ for $v_1 : \tau, \ldots, v_n : \tau$. In addition, we introduce the following notation to single out various components of a type environment:

$$\mathit{Nonces}(\Gamma; \Delta) = \{n \mid \Gamma; \Delta \vdash n : \mathit{Nonce}(p)\}$$
$$\mathit{Secrets}(\Gamma; \Delta) = \{a \mid \Gamma; \Delta \vdash a : \mathit{Secret}(\tilde{u})\}.$$

**Ordering on types and effects.** Types and effects are organized in the pre-order relation defined by the rules in Table 3. Rules (IdPublic) and (ChanPublic) imply that trusted identities are public, and so are channel names, which indeed are always leaked upon output. Rule (FreshFrom) states that $\mathit{Fresh}^{p}(\tilde{v})$ has stronger authenticity guarantees than $\mathit{From}^{p}(\tilde{v})$. Rule (NonceChecked) states that a new nonce can safely be promoted to the status "checked": this is sound, as in our our system the effect *Nonce* may only be assigned to names, not to variables. The pre-order on effects is lifted to sets of effects using the standard *upper* powerset (or *Egli-Milner*) construction: the resulting relation is still a pre-order with set union as (total) meet operator. The remaining rules in the table are self-explanatory. In addition, we define *Any* as the top element of the pre-order (on types) and stipulate that $T/\tilde{E} \le T'/\tilde{E}'$ iff $T \le T'$ and $\tilde{E} \le \tilde{E}'$. Finally, we let $\tau = \tau'$ if and only if $\tau \le \tau'$ and $\tau' \le \tau$.

**Typing of values.** The typing rules for values are collected in Table 4. The (Domain) and (Subsumption) rules are standard, and (Tag) is self-explanatory. The two correlation rules are inspired by BAN Logic [8]: (Correlation Fresh) states that if $y$ is a nonce checked by $p$, then any name received by $p$ with $y$ must be fresh; (Correlation From) states that if $y$ is a shared secret between $p$ and $\tilde{u}$, then any name received by $p$ with $y$ must come from a principal in $\tilde{u}$. The (Combine) rule is used to gather the information inferred by the correlation rules.

**Table 4.** Typing of values

| | |
|---|---|
| (Domain) $\dfrac{\Gamma;\Delta \vdash \diamond, \quad \Gamma(u) = \tau \vee \Delta(u) = \tau}{\Gamma;\Delta \vdash u : \tau}$ | (Subsumption) $\dfrac{\Gamma;\Delta \vdash u : \tau, \quad \tau \leq \tau', \quad \Gamma;\Delta \vdash \tau'}{\Gamma;\Delta \vdash u : \tau'}$ |
| (Tag) $\dfrac{\Gamma;\emptyset \vdash u : T, \quad \emptyset;\Delta \vdash u : \tilde{E}}{\Gamma;\Delta \vdash u : T/\tilde{E}}$ | (Correlation Fresh) $\dfrac{\Gamma;\Delta \vdash y : \mathit{Checked}(p), \quad \Gamma;\Delta \vdash x : \mathit{With}^p(y)}{\Gamma;\Delta \vdash x : \mathit{Fresh}^p}$ |
| (Combine) $\dfrac{\Gamma;\Delta \vdash x : \mathit{Fresh}^p, \quad \Gamma;\Delta \vdash x : \mathit{From}^p(\tilde{u})}{\Gamma;\Delta \vdash x : \mathit{Fresh}^p(\tilde{u})}$ | (Correlation From) $\dfrac{\Gamma;\Delta \vdash y : \mathit{Secret}(p,\tilde{u}), \quad \Gamma;\Delta \vdash x : \mathit{With}^p(y)}{\Gamma;\Delta \vdash x : \mathit{From}^p(\tilde{u})}$ |

**Typing of processes.** Processes are always type-checked with respect to a principal identity. The typing judgement for processes has the form $\Gamma;\Delta \vdash_p P$, where $p$ is intended to be the identity of the principal running $P$. We start illustrating the typing of processes with the rules for input/output in Table 5.

Rule (Public Output) governs the communication of public values, which is legal provided that the type of the payload is consistent with the type expected by the channel. Note that the output can be either plain or secret. The (Secret Output) rule requires both the sender and the receiver to be part of the secrecy group declared for each secret included in the message.

As for input, in all rules the continuation process is type-checked against an environment that stores the interdependence of each input variable with all the remaining components of the message received. If the sender is unknown, the payload type declared by the channel is ignored, as the message may come from the intruder. In absence of adequate guarantees about the sender, the input variables associated to public positions can be safely treated as public, while those associated to secret positions must be given type $\mathit{Any}$ (as they might be secret, if the sender is well-typed, or anything when the sender is untyped). On the other hand, if the sender of a message is a known principal, the receiver can trust the payload type of the channel.

The last two rules in Table 5 involve the conditional forms. Following [15], the (If) rule exploits the equality between $u$ and $v$ to refine the types of the two values in the typing for the *then* branch. The notation $\Gamma \sqcap u : V$ indicates the environment $\Gamma, u : V$ if $u \notin \mathit{dom}(\Gamma)$, otherwise the environment $\Gamma \setminus \{u : U\}, u : U \sqcap V$, where $\sqcap$ is the partial meet operator on types. Notice that we only refine the types of $u$ and $v$ and not their effects, as refining the effects would be unsound. To illustrate, given the assumption $u : \mathit{From}^p(q)$, associating the same effect to $v$ would be unsound, as $v$ might come from another principal $r$, even though $u = v$. The (Check) rule implements a nonce verification mechanism, and involves two operations on the effect environment $\Delta$: $\Delta \sqcap u : \tilde{E}$ is defined similarly to $\Gamma \sqcap u : U$, whereas $\Delta[n : \tilde{E}]$ changes the current association of $n$ to $\tilde{E}$. The

**Table 5.** Typing of processes: input/output and conditionals

(Public Output)

$$\frac{\Gamma; \Delta \vdash u : Chan\langle \tilde{T}; \emptyset \rangle, \quad \Gamma; \Delta \vdash \tilde{u} : \tilde{T}, \quad \Gamma; \Delta \vdash v : Prin}{\Gamma; \Delta \vdash_p \overline{u}@v\langle \underline{*} : \tilde{u} \rangle^{\circ}}$$

(Secret Output)

$$\frac{\begin{array}{ll}\Gamma; \Delta \vdash u : Chan\langle \tilde{T}; \tilde{U} \rangle, & \forall i\, (U_i = Secret(\tilde{v}_i) \wedge p, v \in \tilde{v}_i), \\ \Gamma; \Delta \vdash \tilde{u} : (\tilde{T}, \tilde{U}), & \Gamma; \Delta \vdash v : Prin\end{array}}{\Gamma; \Delta \vdash_p \overline{u}@v\langle \underline{*} : \tilde{u} \rangle^{\bullet}}$$

(Non-certified Input)

$$\frac{\begin{array}{l}\Gamma; \Delta \vdash a : Chan\langle \tilde{T}; \tilde{U} \rangle, \quad |\tilde{x}| = |\tilde{T}| \wedge |\tilde{y}| = |\tilde{U}|, \\ \Gamma, \tilde{x} : Public, \tilde{y} : Any; \Delta, \tilde{x} : With^{p}(\tilde{x}, \tilde{y}), \tilde{y} : With^{p}(\tilde{x}, \tilde{y}) \vdash_p P\end{array}}{\Gamma; \Delta \vdash_p a(- : \tilde{x}, \tilde{y})^{\circ}.P}$$

(Trusted Input)

$$\frac{\begin{array}{l}\Gamma; \Delta \vdash a : Chan\langle \tilde{T}; \tilde{U} \rangle, \quad \Gamma; \Delta \vdash u : Prin, \quad |\tilde{x}| = |\tilde{T}| \wedge |\tilde{y}| = |\tilde{U}|, \\ \Gamma, \tilde{x} : \tilde{T}, \tilde{y} : \tilde{U};\ \Delta, \tilde{x} : \{Fresh^{p}(u), With^{p}(\tilde{x}, \tilde{y})\}, \tilde{y} : \{Fresh^{p}(u), With^{p}(\tilde{x}, \tilde{y})\} \vdash_p P\end{array}}{\Gamma; \Delta \vdash_p a(u : \tilde{x}, \tilde{y})^{\circ}.P}$$

(If)

$$\frac{\Gamma; \emptyset \vdash u : U, \quad \Gamma; \emptyset \vdash v : V, \quad \Gamma \sqcap u : V \sqcap v : U; \Delta \vdash_p P, \quad \Gamma; \Delta \vdash_p Q}{\Gamma; \Delta \vdash_p \text{if } (u = v) \text{ then } P \text{ else } Q}$$

(Check)

$$\frac{\begin{array}{l}\Delta(n) = Nonce(p), \quad \Gamma; \emptyset \vdash u : U, \quad \Gamma; \emptyset \vdash n : V, \\ \Gamma \sqcap u : V \sqcap n : U; (\Delta \sqcap u : Checked(p))[n : Checked(p)] \vdash_p P \qquad \Gamma; \Delta \vdash_p Q\end{array}}{\Gamma; \Delta \vdash_p \text{check } (u = n) \text{ then } P \text{ else } Q}$$

intuition underlying nonce verification is the following: consider the process $c(- : x, y).check\ (x = n)\ then\ P\ else\ Q$, run by the principal $p$, where $n$ has the effect $Nonce(p)$. Then, the continuation $P$ is type-checked in an environment where $n$'s effect is consumed, and turned to $Checked(p)$, and $x$ is deemed $Checked(p)$. Now, since $y : With(x, y)$, we can infer $y : Fresh^{p}$.

The remaining rules for processes and networks are reported in Table 6. The (Parallel) rule splits the $\Delta$ part of the environment between the parallel processes $P$ and $Q$ to avoid that the same nonce is checked by both $P$ and $Q$; the disjoint union $\Delta_1 \uplus \Delta_2$ indicates the environment $\Delta_1 \sqcap \Delta_2$ in case $Nonces(\Delta_1) \cap Nonces(\Delta_2) = \emptyset$, and is undefined otherwise. The condition $Nonce(\Gamma; \Delta) = \emptyset$ in (Recursion) similarly ensures that a nonce is never checked more than once: it is necessary since the body of a recursive process can be

**Table 6.** Other typing rules of processes and networks

(New)
$$\frac{\Gamma, a : T; \Delta' \vdash_p P, \quad T/\tilde{E} \textit{ generative for } p, \quad [\Delta' \triangleq \textit{if } \tilde{E} \neq \emptyset \textit{ then } (\Delta, a : \tilde{E}) \textit{ else } \Delta]}{\Gamma; \Delta \vdash_p (\nu a : T/\tilde{E})P}$$

(Parallel)
$$\frac{\Gamma; \Delta_1 \vdash_p P, \quad \Gamma; \Delta_2 \vdash_p Q}{\Gamma; \Delta_1 \uplus \Delta_2 \vdash_p P|Q}$$

(Recursion)
$$\frac{\mathit{Nonces}(\Gamma; \Delta) = \emptyset, \quad \Gamma, X : \mathit{Proc}; \Delta \vdash_p P}{\Gamma; \Delta \vdash_p \text{rec } X.P}$$

(Principal)
$$\frac{\Gamma; \Delta \vdash_p P}{\Gamma; \Delta \vdash p[\![P]\!]}$$

(Cache)
$$\frac{\Gamma; \Delta \vdash \diamond}{\Gamma; \Delta \vdash \bar{c}@q\langle \underline{p} : \tilde{m} \| \tilde{n} \rangle_i^\circ}$$

(Network Parallel)
$$\frac{\Gamma; \Delta_1 \vdash M, \quad \Gamma; \Delta_2 \vdash N}{\Gamma; \Delta_1 \uplus \Delta_2 \vdash M|N}$$

(Zero)
$$\frac{\Gamma; \Delta \vdash \diamond}{\Gamma; \Delta \vdash_p 0}$$

(Proc)
$$\frac{\Gamma; \Delta \vdash X : \mathit{Proc}}{\Gamma; \Delta \vdash_p X}$$

(Network Zero)
$$\frac{\Gamma; \Delta \vdash \diamond}{\Gamma; \Delta \vdash \mathbf{0}}$$

(Network New)
$$\frac{\Gamma, a : T; \Delta' \vdash M, \quad T/\tilde{E} \textit{ generative for } M, \quad [\Delta' \triangleq \textit{if } \tilde{E} \neq \emptyset \textit{ then } (\Delta, a : \tilde{E}) \textit{ else } \Delta]}{\Gamma; \Delta \vdash (\nu a : T/\tilde{E})M}$$

instantiated multiple times, but it is type-checked only once [17]. In the (New) rules we restrict the possible types for new names to generative tagged types to control the way new names are introduced at run-time. The remaining rules are fairly standard.

## 4 Properties of the Type System

We start our analysis of the type system properties with subject reduction.

### 4.1 Subject Reduction

This is a standard result, but its formulation in our type system is more elaborate than usual, due to the structure of our types and effects and our LTS characterization of the operational semantics.

**Substitution.** As we already said, types are preserved during computation, while effects are not. In particular, the authenticity effects *From*, *Fresh* and *With* associated with an input variable are not preserved by the substitution of that variable with the name received.

This is reflected in the following formulation of the substitution lemma, which as usual is crucial in the proof of subject reduction. Given a set of effects $\tilde{E}$, let $|\tilde{E}|$ denote the *effect-erasure* of $E$, that is the subset of $E$ resulting from erasing all occurrences of the effects *From*, *Fresh* and *With* from $\tilde{E}$.

**Lemma 1 (Substitution)**

*(i)* *If* $\Gamma, x : T \sqcap \Gamma'; \Delta, x : \tilde{E} \sqcap \Delta' \vdash u : U/\tilde{F}$ *and* $\Gamma; \Delta \vdash n : T/|\tilde{E}|$, *then* $\Gamma \sqcap \Gamma'\{n/x\}; \Delta \sqcap \Delta'\{n/x\} \vdash u\{n/x\} : (U/|\tilde{F}|)\{n/x\}$;
*(ii)* *If* $\Gamma, x : T \sqcap \Gamma'; \Delta, x : \tilde{E} \sqcap \Delta' \vdash_p P$ *and* $\Gamma; \Delta \vdash n : T/|\tilde{E}|$, *then* $\Gamma \sqcap \Gamma'\{n/x\}; \Delta \sqcap \Delta'\{n/x\} \vdash_p P\{n/x\}$.

Based on this result, we may show that typing is preserved by each of the transitions in our LTS. Since some of the transitions may introduce fresh names, typing the derivative of a transition requires a new type environment that depends on the transition itself. We use the notation $(\Gamma; \Delta)$ *after* $\alpha$ to refer to such environments. Given a judgement $\Gamma; \Delta \vdash M$ and a transition $M \xrightarrow{\alpha} M'$, the environment $(\Gamma; \Delta)$ *after* $\alpha$ has a straightforward, but lengthy definition[3] (cf. Appendix A). To illustrate, assume $\Gamma; \Delta \vdash M$ and consider a transition $M \xrightarrow{c@p(-:\tilde{m},\tilde{n})} M'$, with $\Gamma; \Delta \vdash c : Chan\langle\tilde{T}; \tilde{U}\rangle$, and $|\tilde{m}| = |\tilde{T}|$, $|\tilde{n}| = |\tilde{U}|$. Then $(\Gamma; \Delta)$ *after* $\alpha$ is the environment $\Gamma \sqcap \tilde{m} : Public \sqcap \tilde{n} : Any; \Delta$, which refines the information on the types of the names $\tilde{m}$ and $\tilde{n}$ received.

**Admissible transitions.** A final technical subtlety is that the construction of the type environment $(\Gamma; \Delta)$ *after* $\alpha$ may fail (and the resulting environment be undefined). This may happen, for instance, after the input transition discussed above, as the meet operation involved in the construction of $(\Gamma; \Delta)$ *after* $\alpha$ fails if the names $\tilde{m}$ transmitted on $c$ are already known to the environment at a *Secret* type (*Secret* $\sqcap$ *Public* is undefined). We rule out such transitions as *non-admissible*, in the following sense.

**Definition 2 (Admissible Transition).** *We say that a transition* $M \xrightarrow{\alpha} M'$ *is admissible for* $\Gamma; \Delta$, *written* $\Gamma; \Delta \vdash \alpha$, *if, whenever* $\alpha = c@q(\underline{p} : \tilde{m}, \tilde{n})$ *with* $\Gamma; \Delta \vdash c : Chan\langle\tilde{T}; \tilde{U}\rangle$ *and* $|\tilde{m}| = |\tilde{T}|$, $|\tilde{n}| = |\tilde{U}|$, *one has* $\tilde{m} \sqcap Secrets(\Gamma; \Delta) = \emptyset$ *and* $\underline{p} = -$.

If $M \xrightarrow{\alpha} M'$ is admissible for $(\Gamma; \Delta)$, it is easy to show that $(\Gamma; \Delta)$ *after* $\alpha$ is always defined, as the definition rules out the transitions that would pass secrets for the non-secrets positions of an input prefix.

**Theorem 3 (Subject Reduction).** *Assume* $\Gamma; \Delta \vdash M$, *and let* $M \xrightarrow{\alpha} M'$ *be admissible for* $\Gamma; \Delta$. *Then* $(\Gamma; \Delta)$ *after* $\alpha \vdash M'$.

[3] The notation is loose here, as indeed the definition needs to consider the reduction step $M \xrightarrow{\alpha} M'$ and not just the transition label $\alpha$: hence, strictly speaking, we should rather say $(\Gamma; \Delta)$ *after* $\alpha$ *in* $M \xrightarrow{\alpha} M'$.

It is important to remark that the restriction to admissible transitions does not involve any loss of expressive power for the attacker. Notice to this regard that well-typed principals only have admissible transitions and, by Proposition 5 below, we know that they never leak their secrets. Hence, restricting to admissible transitions only amounts to assume that the attacker cannot impersonate any trusted principal, and does not know the initial secrets shared by the principals. This is a sound initial assumption for any network and, by Theorem 3, it is a property that is preserved by well-typed networks (there is no circularity here, as the proof of Proposition 5 does not rely on Theorem 3).

### 4.2 Secrecy

We first show that well-typed networks do not leak their secrets. Following [10], we first define what it means to leak an unrestricted secret.

**Definition 4 (Revelation).** *Let $N \equiv N' \mid p[\![\overline{c}@q\langle \underline{p} : \tilde{m}\rangle^{\circ} \mid P]\!]$ and take $(\Gamma;\Delta)$ and $s$ such that $\Gamma;\Delta \vdash N$ and $\Gamma;\Delta \vdash s : Secret(\tilde{r})$. We say that $N$ reveals $s$ iff $s = c$, or $s \in \tilde{m}$ and either $q \notin \tilde{r}$ or $\circ \neq \bullet$. We say that $N$ reveals a secret of $(\Gamma;\Delta)$ if $N$ reveals $s$ for some $s \in Secrets(\Gamma;\Delta)$.*

The definition readily extends to the general case when a secret may be restricted. Let $\Gamma;\Delta \vdash N$ with $N \equiv (\nu\tilde{a} : \tilde{\tau})N'$. $N$ leaks a secret iff $N'$ reveals a secret of $\Gamma, \tilde{a} : \tilde{\tau}.T; \Delta, \tilde{a} : \tilde{\tau}.E$. In other words, a network leaks a secret whenever it either outputs it in clear, or sends it to a principal outside the secrecy group, or uses it as a channel (the name of a channel is always leaked upon output).

**Proposition 5 (Group Secrecy).** *Assume $\Gamma;\Delta \vdash M$. Then $M$ does not leak any secret.*

The proof of this proposition follows directly by an inspection of the typing rules. By Theorem 3, we then know that well-typed networks do not leak their secrets at any step of computation. Indeed, as we show next, the type system provides stronger secrecy guarantees, in that it prevents any (possibly) implicit or indirect flow of secret information. As in [1] we formalize strong secrecy in terms of behavioral equivalence, which in turn we define based on the bisimilarity relation that results from our LTS semantics. Given a transition $M \xrightarrow{\alpha} M'$ we let $\hat{\alpha}$ denote $\alpha$ with the type annotations stripped away. Again, we restrict to admissible transitions, with respect to the secrecy assumptions provided by a typing environment.

**Definition 6 (Bisimilarity).** *A symmetric relation $\mathscr{R}$ between networks is a $(\Gamma;\Delta)$-bisimulation if whenever $M \mathscr{R} N$ and $M \xrightarrow{\alpha} M'$ with $\Gamma;\Delta \vdash \alpha$, there exists $N'$ such that $N \xrightarrow{\alpha'} N'$ with $\Gamma;\Delta \vdash \alpha'$, $\hat{\alpha} = \hat{\alpha}'$ and $M' \mathscr{R} N'$. $(\Gamma;\Delta)$-bisimilarity, noted $\sim_{(\Gamma;\Delta)}$, is the largest $(\Gamma;\Delta)$-bisimulation.*

**Theorem 7 (Strong Secrecy).** *Let $\Gamma;\Delta \vdash N$. Then $N \sim_{(\Gamma;\Delta)} N\sigma$ for all injective substitutions $\sigma$ of the names in $Secrets(\Gamma;\Delta)$.*

Notice the technical difference from the original characterization in [1]: in that case secrecy is characterized as the inability to tell networks apart based on the names of type $Any$ they exchange. Our present formulation is directly based on secret names, instead.

### 4.3 Authenticity

As anticipated at the outset, we formalize authenticity by establishing a form of injective agreement between statements and expectations in the style of [13]. We start by introducing a new construct to express the authenticity expectations about an input variable. The syntax of processes is extended as follows, where $E \in \{From^p(\tilde{u}), Fresh^p(\tilde{u})\}$.

$$P, Q, R \ ::= \ \ldots \text{as in §2} \ldots \mid \text{expect}\langle x : E\rangle.P$$

The expect$\langle\cdot\rangle$ prefix is not a binder, hence the variable $x$ in expect$\langle x : E\rangle.P$ must be bound by an enclosing input prefix. The prefix form expect$\langle x : E\rangle.P$ is well-typed in a given type environment if the effect expected for $x$ is consistent with the effects associated with $x$ in the given environment (and the continuation $P$ is well-typed). When $x$ gets substituted by a name, as in expect$\langle m : E\rangle.P$, the prefix is disregarded (as names are never bound to authenticity effects).

**Table 7.** Typing rules for expect$\langle\cdot\rangle$

$$\frac{\Gamma;\Delta \vdash x : E, \quad \Gamma;\Delta \vdash_p P}{\Gamma;\Delta \vdash_p \text{expect}\langle x : E\rangle.P} \qquad \frac{\Gamma;\Delta \vdash_p P}{\Gamma;\Delta \vdash_p \text{expect}\langle m : E\rangle.P}$$

At run-time, expectations play the role of assertions that express the authenticity properties of a message exchange: specifically, the intention is to check that, in any run of a process, each expectation, say expect$\langle m : E\rangle$, can be associated with a previous output of $m$ that validates the authenticity property on the exchange of $m$ as expressed by the effect $E$. In particular, an expectation of an authentic message from $p$ may not only be justified by a certified output from $p$ (as one would certainly expect), but also by an anonymous output that includes in its payload a shared secret between the receiver and $p$, since secrets are not leaked in well-typed networks. Similarly, an expectation of a fresh, authentic message additionally requires the presence of a nonce in case the justifying output is anonymous, since we are interested in preventing replay attacks.

To formalize the justification mechanisms we just illustrated, we annotate run-time network configurations so as to connect each expect$\langle\cdot\rangle$ statement with the input prefix that binds the variable predicated by the statement. Since the run-time input transitions of a network are triggered by corresponding (Replay/Forward) transitions, we create the desired association by annotating the expect prefix with the index $i$ of the $(i)$ transition induced by the input that binds the variable predicated by the prefix. Note that, in doing so, we actually link by the index $i$ each received value predicated by an expect with a previous output containing that value, as desired.

We formalize all this by introducing an indexed version of the LTS from §2, which we derive by modifying the (Input), (Replay) and (Forward) rules in Table 1 as in Table 8, and introducing a new rule for the expect prefix.

**Table 8.** Indexed LTS

(Input)

$$\frac{\sigma = \{\tilde{m}/\tilde{x}\}}{p[\![c(\underline{q} : \tilde{x})^{\circ}.P]\!] \xrightarrow{c@p(\underline{q}:\tilde{m})^{\circ}_{i}} p[\![idx(P, i, \tilde{x})\sigma]\!]}$$

(Expect)

$$\frac{}{p[\![\text{expect}^{(i)}\langle m : E\rangle.P]\!] \xrightarrow{(i)p\ expects\langle m:E\rangle} p[\![P]\!]}$$

(Forward)

$$\frac{N \equiv (\nu\tilde{a} : \tilde{\tau})(\hat{N}|\bar{c}@q\langle p : \tilde{m}\|\tilde{n}\rangle^{\circ}_{i}),\ \ \hat{N} \xrightarrow{c@q(p:\tilde{m})^{\circ}_{i}} N'}{N \xrightarrow{(i)} (\nu\tilde{a} : \tilde{\tau})N'}$$

(Replay)

$$\frac{N \equiv (\nu\tilde{a} : \tilde{\tau})(\hat{N}|\bar{c}@q\langle - : \tilde{m}\|\tilde{n}\rangle^{\circ}_{i}),\ \ \hat{N} \xrightarrow{c@q(-:\tilde{m})^{\circ}_{i}} N'}{N \xrightarrow{(i)} (\nu\tilde{a} : \tilde{\tau})(N'|\bar{c}@q\langle - : \tilde{m}\|\tilde{n}\rangle^{\circ}_{i})}$$

The input label in the premise of the (Replay) and (Forward) rules now conveys the index $i$ of the induced replay/forward transition, while the (Input) rule states that, before applying the substitution $\sigma$, every expect$\langle\cdot\rangle$ in the continuation, whose variable will become instantiated, must be indexed with $i$. The goal is achieved via a function $idx$, defined by structural induction on processes (cf. Appendix A). The indexed occurrences of expect$\langle\cdot\rangle$ type-check just as the unindexed occurrences (cf. Table 7).

We formalize the intended correspondence between expectations and output messages by means of the following, somewhat elaborate definition.

**Definition 8 (Justified Expectation).** *Given a type environment $(\Gamma; \Delta)$, consider the sequence of reductions $N_0 \xrightarrow{\alpha_0} N_1 \xrightarrow{\alpha_1} \cdots \xrightarrow{\alpha_{m-1}} N_m$. Let then $(\Gamma_k; \Delta_k)$ be the environment $(\Gamma; \Delta)$ after $\alpha_0, \ldots, \alpha_{k-1}$ for each $k \in [1..m]$, where $\alpha_k$ is admissible for $\Gamma_k; \Delta_k$, and let $\alpha_j = (i)p\ expects\langle m : E\rangle$. We say that $\alpha_j$ is justified by $\alpha_h$ $(h < j)$ if $\alpha_h = (i, \tilde{b} : \tilde{\tau})\bar{c}@p\langle \underline{q} : \tilde{m}\rangle^{\circ}_{i}$ and either of the following conditions holds:*

- *if $E = From^{p}(\tilde{q})$, then either $\underline{q} \in \tilde{q}$ or $N_{h+1} \equiv (\nu\tilde{a} : \tilde{\tau})(N' \mid \bar{c}@p\langle \underline{q} : \tilde{m}\|\tilde{n}\rangle^{\circ}_{i})$ and there exists $s \in \tilde{m}$ such that $\Gamma_h, \tilde{a} : \tilde{\tau}.T; \Delta_h, \tilde{a} : \tilde{\tau}.E \vdash s : Secret(p, \tilde{r})$ with $\tilde{r} \subseteq \tilde{q}$;*

– *if* $E = Fresh^p(\tilde{q})$, *the conditions of the previous item hold and, when* $\underline{q} = -$, *we additionally require that* $\Gamma_h, \tilde{a} : \tilde{\tau}.T; \Delta_h, \tilde{a} : \tilde{\tau}.E \vdash n : Nonce(p)$ *for some* $n \in \tilde{m}$.

This notion of justification is clearly inspired by the correspondence assertions proposed in [19], and akin to similar definitions employed in companion type systems for authentication and authorization [14,13]: an "expect" can in fact be seen as an *end* and its corresponding output as a *begin*. However, note that the previous definition allows us to characterize authenticity directly as a property of the data exchanged during a protocol rather than indirectly by extracting and interpreting the effects the protocol has on that data.

**Theorem 9 (Authenticity).** *Let* $\Gamma; \emptyset \vdash N$ *and* $N \equiv N_0 \xrightarrow{\alpha_0} N_1 \cdots \xrightarrow{\alpha_{m-1}} N_m$ *be a sequence of reductions with* $\alpha_k$ *admissible for* $(\Gamma_k; \Delta_k)$ $(k \in [1..m])$*. Then every expect label in the reduction sequence is justified by a previous output label in the sequence.*

## 5 Typing a Variant of 2KP

We show the type system at work on a simplified variant of the e-payment protocol 2KP [5] by IBM. This is a significant example, because the protocol relies on two different authentication schemes: a signature mechanism and the presentation of a shared secret. The latter kind of authentication is important, as in real settings it is unlikely that every principal possesses a signing key.

We can describe the protocol as follows. The customer *cust* sends the description *desc* of the order to the merchant *merc* along the channel *init*. The merchant checks that the description received is the expected one and creates a new transaction identifier *tid*. The merchant sends back the description, packaged with *tid*, to the customer via channel *invc*, and then sends a request to the acquirer *bank* along the channel *req*, providing *tid* and the price of the order. At this stage, the customer allows the payment to the merchant by a communication along *paym* with the acquirer, where it provides *tid*, price and credit card information *can*. Finally, the acquirer checks that the two requests (from the customer and the merchant) agree and that the credit card details provided by the customer are right. If so, the acquirer clears the transaction and sends a notification to the customer and the merchant. The protocol can be coded as the network $2KP = N_{cust} \mid N_{merc} \mid N_{bank}$, where each $N_i$ is defined in Table 9. We use composed conditional guards as syntactic sugar for a series of nested conditionals. The $2KP$ network is well-typed under the following assumptions:

$$desc : Public, can : Secret(cust, bank), price : Secret(cust, merc, bank)$$

The type of the communication channels is immediately derived from the types of the exchanged data, while *cust*, *merc* and *bank* must be given type *Prin*. Below, we detail the most interesting aspects in the type derivation for the example.

First, since *merc* is able to certify its messages, *bank* can easily derive that the expedition of $z_{tid}$ is effectively from *merc*, since that variable is closed by a

**Table 9.** 2KP Protocol Specification

$$N_{cust} \triangleq cust[\![\ \overline{init}@merc\langle - : desc\rangle \mid invc(merc : x_{desc}, x_{tid}).\text{if } (desc = x_{desc})$$
$$\text{then } \overline{paym}@bank\langle - : x_{tid}, price, can\rangle^{\bullet} \mid conf(bank : x_{auth}).0\ ]\!]$$
$$N_{merc} \triangleq merc[\![\ init(- : y_{desc}).\text{if } (y_{desc} = desc)$$
$$\text{then } (\nu\ tid : Public)(\overline{invc}@cust\langle * : y_{desc}, tid\rangle \mid$$
$$\overline{req}@bank\langle * : tid, price\rangle^{\bullet}) \mid resp(bank : y_{auth}).0\ ]\!]$$
$$N_{bank} \triangleq bank[\![\ req(merc : z_{tid}, z_{price})^{\bullet}.paym(- : z'_{tid}, z'_{price}, z_{can})^{\bullet}.$$
$$\text{if } (can = z_{can}\ \wedge z_{tid} = z'_{tid}\ \wedge z_{price} = z'_{price})$$
$$\text{then expect}\langle z_{tid} : Fresh^{bank}(merc)\rangle.$$
$$\text{expect}\langle z'_{tid} : From^{bank}(cust)\rangle.$$
$$(\overline{resp}@merc\langle * : z_{tid}\rangle \mid \overline{conf}@cust\langle * : z_{tid}\rangle)\ ]\!]$$

signed input. Once again, notice that this communication mode guarantees the freshness of the message. Secondly, even though $z_{can}$ is closed by a non-certified input, the receiver can use that variable with type $Secret(cust, bank)$ and not with type $Any$ to type-check the continuation, since $z_{can}$ is checked against $can$ and the typing rule for the conditional branch refines the types for the considered values upon a successful match. Finally, although $cust$ has not a mean to certify its messages, the expedition of $z'_{tid}$ must come from $cust$, since $z'_{tid} : With(z_{can})$ and $z_{can} : Secret(cust, bank)$ by the previous point. Note that, even if $z'_{tid} = z_{tid}$ and $z_{tid}$ is fresh, the type-checker cannot assert the freshness of $z'_{tid}$. Even if this may seem limitative in this particular case, given the nature of the tid, this is the sound choice to make, since in general it is unsound to infer the freshness of a piece of data from its equality with a fresh value.

We remark that the type-checking is completely syntax-directed and compositional, yielding a rather effective tool for protocol verification. In spite of this simplicity, the type system turns out to be quite expressive and flexible, using the correlation rules to infer authenticity information and the conditional branches to refine the types of the values.

# 6 Conclusions

The analysis of distributed systems built upon secure channel abstractions has been subject of active research in the recent literature, based on various formalisms: model checking [3], CSP-style traces specifications [12], Strand spaces [16], inductive verification [4] and process calculi [2,11].

The present paper continues on the line of work initiated in [7,6], by introducing a type system to provide static security guarantees for the high-level abstractions for distributed messaging proposed in those papers.

The type system enforces two main security guarantees – strong secrecy and strong authenticity in the presence of a Dolev-Yao intruder – which are comparable to those provided by companion type systems for security. The novelties of our approach are mainly technical, but they also bear conceptual significance. In particular, the ability to characterize authenticity as a property of data itself, which is distinctive of our type system, appears to constitute an important step towards the integration of security types within typing systems for (semi) structured datatypes available in modern programming languages. This kind of integration within languages accommodating more structured interaction primitives such as those available in session description languages and/or choreography languages represent one of the lines of work we plan for our future research.

## References


1. Abadi, M.: Secrecy by typing in security protocols. Journal of the ACM 46(5), 749–786 (1999)
2. Adão, P., Fournet, C.: Cryptographically sound implementations for communicating processes. In: Bugliesi, M., Preneel, B., Sassone, V., Wegener, I. (eds.) ICALP 2006. LNCS, vol. 4052, pp. 83–94. Springer, Heidelberg (2006)
3. Armando, A., Carbone, R., Compagna, L., Cuéllar, J., Tobarra, M.L.: Formal analysis of saml 2.0 web browser single sign-on: breaking the saml-based single sign-on for google apps. In: FMSE, pp. 1–10 (2008)
4. Bella, G., Longo, C., Paulson, L.C.: Verifying second-level security protocols. In: Basin, D., Wolff, B. (eds.) TPHOLs 2003. LNCS, vol. 2758, pp. 352–366. Springer, Heidelberg (2003)
5. Bellare, M., Garay, J.A., Hauser, R., Herzberg, A., Krawczyk, H., Steiner, M., Tsudik, G., Herreweghen, E.V., Waidner, M.: Design, implementation, and deployment of the iKP secure electronic payment system. IEEE Journal on Selected Areas in Communications 18, 611–627 (2000)
6. Bugliesi, M., Focardi, R.: Channel abstractions for network security. Mathematical Structures in Computer Science xx, xxx–xxx (2010)
7. Bugliesi, M., Focardi, R.: Language based secure communication. In: Proceedings of the 21st IEEE Computer Security Foundations Symposium, CSF 2008, Pittsburgh, Pennsylvania, June 23-25, pp. 3–16. IEEE Computer Society, Los Alamitos (2008)
8. Burrows, M., Abadi, M., Needham, R.M.: A logic of authentication. ACM Trans. Comput. Syst. 8(1), 18–36 (1990)
9. Calzavara, S.: Security Types for Distributed Applications. Master's thesis, Università Ca' Foscari di Venezia (2009)
10. Cardelli, L., Ghelli, G., Gordon, A.D.: Secrecy and group creation. Inf. Comput. 196(2), 127–155 (2005)
11. Corin, R., Deniélou, P.M., Fournet, C., Bhargavan, K., Leifer, J.J.: Secure implementations for typed session abstractions. In: 20th IEEE Computer Security Foundations Symposium, CSF 2007, Venice, Italy, July 6-8, pp. 170–186. IEEE Computer Society, Los Alamitos (2007)
12. Dilloway, C., Lowe, G.: Specifying secure transport channels. In: CSF, pp. 210–223 (2008)
13. Fournet, C., Gordon, A.D., Maffeis, S.: A type discipline for authorization policies. ACM Trans. Program. Lang. Syst. 29(5) (2007)

14. Gordon, A.D., Jeffrey, A.: Types and effects for asymmetric cryptographic protocols. Journal of Computer Security 12(3-4), 435–483 (2004)
15. Hennessy, M., Rathke, J.: Typed behavioural equivalences for processes in the presence of subtyping. Mathematical Structures in Computer Science 14(5), 651–684 (2004)
16. Kamil, A., Lowe, G.: Specifying and modelling secure channels in strand spaces. In: Workshop on Formal Aspects of Security and Trust, FAST (2009)
17. Kobayashi, N., Pierce, B.C., Turner, D.N.: Linearity and the pi-calculus. ACM Trans. Program. Lang. Syst. 21(5), 914–947 (1999)
18. Merro, M., Sangiorgi, D.: On asynchrony in name-passing calculi. Mathematical Structures in Computer Science 14(5), 715–767 (2004)
19. Woo, T.Y.C., Lam, S.S.: A semantic model for authentication protocols. In: IEEE Symposium on Security and Privacy, vol. 178 (1993)

# A Appendix

**The function *after*.** The function $(\Gamma;\Delta)$ *after* $\alpha$ *in* $(M \xrightarrow{\alpha} M')$ is partially defined as follows:

- if $\alpha = c(- : \tilde{m}, \tilde{n})$ with $\Gamma;\Delta \vdash c : Chan\langle\tilde{T};\tilde{U}\rangle$, $|\tilde{m}| = |\tilde{T}|$ and $|\tilde{n}| = |\tilde{U}|$, then $(\Gamma;\Delta)$ *after* $\alpha$ *in* $(M \xrightarrow{\alpha} M') = (\Gamma \sqcap \tilde{m} : Public \sqcap \tilde{n} : Any; \Delta)$;
- if $\alpha = c(p : \tilde{m}, \tilde{n})$ with $\Gamma;\Delta \vdash c : Chan\langle\tilde{T};\tilde{U}\rangle$, $|\tilde{m}| = |\tilde{T}|$ and $|\tilde{n}| = |\tilde{U}|$, then $(\Gamma;\Delta)$ *after* $\alpha$ *in* $(M \xrightarrow{\alpha} M') = (\Gamma \sqcap \tilde{m} : \tilde{T} \sqcap \tilde{n} : \tilde{U}; \Delta)$;
- if $\alpha = (i, \tilde{b} : \tilde{\tau})\overline{c}@p\langle \underline{q} : \tilde{m}\rangle_i^\circ$ with $b_j : \tau_j = T_j/\tilde{E}_j$ for each $j$, then $(\Gamma;\Delta)$ *after* $\alpha$ *in* $(M \xrightarrow{\alpha} M') = (\Gamma, \tilde{b} : \tilde{T}; \Delta')$ with $\Delta' = \Delta \cup \{b_j : Nonce(q) \mid \tilde{E}_j = Nonce(q)\}$;
- if $\alpha = (i)$, then
  $(\Gamma;\Delta)$ *after* $\alpha$ *in* $(M \xrightarrow{\alpha} M') = (\Gamma \sqcap \tilde{m} : Public \sqcap \tilde{n} : Any; \Delta)$ if $i \in fn(M')$,
  $(\Gamma;\Delta)$ *after* $\alpha$ *in* $(M \xrightarrow{\alpha} M') = (\Gamma \sqcap \tilde{m} : \tilde{T} \sqcap \tilde{n} : \tilde{U}; \Delta)$ otherwise.

The definition exploits the fact that a message cached at $i$ is consumed by a transition $(i)$ if and only if it is signed by a principal.

**The function *idx*.** The function $idx(P, i, \tilde{y})$ is defined by induction on the structure of the process $P$ as follows:

- $idx(\text{expect}\langle x : E\rangle.P, i, \tilde{y}) = \text{expect}^{(i)}\langle x : E\rangle.idx(P, i, \tilde{y})$, if $x \in \tilde{y}$;
- $idx(\text{expect}\langle x : E\rangle.P, i, \tilde{y}) = \text{expect}\langle x : E\rangle.idx(P, i, \tilde{y})$, if $x \notin \tilde{y}$;
- $idx(\overline{u}@v\langle \underline{*} : \tilde{u}\rangle^\circ, i, \tilde{y}) = \overline{u}@v\langle \underline{*} : \tilde{u}\rangle^\circ$;
- $idx(a(\underline{u} : \tilde{x})^\circ.P, i, \tilde{y}) = a(\underline{u} : \tilde{x})^\circ.idx(P, i, \tilde{y})$;
- $idx(0, i, \tilde{y}) = 0$;
- $idx(P|Q, i, \tilde{y}) = idx(P, i, \tilde{y})|idx(Q, i, \tilde{y})$;
- $idx(\text{test}(u = v) \text{ then } P \text{ else } Q, i, \tilde{y}) = \text{test}(u = v) \text{ then } idx(P, i, \tilde{y}) \text{ else } idx(Q, i, \tilde{y})$;
- $idx(\text{rec } X.P, i, \tilde{y}) = \text{rec } X.idx(P, i, \tilde{y})$;
- $idx(X, i, \tilde{y}) = X$;
- $idx((\nu a : \tau)P, i, \tilde{y}) = (\nu a : \tau)idx(P, i, \tilde{y})$.

# Modular Plans for Secure Service Composition*

Gabriele Costa[1,2], Pierpaolo Degano[2], and Fabio Martinelli[1]

[1] Istituto di Informatica e Telematica – Consiglio Nazionale delle Ricerche
[2] Dipartimento di Informatica – Università di Pisa

**Abstract.** Service Oriented Computing (SOC) is a programming paradigm aiming at characterising Service Networks. Services are entities waiting for clients requests and they often result from the composition of many services.

We address here the problem of statically guaranteeing security of open services, i.e. services with unknown components. Security constraints are expressed by local policies that service components must obey.

We present here a type and effect system that safely over-approximates, in the form of history expressions, the possible run-time behaviour of open services, collecting partial information on the behaviours of their components. From a history expression, we then extract a plan that drives executions that never rise security violations.

Finally, we show how partial plans satisfying security requirements can be put together to obtain a safe orchestration plan.

## 1 Introduction

In the last decade, *history-based security* [1] has emerged as a powerful approach to guarantee that program do not misbehave. Histories, i.e. execution traces, are sequences of relevant actions generated by running programs. Hence, a *security policy* consists in a distinction between accepted and rejected traces. A program is considered secure if all its executions obey the given security policies. Many techniques use histories for deciding whether a program is secure or not. Mainly, two distinct methods exist: *run-time enforcement* and *static verification* (e.g. see [20,10,19,15]).

Briefly, policy enforcement consists in applying a monitor to the running program. Whenever the monitor target tries to perform an action, the current trace is checked against the enforced policy. A security violation, i.e. an attempt to extend the actual trace to a forbidden one, activates some emergency operation, e.g. the program termination. Instead, static verification aims to prove program security regardless of any possible execution scenario. Roughly, one proves that the program can only produce policy-compliant traces by only looking at the program text. Some authors use a mixed approach (e.g. [17]) that combines a static check with a dynamic one in case the first fails. Often, security policies

* Work partially supported by EU-funded project "SENSORIA", by EU-funded project "CONSEQUENCE" and by EU-funded project "CONNECT".

A. Armando and G. Lowe (Eds.): ARSPA-WITS 2010, LNCS 6186, pp. 41–58, 2010.

are expressed as global safety properties of systems and in this case execution monitors rely on finite state automata for detecting illegal traces.

Recently, [3] proposed a more flexible approach in which so-called *local policies* only guard portions of code and have a local scope. Originally, local policies have been coupled with an extension on the $\lambda$-calculus used to specify services [4]. Then, also Java has been extended [2] with local policies showing the feasibility of this approach on a real-world language.

In this paper, we use *right-bounded* local policies, a variant of those defined in [3]; for brevity we will omit in the following "right-bounded" whenever unambiguous. The main difference between the two versions is that in the original one an active policy is checked on the whole past execution history, while in our proposal it is checked on the history produced since the policy is activated (see Tab. 2). In the next section we shall introduce only intuitively *usage automata* that are used to specify local policies. Usage automata are a variant of nondeterministic finite state automata, parameterized over system resources. More details and the formal definition are in [6,7].

The approach can be summarized as follows. The specification of a system already contains the local policies to be obeyed. Compliance is then established by model-checking a suitable, safe abstraction of the system behaviour (for the $\lambda$-calculus this is done through a type and effect system, for Java through a control flow analysis).

Systems may behave differently according to how requests are resolved into services. The association between requests and services, called *plan*, drives the execution at run-time. If the plan determines an abstract behaviour passing the model-checking phase (the plan is viable) then the original code can be run securely with no monitoring.

The above approach only deals with closed networks, i.e. with services whose components are fully specified a priori. However, services are built incrementally and components may appear and disappear dynamically. It is important then to also analyse *open* networks, i.e. networks having unspecified participants. As a matter of fact, service-oriented paradigms aim to guarantee compositional properties and should be independent from the actual implementation of (possibly unknown) parties. Moreover, closed networks orchestrated by a global, composition plan require to be completely reorganized whenever a service falls or a new one rises.

Here, we extend the results of [4,5] on open networks. In particular, we will single out *partial* plans that only involve parts of the known network and that however can be safely adopted within any operating context. We also show how these partial plans can be combined together, along with the composition of the services they come from. As expected, composability of viable plans is subject to some constraints, and we also outline a possible way to efficiently check when these constraints are satisfied.

The paper is structured as follows. Section 2 introduces our motivating example. To carry on our investigation in a pure framework, we use here an extension of $\lambda^{req}$[4], the syntax and semantics of which are in Section 3. Section 4 introduces history expressions and our type and effect system. In Section 5 we provide our results on plans compositionality and propose a way to efficiently check their validity. Finally, Section 6 concludes the paper.

## 2 An Example

In this section we introduce our working example. Figure 1 shows a simple service network for travel booking. Rounded boxes denote service locations (dashed lines contain homogeneous services, i.e. services offering similar functionalities). Clients contact the travel agency providing a credit card number for payments and receive back a receipt. Every instance of the travel agency books exactly one room and one flight. The responsibility of doing an actual reservation is delegated to booking services. Each booking service receives a card number and uses it for paying a reservation. Payment services are in charge for authorising a purchase. A payment service charges the needed amount on the credit card (possibly after checking some credentials of the card number), and returns `TRUE`. Otherwise, it answers `FALSE` if a failure occurs.

Each service has its own security requirements expressed through a corresponding usage automaton. For example, a booking service would like to "perform at least one availability check before each payment". This is represented by Fig. 2b: every action but `check`(x) and `charge`(x) is allowed and leaves the automaton in state 0 (self-loops on actions not labelling existing arcs are omitted in Fig. 2). After a check, any action is permitted in state 1, including charging. Instead, a charge action in state 0 leads to the offending state 2. Additionally, booking service can be forbidden to check more than once ($\varphi_{\mathtt{BH}}$). Similarly, the travel agency can declare different rules focussing on different aspects, e.g. "never book two times the same service (hotel or flight)" ($\varphi_{\mathtt{TA}}$).

Clients are unspecified, so the network is open. However, clients do not affect at all the security policies introduced so far. We can therefore check secure this open network.

As a matter of fact, services only put security constraints on their own traces and on those of the services they invoke. This is because our policies are

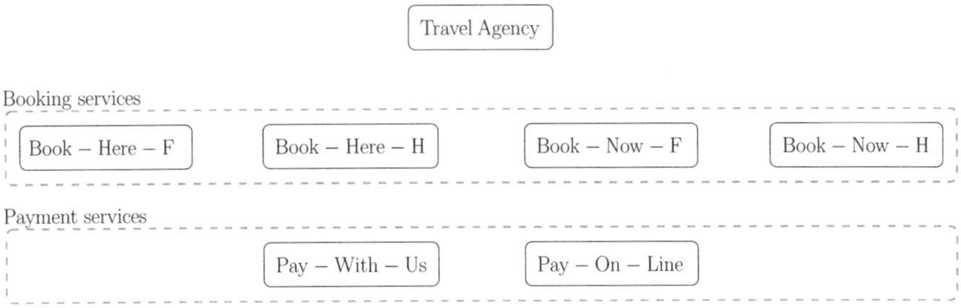


**Fig. 1.** A travel booking network

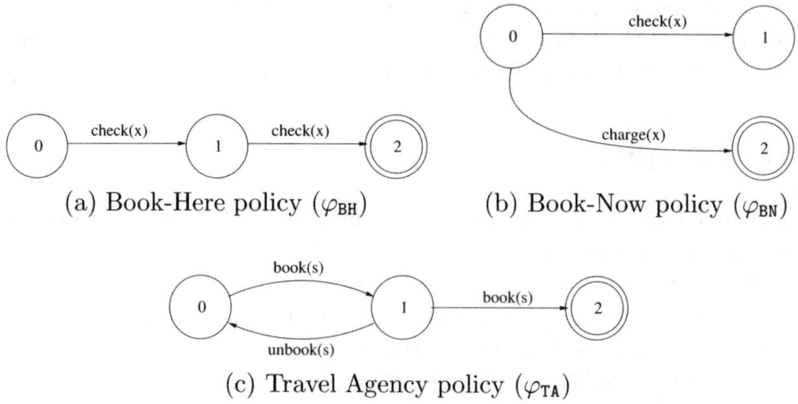


**Fig. 2.** Security policies as usage automata (self-loops are omitted)

right-bounded and so their scope spans from their activation until their deactivation points. Note that in this way, the services we model cannot discriminate against clients. Everyone can invoke a service, because service behaviour is client-independent.

# 3 Service Network

The programming model for service composition based on $\lambda^{req}$ was first introduced in [4]. Its syntax resembles the classical call-by-value $\lambda$-calculus with two main differences: *security framing* and a call-by-contract *service request*.

Service networks are set of services. Each service $e$ is hosted in a location $\ell$. As expected, we assume that there exists a public *service repository* $\mathtt{Srv}$. An element of $\mathtt{Srv}$ has the form $e_\ell : \tau \xrightarrow{H} \tau'$, where $e_\ell$ is the code of the service, $\ell$ is a unique service location (sometimes used to denote the service itself), $\tau \to \tau'$ is the type of $e_\ell$, and $H$ is the effect of $e_\ell$ (see Section 4.1).

## 3.1 Syntax

The syntax of $\lambda^{req}$ is in Table 1. The expression $*$ represents a fixed, closed, event-free value. Resources, ranged over by $r, r'$, belong to finite, statically defined classes $\mathcal{R}, \mathcal{R}'$. Access events $\alpha, \beta$ are side effects, parametrized over resources.

Function abstraction and application follow the classical syntax (we use $z$ in $\lambda_z x.e$ as a binding to the function in $e$). Security framing applies the scope of a policy $\varphi$ to a program $e$. Service request requires more attention. We state that services can not be directly accessed (for instance using a public name or address). Clients invoke services through their public interface, i.e. their type. The label $\rho$ is a unique identifier associated with the request. A policy $\varphi$ is attached to the request in a call-by-contract fashion: the invoked service must

**Table 1.** Syntax of $\lambda^{req}$

| | | |
|---|---|---|
| $e, e' ::=$ | | |
| | $*$ | unit |
| | $r$ | resource |
| | $x$ | variable |
| | $\alpha(e)$ | access event |
| | $\texttt{if}\, g\, \texttt{then}\, e \;\; \texttt{else} \;\; e'$ | conditional |
| | $\lambda_z x.e$ | abstraction |
| | $e\, e'$ | application |
| | $\varphi[e]$ | security framing |
| | $\texttt{req}_\rho\, \tau \xrightarrow{\varphi} \tau'$ | service request |

obey the policy $\varphi$. Since both $\tau$ and $\tau'$ can be higher-order types, we can model simple value-passing interaction, as well as mobile code scenarios.

We use $v$ to denote values, i.e. resources, variables, abstractions and requests. Moreover, we introduce the usual abbreviations: $\lambda x.e = \lambda_z x.e$ with $z \notin fv(e)$, $\lambda.e = \lambda x.e$ with $x \notin fv(e)$ and $e; e'$ for $(\lambda.e')e$.

Here we make explicit the conditions of branching, similarly to [11]. Briefly, we check equality between resources, and we have negation and conjunction.

**Definition 1.** *(Syntax of guards)*

$$g, g' ::= true \mid [\bar{x} = \bar{y}] \mid \neg g \mid g \wedge g' \qquad (\bar{x}, \bar{y} \textit{ range over variables and resources})$$

We use $false$ as an abbreviation for $\neg true$, $[\bar{x} \neq \bar{y}]$ for $\neg [\bar{x} = \bar{y}]$ and $g \vee g'$ for $\neg(\neg g \wedge \neg g')$. We also define as expected an *evaluation function* $\mathcal{B}$ mapping guards into boolean values, namely $\{tt, ff\}$. E.g. $\mathcal{B}([\bar{x} = \bar{x}]) = tt$ and $\mathcal{B}([\bar{x} = \bar{y}]) = ff$ if $\bar{x} \neq \bar{y}$. In our model we assume resources to be uniquely identified by their (global) name, i.e. $r$ and $r'$ denote the same resource if and only if $r = r'$. Moreover, we use $[\bar{x} \in D]$ for $\bigvee_{d \in D}[\bar{x} = d]$.

*Example 1.* We specify the services Travel-Agency, Book-Here-$S$, Book-Now-$S$ ($S \in \{F, H\}$), Pay-On-Line and Pay-With-Us in Fig. 1, through $e_{\texttt{TA}}$, $e_{\texttt{BH-S}}$, $e_{\texttt{BN-S}}$, $e_{\texttt{POL}}$ and $e_{\texttt{PWU}}$ (resp.) as follows.

$$e_{\texttt{PWU}} = \lambda x.\texttt{if}\ [x \in \mathcal{C}]\ \texttt{then}\ \texttt{charge}(x); \texttt{TRUE}\ \texttt{else}\ \texttt{FALSE}$$

$$e_{\texttt{POL}} = \lambda x.\texttt{if}\ [x \in \mathcal{C}']\ \texttt{then}\ \texttt{check}(x); \texttt{charge}(x); \texttt{check}(x); \texttt{TRUE}\ \texttt{else}\ \texttt{FALSE}$$

$$e_{\texttt{BH-S}} = \lambda x.(\lambda y.\texttt{if}\ [y = \texttt{TRUE}]\ \texttt{then}\ \texttt{book}(S)\ \texttt{else}\ *) \\ ((\texttt{req}_\rho\ Card \xrightarrow{\varphi_{\texttt{BH}}} Bool)x)$$

$$e_{\texttt{BN-S}} = \lambda x.\texttt{book}(S); (\lambda y.\texttt{if}\ [y = \texttt{FALSE}]\ \texttt{then}\ \texttt{unbook}(S)\ \texttt{else}\ *) \\ ((\texttt{req}_{\rho'}\ Card \xrightarrow{\varphi_{\texttt{BN}}} Bool)x)$$

$$e_{\texttt{TA}} = \lambda x.\varphi_{\texttt{TA}}\big[(\texttt{req}_{\bar{\rho}}\ Card \to \mathbf{1})x; (\texttt{req}_{\bar{\rho}'}\ Card \to \mathbf{1})x; rcpt\big]$$

Briefly, $e_{\mathtt{PWU}}$ receives a card number $x$, verifies whether it is a registered one (i.e. $[x \in \mathcal{C}]$) and charges on $x$. Service $e_{\mathtt{POL}}$ works similarly, but verifies money availability (event `check`) before and after the operation.

Booking services $e_{\mathtt{BH-S}}$ require a payment and then, if it has been authorised, book the hotel (flight). On the contrary, $e_{\mathtt{BN-S}}$ book the hotel (flight) and then cancel the reservation if the payment has been refused. Both $e_{\mathtt{BH-S}}$ and $e_{\mathtt{BN-S}}$ require the behaviour of the invoked service to comply with the policies $\varphi_{\mathtt{BH}}$ and $\varphi_{\mathtt{BN}}$.

Finally $e_{\mathtt{TA}}$ simply calls two booking service instances and releases a receipt (*rcpt* of type *Rec*) to the client. Note that now the travel agency applies its policy $\varphi_{\mathtt{TA}}$ to the sequential composition of service requests.

### 3.2 Operational Semantics

Clearly, the run-time behaviour of a network of services depends on the way they interact. As we already mentioned, requests do not directly refer to a specific service that will be actually invoked during the execution, but to its behaviour, i.e. its type and effect (defined below), only. A *plan* resolves the requests by associating them with services locations. Needless to say, different plans lead to different executions. A service network can have many, one or even no valid plans. A plan is said to be *valid* if and only if the executions it drives complies with all the active security policies. More precisely, an execution trace $\eta$ is valid w.r.t. a policy $\varphi$, in symbols $\eta \models \varphi$, if and only if it is not a word in the language of the security automaton of $\varphi$.

As expected, we assume that services can not be composed in a circular way. This condition amounts to say that there exists a partial order relation $\prec$ over services. We define $\mathtt{Srv}\rfloor_\ell = \{e_{\ell'} : \tau \in \mathtt{Srv} \mid \ell \prec \ell'\}$ as the sub-network that can be seen from a service hosted at $\ell$.

A computational step of a program is a transition from a source configuration to a target one. In our model, configurations are pairs $\eta, e$ where $\eta$ is the execution *history*, that is the sequence of action events done so far ($\varepsilon$ being the empty one), and $e$ is the expression under evaluation. Actually, the syntax of histories and expressions is slightly extended with markers $[^m_\varphi$ as explained in the comment to the rule for framing. Note that the automaton for a policy $\varphi$ will simply ignore these markers.

Formally, a plan is a (partial) mapping from request identifiers $(\rho, \rho', \ldots)$ to service locations $(\ell, \ell', \ldots)$ defined as

$$\pi, \pi' ::= \emptyset \mid \{\rho \mapsto \ell\} \mid \pi; \pi'$$

An empty plan $\emptyset$ is undefined for any request, while a singleton $\{\rho \mapsto \ell\}$ is only defined for $\rho$. Plan composition $\pi; \pi'$ combines two plans. It is defined if and only if for all $\rho$ such that $\rho \in \mathit{dom}(\pi) \cap \mathit{dom}(\pi') \Rightarrow \pi(\rho) = \pi'(\rho)$, i.e. the same request is never resolved by different services. Two such plans are called *modular*.

**Table 2.** Operational semantics of $\lambda^{req}$

$$(\texttt{S-Ev}_1)\quad \frac{\eta, e \to_\pi \eta', e'}{\eta, \alpha(e) \to_\pi \eta', \alpha(e')} \qquad (\texttt{S-Ev}_2)\quad \eta, \alpha(r) \to_\pi \eta\alpha(r), *$$

$$(\texttt{S-If})\quad \eta, \texttt{if}\ g\ \texttt{then}\ e_{tt}\ \texttt{else}\ e_{ff} \to_\pi \eta, e_{\mathcal{B}(g)} \qquad (\texttt{S-App}_1)\quad \frac{\eta, e_1 \to_\pi \eta', e_1'}{\eta, e_1 e_2 \to_\pi \eta', e_1' e_2}$$

$$(\texttt{S-App}_3)\quad \eta, (\lambda_z x.e)v \to_\pi \eta, e\{v/x, \lambda_z x.e/z\} \qquad (\texttt{S-App}_2)\quad \frac{\eta, e_2 \to_\pi \eta', e_2'}{\eta, v e_2 \to_\pi \eta', v e_2'}$$

$$(\texttt{S-Frm}_1)\quad \eta, \varphi[e] \to_\pi \eta[^m_\varphi, \varphi^m[e] \quad m \text{ fresh} \qquad (\texttt{S-Frm}_2)\quad \eta[^m_\varphi\eta', \varphi^m[v] \to_\pi \eta\eta', v$$

$$(\texttt{S-Frm}_3)\quad \frac{\eta[^m_\varphi\eta', e \to_\pi \eta[^m_\varphi\eta'', e' \quad \eta'' \models \varphi}{\eta[^m_\varphi\eta', \varphi^m[e] \to_\pi \eta[^m_\varphi\eta'', \varphi^m[e']}$$

$$(\texttt{S-Req})\quad \frac{e_{\bar\ell} : \tau \xrightarrow{H} \tau' \in \texttt{Srv}\rfloor_\ell \qquad \pi(\rho) = \bar\ell \qquad H \models \varphi}{\eta, (\texttt{req}_\rho\, \tau \xrightarrow{\varphi} \tau')v \to_\pi \eta, e_{\bar\ell} v}$$

Given a plan $\pi$ we evaluate $\lambda^{req}$ expressions, i.e. services, accordingly to the rules of the operational semantics in Table 2. Actually, a transition should be also labelled by the location $\ell$ hosting the expression under evaluation. For readability, we omit this label.

Briefly, an action $\alpha(r)$ is appended to the current history (possibly after the evaluation of its parameter), a conditional branching chooses between two possible executions (depending on its guard $g$) and application works as usual. The rule ($\texttt{S-Frm}_1$) opens an instance of framing $\varphi[e]$ and records the activation in the history with a marker $[^m_\varphi$, and in the expression with $\varphi^m[e]$ (to keep different instantiations apart we use a fresh $m$). The rule ($\texttt{S-Frm}_2$) simply deactivates the framing and correspondingly purges the relevant marker from the history. The rule ($\texttt{S-Frm}_3$) checks whether the $m$-th instantiation of $\varphi$ is respected by the history since it has been activated (recall that the usage automaton for $\varphi$ ignores the markers $[^{m'}_{\varphi'}$, where of course $m' \neq m$). This is how our right-bounded local mechanism is implemented. A service request firstly retrieves the service $e_{\bar\ell}$ that the current plan $\pi$ associates with $\rho$, and that belongs to $\texttt{Srv}\rfloor_\ell$, i.e. visible from the present evaluation location $\ell$ (omitted in the rule, as stipulated above). Then, the effect of the selected service is checked against the policy $\varphi$ required by the client. If successful, the service is finally applied to the value provided by the client.

*Example 2.* Consider the service *Book-Here-F* as implemented in Example 1. If it is invoked with parameter $c \in \mathcal{C}$ starting from an empty trace, its execution under the plan $\pi = \{\rho \mapsto \texttt{PWU}\}$ is:

$$
\begin{aligned}
&\varepsilon, (e_{\text{BH}-\text{F}}\ c) \\
&\quad \rightarrow_{\pi} \varepsilon, (\lambda_z y.\mathtt{if}\ [y = \mathtt{TRUE}]\ \mathtt{then}\ \mathtt{book}(F)\ \mathtt{else}\ *)((\mathtt{req}_{\rho}\ Card \xrightarrow{\varphi_{\text{BH}}} Bool)c) \\
&\quad \rightarrow_{\pi} \varepsilon, (\lambda_z y.\mathtt{if}\ [y = \mathtt{TRUE}]\ \mathtt{then}\ \mathtt{book}(F)\ \mathtt{else}\ *)((e_{\text{PWU}})c) \\
&\quad \rightarrow_{\pi} \varepsilon, (\lambda_z y.\mathtt{if}\ [y = \mathtt{TRUE}]\ \mathtt{then}\ \mathtt{book}(F)\ \mathtt{else}\ *) \\
&\qquad\quad (\mathtt{if}\ [c \in \mathcal{C}]\ \mathtt{then}\ \mathtt{charge}(c); \mathtt{TRUE}\ \mathtt{else}\ \mathtt{FALSE}) \\
&\quad \rightarrow_{\pi} \varepsilon, (\lambda_z y.\mathtt{if}\ [y = \mathtt{TRUE}]\ \mathtt{then}\ \mathtt{book}(F)\ \mathtt{else}\ *)(\mathtt{charge}(c); \mathtt{TRUE}) \\
&\quad \rightarrow_{\pi} \mathtt{charge}(c), (\lambda_z y.\mathtt{if}\ [y = \mathtt{TRUE}]\ \mathtt{then}\ \mathtt{book}(F)\ \mathtt{else}\ *)(\mathtt{TRUE}) \\
&\quad \rightarrow_{\pi} \mathtt{charge}(c), \mathtt{if}\ [\mathtt{TRUE} = \mathtt{TRUE}]\ \mathtt{then}\ \mathtt{book}(F)\ \mathtt{else}\ * \\
&\quad \rightarrow_{\pi} \mathtt{charge}(c), \mathtt{book}(F) \\
&\quad \rightarrow_{\pi} \mathtt{charge}(c)\mathtt{book}(F), *
\end{aligned}
$$

*Example 3.* Let $z = \lambda_z x.\varphi[\alpha; z(x)]$ and let $\varphi$ be the policy saying that "a single $\alpha$ is allowed". Then, we have the following computation (under the empty plan).

$$\varepsilon, (z\ *) \rightarrow_{\emptyset} \varepsilon, \varphi[\alpha; z(*)] \rightarrow_{\emptyset} [^1_{\varphi}, \varphi^1[\alpha; z(*)] \rightarrow_{\emptyset} [^1_{\varphi}\alpha, \varphi^1[z(*)]$$

Note that the last transition is possible because $\alpha \models \varphi$. Then the computation proceeds as follows.

$$\rightarrow_{\emptyset} [^1_{\varphi}\alpha, \varphi^1[\varphi[\alpha; z(*)]] \rightarrow_{\emptyset} [^1_{\varphi}\alpha[^2_{\varphi}, \varphi^1[\varphi^2[\alpha; z(*)]]$$

This configuration is stuck. Indeed, a further step would lead to the configuration $[^1_{\varphi}\alpha[^2_{\varphi}\alpha, \varphi^1[\varphi^2[z(*)]]$. In spite of the fact that the second instance of $\varphi$ is satisfied by the suffix $\alpha$ of the history after the marker $[^2_{\varphi}$, the first instance is not: $\alpha[^2_{\varphi}\alpha \not\models \varphi$ (recall that the marker $[^2_{\varphi}$ is invisible to $\varphi$).

## 4 Type and Effect System

We now introduce the type and effect system for $\lambda^{req}$. Our system builds upon [4] introducing two new rules: guarded effects and a new typing rule, namely *strengthening*.

### 4.1 History Expressions

History expressions are used to denote sets of histories. They are defined through the abstract syntax of Table 3, which extends the syntax introduced in [4].

A history expression can be empty ($\varepsilon$), a single access event to some resource ($\alpha(r)$) or it can be obtained either through sequential composition ($H \cdot H'$) or non-deterministic choice ($H + H'$). Moreover, we use safety framing $\varphi[H]$ for specifying that all the execution histories represented by $H$ are under the scope of the policy $\varphi$. Additionally, $\mu h.H$ (where $\mu$ binds the free occurrences of $h$ in $H$) represents recursive history expressions. Finally, we introduce guarded histories $gH$ (where $g$ respects the syntax of guards given in Def. 1).

**Table 3.** Syntax of history expressions

| | | |
|---|---|---|
| $H, H' ::=$ | | |
| | $\varepsilon$ | empty |
| | $h$ | variable |
| | $\alpha(r)$ | access event |
| | $H \cdot H'$ | sequence |
| | $H + H'$ | choice |
| | $\varphi[H]$ | security framing |
| | $\mu h.H$ | recursion |
| | $gH$ | guard |

**Table 4.** Semantics of history expressions

$$[\![\varepsilon]\!]^{\sigma}_{\delta} = \emptyset \qquad [\![h]\!]^{\sigma}_{\delta} = \delta(h)$$

$$[\![\alpha(r)]\!]^{\sigma}_{\delta} = \{\alpha(r)\} \qquad [\![H \cdot H']\!]^{\sigma}_{\delta} = [\![H]\!]^{\sigma}_{\delta}[\![H']\!]^{\sigma}_{\delta}$$

$$[\![H + H']\!]^{\sigma}_{\delta} = [\![H]\!]^{\sigma}_{\delta} \cup [\![H']\!]^{\sigma}_{\delta} \qquad [\![gH]\!]^{\sigma}_{\delta} = \begin{cases} [\![H]\!]^{\sigma}_{\delta} & \text{if } \sigma \models g \\ \emptyset & \text{otherwise} \end{cases}$$

$$[\![\varphi[H]]\!]^{\sigma}_{\delta} = \varphi[[\![H]\!]^{\sigma}_{\delta}] \qquad [\![\mu h.H]\!]^{\sigma}_{\delta} = \bigcup_{n>0} f^n(!)$$

$$\text{where } f(X) = [\![H]\!]^{\sigma}_{\delta\{X/h\}}$$

The *denotational semantics* of history expressions (Table 4) maps a history expression $H$ to a set of histories $\mathcal{H}$. The domain $\mathcal{H}$ is the lifted complete partial order of sets of histories [21]. Sets are ordered by (lifted) inclusion $\subseteq_\perp$ (where $\forall \mathcal{H}.\perp \subseteq_\perp \mathcal{H}$ and $\mathcal{H} \subseteq_\perp \mathcal{H}'$ whenever $\eta \in \mathcal{H} \Rightarrow \eta \in \mathcal{H}'$).

We first need a couple of standard, auxiliary notions. An environment $\delta$ binds variables $(h, h', \ldots)$ to history expressions $(H, H', \ldots)$ and a substitution $\sigma$ maps variable names $(x, y, \ldots)$ to variable names or resources $(x, y, \ldots$ or $r, r', \ldots)$. Given $\delta$ and $\sigma$, the semantic function maps a history expression to a corresponding set. As expected, $\varepsilon$ denotes the empty set under any configuration and $\alpha(r)$ denotes the singleton containing only $\alpha(r)$. The semantics of a sequential composition $H \cdot H'$, of non-deterministic choice $H + H'$ and of $\varphi[H]$ is obvious. The semantics for $gH$ is a little more tricky. We assert $gH$ to define two distinct sets: $[\![H]\!]^{\sigma}_{\delta}$, if $\sigma$ *satisfies* $g$ (we write $\sigma \models g$ if and only if $\mathcal{B}(g\sigma) = tt$), or $\emptyset$ otherwise. The semantics of $\mu h.H$ is the least fixed point of the function $f$ (see [3] for further details).

## 4.2 Typing Relation

Before introducing a type and effect system for our calculus, we define the relation $\sqsubseteq_\sigma$ as the partial order between history expressions

$$H \sqsubseteq_\sigma H' \text{ if and only if } [\![H]\!]^\sigma_\emptyset \subseteq_\perp [\![H']\!]^\sigma_\emptyset$$

We write $H \sqsubseteq H'$ when $\forall \sigma. H \sqsubseteq_\sigma H'$.

Types and type environments are introduced in Table 5. Type environments are defined in a standard way as mappings from variables to types. Types can be either base types, i.e. unit or resources, or higher-order types $\tau \xrightarrow{H} \tau'$ annotated with the history expression $H$.

A typing judgement (Table 6) has the form $\Gamma, H \vdash_g e : \tau$ and means that the expression $e$ is associated with the type $\tau$ and the history expression $H$. The proposition $g$ records information about the branching path collected during the typing process.

Rules (T−Unit, T−Res, T−Var) for $*$, resources and variables are straightforward. An event has type **1** and produces a history that is the one obtained from the evaluation of its parameter increased with the event itself (T−Ev). Note that, since the class of resources is finite, an event only has finitely many instantiations. An abstraction has an empty effect and a functional type carrying a *latent*

**Table 5.** Types and type environments

$$\tau, \tau' ::= \mathbf{1} \mid \mathcal{R} \mid \tau \xrightarrow{H} \tau' \qquad\qquad \Gamma, \Gamma' ::= \emptyset \mid \Gamma; x : \tau$$

**Table 6.** Typing relation

$$(\texttt{T-Unit})\ \Gamma, \varepsilon \vdash_g * : \mathbf{1} \qquad (\texttt{T-Res})\ \Gamma, \varepsilon \vdash_g r : \mathcal{R} \qquad (\texttt{T-Var})\ \Gamma, \varepsilon \vdash_g x : \Gamma(x)$$

$$(\texttt{T-Abs})\ \frac{\Gamma; x : \tau; z : \tau \xrightarrow{H} \tau', H \vdash_g e : \tau'}{\Gamma, \varepsilon \vdash_g \lambda_z x.e : \tau \xrightarrow{H} \tau'} \qquad (\texttt{T-Ev})\ \frac{\Gamma, H \vdash_g e : \mathcal{R}}{\Gamma, H \cdot \sum_{r \in \mathcal{R}} \alpha(r) \vdash_g \alpha(e) : \mathbf{1}}$$

$$(\texttt{T-App})\ \frac{\Gamma, H \vdash_g e : \tau \xrightarrow{H''} \tau' \quad \Gamma, H' \vdash_g e' : \tau}{\Gamma, H \cdot H' \cdot H'' \vdash_g e\, e' : \tau'} \qquad (\texttt{T-Frm})\ \frac{\Gamma, H \vdash_g e : \tau}{\Gamma, \varphi[H] \vdash_g \varphi[e] : \tau}$$

$$(\texttt{T-If})\ \frac{\Gamma, H \vdash_{g \wedge g'} e : \tau \quad \Gamma, H \vdash_{g \wedge \neg g'} e' : \tau}{\Gamma, H \vdash_g \texttt{if } g' \texttt{ then } e \texttt{ else } e' : \tau} \qquad (\texttt{T-Wkn})\ \frac{\Gamma, H \vdash_g e : \tau \quad H \sqsubseteq H'}{\Gamma, H' \vdash_g e : \tau}$$

$$(\texttt{T-Req})\ \frac{I = \{H \mid e_{\ell'} : \tau \xrightarrow{H} \tau' \in \texttt{Srv}\rfloor_\ell \wedge H \models \varphi\}}{\Gamma, \varepsilon \vdash_g \texttt{req}_\rho\, \tau \xrightarrow{\varphi} \tau' : \tau \xrightarrow{\sum_{i \in I} H_i} \tau'} \qquad (\texttt{T-Str})\ \frac{\Gamma, H \vdash_g e : \tau \quad g \Rightarrow g'}{\Gamma, g' H \vdash_g e : \tau}$$

*effect*, i.e. the effect that will be produced when the function is actually applied (T−Abs). The application moves the latent effect to the actual history expression and concatenates it with the actual effects according the call-by-value semantics (T−App). Security framing extends the scope of the property $\varphi$ to the effect of its target (T−Frm). The rule for conditional branching says that if we can type $e$ and $e'$ to the same $\tau$ generating the same effect $H$, then we can extend $\tau$ and $H$ to be the type and effect of the whole expression (T−If). Moreover, in typing the sub-expressions we take into account $g'$ and its negation, respectively. Similarly to abstractions, service requests have an empty effect (T−Req). However, the type of a request is obtained as the composition of all the types of the possible servers. In particular, the resulting latent effect is the (unguarded) non-deterministic choice among them. Observe that we only accept exact matching for input/output types (see [4] for a different composition of types). The last two rules are for weakening and strengthening. The first (T−Wkn) states that is always possible to make a generalisation of the effect inferred from an expression $e$. Finally, (T−Str) applies a guard $g'$ to an effect $H$ provided that $g \Rightarrow g'$ (if and only if $\forall\, \sigma.\sigma \models g \Rightarrow \sigma \models g'$). This rule says that we can use the information stored in $g$ for wrapping an effect in a guarded context.

Referring to the type system introduced above, we assert the following statement to be always respected by services in Srv

$$\boxed{e_\ell : \tau \xrightarrow{H} \tau' \in \mathtt{Srv} \Longrightarrow \emptyset, \varepsilon \vdash_{tt} e_\ell : \tau \xrightarrow{H} \tau'}$$

This assumption guarantees that Srv records are always consistent with our type system.

*Example 4.* Let $e_{\mathtt{PWU}}$ be the service introduced in Example 1, then the following derivation is possible (dots stands for trivial or symmetrical derivations)

$$\dfrac{\dfrac{\dfrac{\vdots}{x : Card, [x \in \mathcal{C}]\, \mathtt{charge}(\mathcal{C}) \vdash_{[x\in\mathcal{C}]} \mathtt{charge}(x); \mathtt{TRUE} : Bool} \quad \vdots}{x : Card, [x \in \mathcal{C}]\, \mathtt{charge}(\mathcal{C}) \vdash_{true} \mathtt{IF} : Bool}}{\emptyset, \varepsilon \vdash_{true} e_{\mathtt{PWU}} : Card \xrightarrow{[x\in\mathcal{C}]\mathtt{charge}(\mathcal{C})} Bool}$$

where $\mathtt{charge}(\mathcal{C}) = \sum_{c\in\mathcal{C}} \mathtt{charge}(c)$ and
$\mathtt{IF} = \mathtt{if}\ [x \in \mathcal{C}]\ \mathtt{then}\, \mathtt{charge}(x); \mathtt{TRUE}\, \mathtt{else}\, \mathtt{FALSE}$.

Similarly, we observe that

$$\emptyset, \varepsilon \vdash_{true} e_{\mathtt{POL}} : Card \xrightarrow{[x\in\mathcal{C}']\mathtt{check}(\mathcal{C}')\mathtt{charge}(\mathcal{C}')\mathtt{check}(\mathcal{C}')} Bool$$

*Example 5.* Consider now $e_{\mathtt{BH-S}}$ from Example 1. For the rightmost expression we can derive

$$\dfrac{x : Card, \varepsilon \vdash_{true} \mathtt{req}_\rho\, Card \xrightarrow{\varphi_{\mathtt{BH}}} Bool : \tau \qquad x : Card, \varepsilon \vdash_{true} x : Card}{x : Card, H \vdash_{true} (\mathtt{req}_\rho\, Card \xrightarrow{\varphi_{\mathtt{BH}}} Bool)x : Bool}$$

where

$$\tau = Card \xrightarrow{[x \in \mathcal{C}]\mathtt{charge}(\mathcal{C})} Bool$$

Moreover we can derive

$$\dfrac{\dfrac{\Gamma, \mathtt{book}(S) \vdash_{[y=\mathtt{TRUE}]} \mathtt{book}(S) : \mathbf{1}}{\Gamma, [y = \mathtt{TRUE}]\mathtt{book}(S) \vdash_{[y=\mathtt{TRUE}]} \mathtt{book}(S) : \mathbf{1}} \quad \dfrac{\Gamma, \varepsilon \vdash_{[y \neq \mathtt{TRUE}]} * : \mathbf{1}}{\Gamma, [y = \mathtt{TRUE}]\mathtt{book}(S) \vdash_{[y \neq \mathtt{TRUE}]} * : \mathbf{1}}}{\Gamma, [y = \mathtt{TRUE}]\mathtt{book}(S) \vdash_{true} \mathtt{if}\ [y = \mathtt{TRUE}]\ \mathtt{then}\ \mathtt{book}(S)\ \mathtt{else}\ * : \mathbf{1}}$$

where $\Gamma = x : Card; y : Bool$. Combining the two we obtain

$$\emptyset, \varepsilon \vdash_{true} e_{\mathtt{BH-S}} : Card \xrightarrow{[x \in \mathcal{C}]\mathtt{charge}(\mathcal{C}) \cdot [y=\mathtt{TRUE}]\mathtt{book}(S)} \mathbf{1}$$

Similarly, the result of typing $e_{\mathtt{BN-S}}$ is

$$\emptyset, \varepsilon \vdash_{true} e_{\mathtt{BN-S}} : Card \xrightarrow{\mathtt{book}(S) \cdot \left[x \in \mathcal{C}'\right]\mathtt{check}(\mathcal{C}')\mathtt{charge}(\mathcal{C}')\mathtt{check}(\mathcal{C}')[y=\mathtt{FALSE}]\mathtt{unbook}(S)} \mathbf{1}$$

*Example 6.* Consider now the term $e_{\mathtt{TA}}$. The following derivation is possible

$$\dfrac{\dfrac{\vdots}{x : Card, \varepsilon \vdash_{true} \mathtt{req}_{\bar{\rho}}\ Card \to \mathbf{1} : Card \xrightarrow{H+H'} \mathbf{1}} \quad \dfrac{}{x : Card, \varepsilon \vdash_{true} x : Card}}{x : Card, H + H' \vdash_{true} (\mathtt{req}_{\bar{\rho}}\ Card \to \mathbf{1})x : \mathbf{1}}$$

where

$$H = [x \in \mathcal{C}]\mathtt{charge}(\mathcal{C}) \cdot [y = \mathtt{TRUE}]\mathtt{book}(S)$$

$$H' = \mathtt{book}(S) \cdot [x \in \mathcal{C}']\,\mathtt{check}(\mathcal{C}')\mathtt{charge}(\mathcal{C}')\mathtt{check}(\mathcal{C}') \cdot [y = \mathtt{FALSE}]\mathtt{unbook}(S)$$

Then, we can type the whole service to

$$\emptyset, \varepsilon \vdash_{true} e_{\mathtt{TA}} : Card \xrightarrow{\varphi_{\mathtt{TA}}\left[(H+H') \cdot (H+H')\right]} Rec$$

Our type and effect system produces history expressions that approximate the run-time behaviour of programs. The soundness of our approach relies on producing *safe* history expressions, i.e. any trace produced by the execution of an expression $e$ (under any valid plan) is denoted by the history expression obtained typing $e$. To prove type and effect safety we need the following lemmata. Lemma 1 states that type and effect inference is closed under logical implication for guards, and Lemma 2 says that history expressions are preserved by programs execution.

**Lemma 1.** *If $\Gamma, H \vdash_g e : \tau$ and $g' \Rightarrow g$ then $\Gamma, H \vdash_{g'} e : \tau$*

**Lemma 2.** ***(Subject reduction)*** *Let $\Gamma, H \vdash_g e : \tau$ and $\eta, e \to_\pi^* \eta', e'$. For each $g'$ such that $g' \Rightarrow g$, if $\Gamma, H' \vdash_{g'} e' : \tau$ then $\forall \sigma . \sigma \models g' \Longrightarrow \eta' [\![ H' ]\!]^\sigma_\emptyset \subseteq \eta [\![ H ]\!]^\sigma_\emptyset$*

Then, the soundness of our approach is established through the following theorem, where we use $\eta$ for both a history generated by the operational semantics and a history belonging to the denotational semantics of a history expression $H$. To compare histories of the two kinds, given $\eta \in [\![H]\!]^{\sigma}_{\emptyset}$ we write $\eta^{-\Phi}$ for $\eta$ where all the security framings $\varphi[]$ have been removed, as defined below:

$$\varepsilon^{-\Phi} = \varepsilon \qquad (\alpha\eta)^{-\Phi} = \alpha(\eta^{-\Phi}) \qquad \varphi[\eta]^{-\Phi} = \eta^{-\Phi}$$

We can now state our type safety theorem.

**Theorem 1.** ***(Type safety)*** *If $\Gamma, H \vdash_{true} e : \tau$ and $\varepsilon, e \rightarrow^{*}_{\pi} \eta', v$, then $\forall\, \sigma.\ \exists\, \eta \in [\![H]\!]^{\sigma}_{\emptyset}$ such that $\eta' = \eta^{-\Phi}$.*

The type and effect system of [3] has no rule for strengthening like our rule (T−Str). The presence of this rule in our system makes it possible to discard some of the denoted traces. These traces correspond to executions that, due to the actual instantiation of formal parameters, can not take place. Consequently, our type and effect system produces more compact history expressions than those of [3]. This has several advantages, and we mention here a couple of them. First, having small history expression reduces the search space contributing to speed up verification algorithms. Secondly, it removes possible false negatives raising from traces that violate the active policy but will never be produced at run-time.

History expressions validity guarantees that no security violations can happen at run-time. We define it as follows.

**Definition 2.** *(Validity of History Expressions)*

$$H \models \varphi \text{ if and only if } \forall\, \sigma \text{ and } \forall\, \varphi \text{ occurring in } H,\ \forall\, \eta \in [\![H]\!]^{\sigma}_{\emptyset} : \eta \models \varphi.$$

We say that a history expression $H$ is *valid* if and only if $\forall \eta \in [\![H]\!]$ and $\forall \varphi$ occurring in $H$ then $\eta \models \varphi$. Note in passing that validity of histories is not compositional being our framework a history-dependent one. E.g. if $\varphi$ says "never $\alpha$" from the validity of $\alpha$ and of $\varphi[\beta]$ it does not follow $\alpha\beta \models \varphi$. As a matter of fact, the validity of $H$ is established through model-checking in polynomial time [8].

## 5 Modular Plans

In this section we introduce the main contribution of this work, i.e. how plans can be composed.

### 5.1 Properties of Plans

In Section 3.2 we saw how plans drive the execution of services turning service requests into actual service invocations. We can also interpret plans as a substitution strategy of request expressions. We can therefore inline $e_\ell$ for $\texttt{req}_\rho\, \tau$

whenever $\pi(\rho) = \ell$ (note that recursion is not a problem here because the binding request-service defined by $\pi$ is static). We call this semantics preserving process *flattening*, and *flat* a service without requests.

**Definition 3.** *(Flattening)*

$$* \mid_\pi = * \qquad r \mid_\pi = r \qquad x \mid_\pi = x$$

$$\alpha(e) \mid_\pi = \alpha(e \mid_\pi) \qquad (\lambda_z x.e) \mid_\pi = \lambda_z x.e \mid_\pi \qquad (e\, e') \mid_\pi = e \mid_\pi \; e' \mid_\pi$$

$$\varphi[e] \mid_\pi = \varphi[e \mid_\pi] \qquad (\texttt{if}\ g\ \texttt{then}\ e\ \texttt{else}\ e') \mid_\pi = \texttt{if}\ g\ \texttt{then}\ e \mid_\pi\ \texttt{else}\ e' \mid_\pi$$

$$(\texttt{req}_\rho\, \tau \to \tau') \mid_\pi = \begin{cases} \texttt{req}_\rho\, \tau \to \tau' & \text{if } \pi(\rho) = \bot \\ e_\ell \mid_\pi & \text{if } \pi(\rho) = \ell \end{cases}$$

Flattening an expression $e$ with larger plans makes smaller the set of histories associated with $e$. This property is stated by the following theorem.

**Theorem 2.** *Given two plans $\pi$ and $\pi'$, if $\Gamma, H \vdash_g e \mid_\pi : \tau$ and $\Gamma, H' \vdash_g e \mid_{\pi;\pi'} : \tau$ then $H' \sqsubseteq H$*

To securely compose plans we must guarantee that the resulting plan preserves validity. Hence, we introduce the key concept of plan *completeness.* A plan $\pi$ is complete w.r.t. a service $e$ if it is valid and makes $e$ flat.

**Definition 4**

*Given a closed term $e$, a plan $\pi$ is said to be* complete *for $e$ if and only if*

1. *$e \mid_\pi$ is flat and*
2. *if $\emptyset, H \vdash_{true} e \mid_\pi : \tau$ then $H$ is valid.*

Complete, modular plans for services can be composed preserving completeness, as stated below.

**Lemma 3.** *Given two terms $e$,$e'$ and two modular plans $\pi$,$\pi'$ complete for $e$ and $e'$, respectively, then $\pi; \pi'$ is complete for both $e$ and $e'$.*

We present now a way of incrementally building services in a secure manner. We first state a theorem characterising our notion of composition. As expected, we cannot aim at a full compositionality because history validity itself is not compositional. The lemma above helps in finding conditions that permit to obtain secure services by putting together components already proved secure. We shall then outline a way of efficiently reuse the proofs of validity already known for components, so to incrementally prove the validity of a plan for the composed service. (Recall that services are closed expressions, typable in an empty environment.)

**Theorem 3.** *Let $\pi_i$ be modular plans complete for services $e_i$, and let $\emptyset, H_i \vdash_{g_i} e_i : \tau_i$, $i = 0, 1$. Then,*

- $\pi_0; \pi_1$ *is complete for both* $\alpha(e_0)$ *and* $\texttt{if}\ g\ \texttt{then}\ e_0\ \texttt{else}\ e_1$
- $\forall\varphi$, *if* $H_0 \models \varphi$ *then*
  - $\pi_0; \pi_1$ *is complete for* $\varphi[e_0]$
  - $\{\rho \mapsto \ell_0\}; \pi_0$ *is complete for* $\texttt{req}_\rho\, \tau \xrightarrow{\varphi} \tau'$, *where* $\ell_0$ *hosts* $e_0$
- *if* $\tau_0 = \tau_1 \xrightarrow{H_0'} \tau'$ *and* $H_0 \cdot H_1 \cdot H_0'$ *is valid, then* $\pi_0; \pi_1$ *is complete for* $e_0 e_1$

We now sketch a procedure for checking the validity of the composition of histories that occurs when applying a service to another one (third item above). First, notice that $H_0 \cdot H_1 \cdot H_0'$ is valid if and only if (i) $H_0$ is valid, (ii) $\forall\varphi$ in $H_1$, $H_0 \cdot H_1 \models \varphi$ and (iii) $\forall\varphi'$ in $H_0'$, $H_0 \cdot H_1 \cdot H_0' \models \varphi'$. Item (i) holds by hypothesis (as well as $H_1 \models \varphi$ and $H_0' \models \varphi'$). So, it suffices to define a method for checking validity of the sequential composition of two histories $H \cdot H'$ w.r.t. a policy $\varphi$.

To check validity of $H \cdot H'$ w.r.t. $\varphi$, we look for a usage policy $\psi$ that rejects any trace $\eta$ that, once extended with any $\eta'$ of $H'$, leads to a violation of $\varphi$, i.e. $\eta\eta' \not\models \varphi$. Clearly for $H \cdot H' \models \varphi$, $\eta$ should not be trace of $H$ if $\eta \not\models \psi$.

We proceed as follows, recalling that $\varphi$ is a regular language, the strings of which are rejected by a finite-state automaton $A$. We first build $A^R$, the automaton that rejects the reverse strings $\eta^R$, for $\eta$ not in the language of $A$. Note that $\eta \not\models \varphi$ if and only if $\eta^R$ belongs to the language of $A^R$. Now, mark all the states $q$ of $A^R$ reachable with $\eta^R$ for all $\eta$ denoted by $H'$. For all such $q$, build a new automaton $A^R_q$ equal to $A^R$, except that its initial state is $q$. Let $\eta^R_q$ belong to the language of $A^R_q$, for some $q$. This implies that there exists $\eta$ denoted by $H'$ such that $\eta^R \cdot \eta^R_q$ belongs to the language of $A^R$. Consequently, $\eta_q \cdot \eta \not\models \varphi$. The required policy $\psi$ is given by the reverse of the union of the languages accepted by the automata $A^R_q$ specified above, for all relevant $q$.

For example, let $H' = \texttt{charge}(x) + \texttt{check}(x)$ and $\varphi = \varphi_{\texttt{BH}}$ (see Fig. 2a). Applying the procedure introduced above, we find $\psi =$ "never $\texttt{check}$(x)".

*Example 7.* Consider again the service network of Section 2 typed in Section 4. Let $H_{\texttt{PWU}}$, $H_{\texttt{POL}}$, $H_{\texttt{BH}}$, $H_{\texttt{BN}}$ and $H_{\texttt{TA}}$ their latent effects.

Consider now the three service policies defined in Figure 2. It is immediate to verify that the plans $\pi_1 = \{\rho \mapsto \texttt{PWU}\}$ and $\pi_4 = \{\rho' \mapsto \texttt{POL}\}$ are modular and complete for Book-Here-F and Book-Now-H, respectively.

We try to obtain the service Travel Agency by sequentially composing the above two components (recall that sequentialization is a simple form of application). To guarantee security we have to prove the validity of $H_{\texttt{BH-F}} \cdot H_{\texttt{BN-H}}$ (or vice versa). However, state 2 of $\varphi_{\texttt{BN}}$ is reachable through a prefix of a history in the semantics of $H_{\texttt{BH-F}}$, e.g. $\texttt{charge}(x)\texttt{book}(F)$ originated when $x \in \mathcal{C}$. Similarly, for $H_{\texttt{BN-F}} \cdot H_{\texttt{BH-H}}$.

Instead, if we consider $H_{\texttt{BH-F}} \cdot H_{\texttt{BH-H}}$ no violations can occur (neither service performs a check). Now, the composed service is secure because it is compliant with the policy $\varphi_{\texttt{TA}}$.

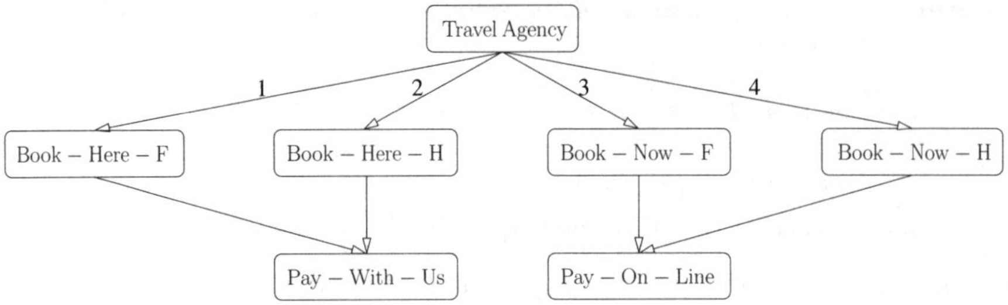


**Fig. 3.** A travel booking network

Similarly for the three cases $H_{\mathtt{BH-H}} \cdot H_{\mathtt{BH-F}}$, $H_{\mathtt{BN-F}} \cdot H_{\mathtt{BN-H}}$ and $H_{\mathtt{BN-H}} \cdot H_{\mathtt{BN-F}}$.

Finally, although $H_{\mathtt{BH-F}} \cdot H_{\mathtt{BH-F}}$ (and the analogous three compositions) can be proved secure, it does not obey $\varphi_{\mathtt{TA}}$.

## 6 Conclusion and Related Work

In this paper we presented a framework for secure service composition. Services are implemented in $\lambda^{req}$ [3], a service-oriented version of the call-by-value $\lambda$-calculus. Security properties are defined through usage automata and locally applied to pieces of code using a proper operator, namely security framing. A type and effect system extracts a history expression from a service. Since it considers service assertions on resources, our type and effect system can also deal with open service networks, i.e. networks where one or more services are unspecified. History expressions are safe approximation of a program, i.e. they denote every possible sequence of security relevant actions fired at run-time. Moreover, history expressions can be model-checked against local policies. The result of this process is a policy compliance proof, if it exists, guaranteeing that no security violation will happen at run-time. We used this technique for generating viable composition plans. Plans produced in this way drive the service execution respecting the security constraints. Additionally, we showed a composition strategy for plans. If two or more plans satisfy the necessary conditions they can be composed in a wider plan. Then, we defined a simple procedure for verifying the validity of composed plans.

This work is a first step toward a bottom-up composition strategy for service network. Many further directions can be investigated. An interesting result could be obtained by exploiting the correspondence between history expressions and basic process algebras (BPAs [9]). Using an approach similar to [11], we could define a symbolic transition system (STS). STSs offer many interesting properties and allow for a fine-grained analysis of security properties.

Another possible improvement consists in extending out programming model introducing a concurrent composition of services. This scenario poses several issues increasing the complexity of our framework. Mainly, the well known state explosion problem could make the model checking step practically infeasible.

To the best of our knowledge, there are no proposals for the secure composition of services within a linguistic framework. Below we briefly survey on a few related work.

In [12] the authors present a framework for contract-based creation of choreographies. Roughly, they use a contract system for finding a match between contracts and choreographies. In this way they verify whether a given contract, declared by a service joining the network, is consistent with the current choreography. However, this framework exploits a global knowledge about the network structure while our model also deals with open networks.

Castagna et al. [14] use a variant of CCS with internal and external choice operators [18] for defining service contracts. A subcontract relation guarantees that the choreography always respects the contracts of both client and service. Nevertheless, this approach assumes that clients always know the request contract and it is focused on finding a satisfactory composition with some available service. Since the composition depends on the possible instantiations of a service, such a contract could be unavailable during the analysis phase. In this sense, our technique overcomes this limitation by producing valid plans independently from the actual instantiation of resources.

Busi et al. [13] propose an analysis of service orchestration and choreography. In their work, the validity of the service orchestration is a consequence of its conformance with respect to the intended choreography. The main difference with our work consists in the approach to choreography. Indeed, they start from a pre-defined choreography and verify the validity of an orchestration. Instead, our approach aims at checking partial service composition without relying on any global orchestrator.

In [16] a framework for the synthesis of orchestrators is presented. This technique consists in automatically producing an orchestrator guaranteeing that the service composition respects the desired security policy. This approach defines a composition that complies with the policy of a client. Since our method produces partial compositions that respect all the involved policies (of both clients and servers), it seems to be more general. However, as [16] generates dynamic orchestrators, the two systems work under completely different assumptions.

## References


1. Abadi, M., Fournet, C.: Access control based on execution history. In: NDSS (2003)
2. Bartoletti, M., Costa, G., Degano, P., Martinelli, F., Zunino, R.: Securing Java with local policies. Journal of Object Technology (JOT) (2008)
3. Bartolett, M., Degano, P., Ferrari, G.L.: History-based access control with local policies. In: Sassone, V. (ed.) FOSSACS 2005. LNCS, vol. 3441, pp. 316–332. Springer, Heidelberg (2005)
4. Bartoletti, M., Degano, P., Ferrari, G.L.: Planning and verifying service composition. Journal of Computer Security (JCS) 17(5), 799–837 (2009); Abridged version In: Proc. 18th Computer Security Foundations Workshop (CSFW) (2005)
5. Bartoletti, M., Degano, P., Ferrari, G.L., Zunino, R.: Secure service orchestration. In: Aldini, A., Gorrieri, R. (eds.) FOSAD 2007. LNCS, vol. 4677, pp. 24–74. Springer, Heidelberg (2007)

6. Bartoletti, M., Degano, P., Ferrari, G.L., Zunino, R.: Types and effects for resource usage analysis. In: Seidl, H. (ed.) FOSSACS 2007. LNCS, vol. 4423, pp. 32–47. Springer, Heidelberg (2007)
7. Bartoletti, M., Degano, P., Ferrari, G.L., Zunino, R.: Local policies for resource usage analysis. ACM Trans. Program. Lang. Syst. 31(6), 1–43 (2009)
8. Bartoletti, M., Degano, P., Ferrari, G.L., Zunino, R.: Model checking usage policies. In: Kaklamanis, C., Nielson, F. (eds.) TGC 2008. LNCS, vol. 5474, pp. 19–35. Springer, Heidelberg (2009)
9. Bergstra, J.A., Klop, J.W.: Algebra of communicating processes with abstraction. Theor. Comput. Sci. 37, 77–121 (1985)
10. Besson, F., Jensen, T.P., Le Métayer, D.: Model checking security properties of control flow graphs. Journal of Computer Security 9(3), 217–250 (2001)
11. Boreale, M., De Nicola, R.: A symbolic semantics for the pi-calculus. Inf. Comput. 126(1), 34–52 (1996)
12. Bravetti, M., Lanese, I., Zavattaro, G.: Contract-driven implementation of choreographies. In: Kaklamanis, C., Nielson, F. (eds.) TGC 2008. LNCS, vol. 5474, pp. 1–18. Springer, Heidelberg (2009)
13. Busi, N., Gorrieri, R., Guidi, C., Lucchi, R., Zavattaro, G.: Choreography and orchestration: A synergic approach for system design. In: Benatallah, B., Casati, F., Traverso, P. (eds.) ICSOC 2005. LNCS, vol. 3826, pp. 228–240. Springer, Heidelberg (2005)
14. Castagna, G., Gesbert, N., Padovani, L.: A theory of contracts for web services. ACM Trans. Program. Lang. Syst. 31(5) (2009)
15. Ligatti, J., Bauer, L., Walker, D.: Edit automata: enforcement mechanisms for run-time security policies. Int. J. Inf. Sec. 4(1-2), 2–16 (2005)
16. Martinelli, F., Matteucci, I.: Synthesis of web services orchestrators in a timed setting. In: Dumas, M., Heckel, R. (eds.) WS-FM 2007. LNCS, vol. 4937, pp. 124–138. Springer, Heidelberg (2008)
17. Martinelli, F., Matteucci, I.: Synthesis of local controller programs for enforcing global security properties. In: ARES, pp. 1120–1127 (2008)
18. De Nicola, R., Hennessy, M.: Ccs without tau's. In: Ehrig, H., Levi, G., Montanari, U. (eds.) TAPSOFT 1987. LNCS, vol. 249, Springer, Heidelberg (1987)
19. Schneider, F.B.: Enforceable security policies. ACM Trans. Inf. Syst. Secur. 3(1), 30–50 (2000)
20. Skalka, C., Smith, S.F.: History effects and verification. In: Chin, W.-N. (ed.) APLAS 2004. LNCS, vol. 3302, pp. 107–128. Springer, Heidelberg (2004)
21. Winskel, G.: The formal semantics of programming languages. MIT Press, Cambridge (1993)

# A Type System for Access Control Views in Object-Oriented Languages

Mário Pires and Luís Caires

CITI and Faculdade de Ciência e Tecnologias, Universidade Nova de Lisboa

**Abstract.** Access control to objects in common object-oriented languages is statically verified but cannot be changed at run-time. However, dynamic authorization is required by most applications and it would be desirable to check more flexible access control policies also statically, at least partially. In this work, we introduce a model where "views" to object references represent the current access control policy of a principal for a given object, and first class authorizations support dynamic modification of those policies. To demonstrate our concepts, we have developed a core language, equipped with a provably correct type and effect system capable of detecting unauthorized method calls at compile-time, and defined and implemented a typechecking algorithm.

## 1 Introduction

Computer security is often ensured by resorting to special programming idioms and techniques. However, programming errors are common, which in the context of increasingly demanding security requirements may easily lead to security breaches. Language-based security [14,19] approaches the enforcement of software security by imposing rules to program structure, preferably in a way that is usually amenable to compile-time verification. In this work, we focus on access control, a mechanism to guarantee that resources are only used by authorized principals, conforming to other confidentiality and integrity requirements.

Language-based access control is frequently enforced with type-based verifications. In this context, type systems are extremely useful. In general, types prevent the occurrence of errors during a program execution by forcing the developer to produce programs in conformance with some typing discipline. If we are interested in verifying security properties, types may also be used to statically impose security constraints, that will ensure that all runs of a program comply with certain security properties, so that their violation will be seen as an execution error. In this work, we introduce a model where "views" to object references represent the current access control policy of a principal for a given object, and first class authorizations support dynamic modification of such policies. This idea of decoupling the verification of access policies from the protected object to the (dynamically changing) user-object relationships has not been much explored before: our aim is then to develop a type-based analysis for such model.

The simplest access control mechanism available in object-oriented languages is usually based on the visibility modifiers public and private (among others) [11,

A. Armando and G. Lowe (Eds.): ARSPA-WITS 2010, LNCS 6186, pp. 59–76, 2010.

```
class File {
    public void open() {...}
    public void read() {...}
    public void write() {...}
    public void close() {...}
    private void seek() {...}
}
void create(){
    File f = new File();
    DoRead(f);
}
void DoRead(File f){
    f.open(); f.read(); f.write(); f.close();
}
```

**Fig. 1.** Motivating Example

section 6.6]. These modifiers restrict where objects' methods can be called; either anywhere or only within a class. A motivating example is presented in Figure 1, where we have a skeleton of a class `File` with the usual methods public open, read, write and close, and a private method `seek`() (for example). We also have a method `DoRead`() that receives an object instance of that class. As the name of the method implies, it should only read the file. However, since method `write`() is public, the respective call in `DoRead`() is not considered an error. This restriction could only be verified in run-time and each time a method would be called. Also, if we want to add permissions for different clients to read or write the file, we end up creating more dynamic checks to validate the respective calls. If we think that some methods once executed cannot be undone, these validations had to be even more complex, slowing down the method execution time.

As we can see, this simple example raises some issues. The goal of the type system developed in this work is to solve these problems during compile-time. If a program typechecks, it can safely execute with a minimum of run-time verifications to ensure that objects are used according to the authorized policy. To that end, we introduce two new values to the language that, used together, achieve this goal: access views and authorizations.

Our approach is based on moving the (unique) access control policy for each object to a setting where a different access control policy may be available for each client of an object, under control of the programmer (with assistance from the type system), as explained below. First, we change where access control is imposed: from the object's perspective (visibility modifiers) to the client's perspective (access privileges). So, *Access Views* are protected references; a pair with the usual reference and an access policy - the client's privileges over the object. Second, we add first class *Authorizations* to enable dynamic modification of access views' policies. They can be seen as security tokens that grant access to an object and can be stored in structures, passed between processes or be an argument for a method call. Furthermore, authorizations are created with

```
class File : { (open; (read + write)* ; close)* } {
   void open() {...}
   void read() {...}
   void write() {...}
   void close() {...}
   void seek() {...}
}
void create(){
   File f = new File;
   Auth readOnly = authorization(f, {open; read*; close});
   Auth writeOnly = authorization(f, {open; write*; close});
   DoRead(f,readOnly);
}
void DoRead(File f, Auth a){
   authorize f:a
   case {open; read*; close} :
       { f.open();  f.read(); f.read(); f.close() }
   case error: { }
}
```

**Fig. 2.** Modified Example

cryptographic techniques, being impossible to forge or replicate. The previous example is now rewritten in Figure 2.

As explained above, visibility modifiers are not needed in method declarations. Instead, the developer defines a maximal class policy that reflects the most permissive access privilege. Moreover, the object creator, who has maximal privilege over it, can delegate various authorizations with different policies using the programming primitive *authorization*, granting rights to access the object to whoever can obtain those authorizations. To apply an authorization and change an access view's policy, we use the primitive *authorize*. This primitive invokes a run-time verification that the given authorization validates the intended policy for the object. On the other hand, the type system statically verifies that all methods are only called according to the current access view policy.

To enforce the use of authorizations, any receiving access view has an empty (less permissive) policy, i.e., one does not have privileges over method arguments and results of method calls. So, to access any objects, one needs to apply valid authorizations, changing the policies of access views.

As in the example, we can verify that method `DoRead()` uses the file as the intended protocol. If a method were called outside an *authorize* block by a non-creator client, it would be considered an unauthorized method call and detected by the typechecker as a typing error. Also, notice that the method `seek()` is not present in the maximal class policy. So, since even the object's creator cannot call it, the method is private to the class.

As explained in the next sections, our type system is generic in the sense that it works with a family of interesting policy languages (Definition 1).

For further examples and explanation of concepts presented on this paper, as well as complete proofs of theorems, see [17]. A sketch of a distributed file system is also shown in that document, where files are protected using access views and clients have authorizations associated with them in order to access each file. Other applications of our type system could be to control the access to a web-service. Each client would receive the service's reference protected with a usage policy (an access view) and would have to apply an authorization in order to use it, allowing the same web-service to be used differently by distinct clients.

This work's contributions are the following. We introduce access views, that describe the usage discipline of an object from the client perspective, not from the object perspective, which is the key new idea explored in the work. This allows to verify statically the usage of an object by different clients with different privileges over that object. Also, we introduce first class authorizations as tokens to allow dynamic modifications of those privileges within access views. We develop a generic type system with respect to policy languages and defined and implemented a typechecking algorithm for the core language defined in Section 2 on a prototype typechecker [18]. We enforce correct access control to objects with types, developed a type and effect system [15], defined in Section 3, to reflect policy changes, and proved type soundness. In Section 4 we discuss the main challenges that arise from our approach, in Section 5 we compare our solution with some related work and in Section 6 we present some concluding remarks and future work.

## 2 Core Language

Our core language is a simplified object-oriented language, extended with primitives to create and apply authorizations, and related primitive types (access views, authorizations).

Access control policies play a central role in our model. Instead of proposing a concrete language for expressing policies, we identify a set of general conditions a policy language must comply in order to fit our framework, so to keep a degree of generality. A policy $\pi$ is a specification of the privileges to access an object, describing which methods may be invoked at a given moment. Any policy language must come equipped with the following relations:

**Definition 1 (Policy Language Properties)**

1. *Validity, written $M \vdash \pi$, where $M$ is a set of methods. This states the domain of the policy $\pi$, e.g., the set of methods $M$ it refers to.*
2. *Step, written $\pi \xrightarrow{m} \pi'$, where $\pi$ and $\pi'$ are policies and $m$ is a method identifier. To accommodate history-dependent access control, each time a method is called, the access control policy for the object can change. Step precisely specifies how a policy may evolve as an effect of a method call.*
3. *Sub-policy, written $\pi <: \pi'$, where $\pi$ and $\pi'$ are policies. This relation states that $\pi'$ is more permissive than $\pi$. Depending on the particular policy language used, one may define several notions of sub-policy, as far as it is consistent with step, in the following sense (of simulation):*
   *If $\pi_1 <: \pi_2$ and $\pi_1 \xrightarrow{m} \pi_1'$ then $\pi_2 \xrightarrow{m} \pi_2'$ and $\pi_1' <: \pi_2'$.*

We define the *full access policy* to be the policy $\{*\}$ such that $\{*\} \xrightarrow{m} \{*\}$ for all methods $m$. Notice that then $\pi <: \{*\}$ for all $\pi$. It is also useful to define for each class a *maximal class policy*, which represents the maximal privilege an access view can have for an object instance of that class. Finally, the *empty policy* is the policy $\{\emptyset\}$ with no privileges, e.g. $\{\emptyset\} \stackrel{m}{\not\rightarrow}$ for all $m$.

In most examples presented in this paper, we use a regular expression language to describe policies, e.g. $\{\texttt{open}\ ;\ (\texttt{write} + \texttt{read})*\ ;\ \texttt{close}\}$. Other examples of policies languages include: a simple method set, e.g. $\{a, b, c\}$, where step $\{a, b, c\} \xrightarrow{m} \{a, b, c\}$ is possible if the set contains the method identifier $m$, not changing the policy, thus mimicking the use of public modifier when declaring methods $a$, $b$ and $c$ in traditional programming languages; and a slightly different language, where each method has a counter associated with it, e.g. $\{a\ 2, b\ 3, c\ 1\}$, enabling to specify how many times a method can be called.

$$
\begin{array}{lll}
P & ::= & \mathit{defn} * \ \{e\} \\
\mathit{defn} & ::= & \mathit{class}\ cn : \pi\ \mathit{body} \\
\mathit{body} & ::= & \{\ \mathit{field} *\ \ \mathit{method}*\} \\
\mathit{field} & ::= & T_s\ fd = e \\
\mathit{method} & ::= & T_s\ m(V_s\ x)\ \{\ e\ \}
\end{array}
$$

$$
\begin{array}{rl}
e ::= & \mathit{new}\ cn \ \mid\ e.fd \ \mid\ e.fd = e \ \mid\ e.m(e) \\
\mid & \mathit{this} \ \mid\ x \ \mid\ n \ \mid\ a \ \mid\ \mathit{let}\ x\ = e\ \mathit{in}\ e \ \mid\ \mathit{authorization}(e, \pi) \\
\mid & \mathit{authorize}\ e : e\ \ \mathit{case}\ \{\pi\}\ :\ \{e\}\ \ \mathit{case\ error}\mathrm{:}\ \{e\}
\end{array}
$$

$$
\begin{array}{ll}
 & x \in \mathit{variable\ names} \\
cn \in \mathit{class\ names} & n \in \mathbb{N} \\
fd \in \mathit{field\ names} & a \in \mathit{authorization\ names} \\
m \in \mathit{method\ names} & \pi \in \mathit{policies}
\end{array}
$$

**Fig. 3.** Abstract syntax of our core language

The syntax of our language is defined in Figure 3. A program is a set of class declarations and a main expression as the entry point for the program. A class contains a set of mutable fields with initial values, a set of methods and a maximal class policy declaration. A method declaration has just one parameter to simplify the presentation. An expression is either an object creation, a field access, a field update, a method call, a variable binding, an integer, the reserved word `this` as the self reference, a variable or the new primitives authorization and authorize to create and apply authorizations, respectively. Notice that we do not introduce a sequential primitive $(e_1; e_2)$, since it can be encoded with a let primitive ($\mathit{let}\ \_ = e_1\ \mathit{in}\ e_2$). The values of our language are given by

$$
v\ ::=\ n\ \mid\ u\ \mid\ \mathit{this}\ \mid\ a\quad (\mathit{Values})\ .
$$

We do not consider locations as values, since they are only accessible through access views, but they are also created when a new object is created. As such, the values for our language are integers $n$ (representing all basic values), access views $u$, the special access view `this` and authorizations $a$. Both access views and authorizations only appear during evaluation time when variables are evaluated.

Types, as used in the syntax, are given by

$$T_s, V_s \ ::= \ int \ \mid \ cn \ \mid \ Auth \quad (Types) \ .$$

We adopt a nominal type system, where we use class names $cn$ to represent types. In addition to class types, there is the integer type $int$ (representing all basic types) and the new authorization type $Auth$. Note that authorizations do not have static information about the policy. Otherwise, if we had the type $Auth\{\pi\}$, the verification performed by the authorize primitive during run-time would be simpler, since the authorized policy ($\pi$) would be available during the static analysis, but authorizations would be depended on policies and programming would be very restrictive and difficult, e.g., an hashtable of authorizations would be restricted to a single kind of policy. Therefore, our decision was based on the usability of authorizations and, as a consequence, the authorized primitive has an additional overhead during run-time to verify if the new policy is a sub-policy of the authorized one, stored on the authorization. Also, note that at the syntax level, we do not make explicit the information about policies when declaring an object; they will be assigned by the typing rules. Though they are not needed during execution, policies are necessary to define the notion of error (Section 3.2): a method call is an error if the policy does not allow that call.

The semantics of our language is defined as a small-step operational semantics, following a call-by-value evaluation strategy (Figure 4). Let $S$ be a store and $e$ an expression such that $< S \ ; e >$ is a valid configuration, a reduction rule is a single step evaluation of $e$ to an expression $e'$, where the resulting store is $S'$. The judgement has the form $< S \ ; e > \longrightarrow < S' \ ; e' >$.

The store contains the program classes' information and the locations of the objects in run-time to maintain a unique object state. Locations hold objects, since the only mutable elements are object's fields. Objects $\{F_s \ M_s\}$ have two components: a set $F_s$, to associate field names with their values, and a set $M_s$, to store the object's methods information.

$$\begin{array}{llll} F_s & ::= & \emptyset \mid F_s, fd \rightarrow v & (Fields) \\ M_s & ::= & \emptyset \mid M_s, m(x) = e & (Methods) \end{array}$$

Access to locations by running code may only be done through access views, protecting them with an access control policy. For technical convenience, authorizations are also referenced through the store.

$$\begin{array}{lll} S ::= & & (Store) \\ \mid & \emptyset & (empty\ store) \\ \mid & S, c \rightarrow \{F_s \ M_s \ \pi\} & (class\ information) \\ \mid & S, u \rightarrow (l, \ \pi) & (access\ view) \\ \mid & S, l \rightarrow \{F_s \ M_s\} & (location) \\ \mid & S, a \rightarrow [l, \ \pi] & (authorization) \end{array}$$

The operations over stores are defined as follows. We say $Dom(S)$ to denote the domain of $S$, $S(c)$ to denote the value of $c$ stored at $S$, and $S[u \leftarrow (l,\ \pi)]$ to denote the policy modification of access view (or field) $u$ to the policy $\pi$. An expression $e$ is closed in store $S$ if $e$ does not have free variables and if all access views and authorizations occurring in $e$ are elements of $Dom(S)$. We say that $< S\ ;\ e >$ is a valid configuration if $e$ is closed in store $S$.

We now describe some key reduction rules. When a new object is created, by rule [R - Object Creation] a new location and access view with the maximal (most permissive) policy are created for the object. When accessing a field, by rule [R - Field Access], its current policy is lost to a new access view. On the other hand, when updating a field with an access view, rule [R - Field Update - Base] does the opposite: the access view loses its policy to the field. Rule [R - Variable Binding] follows the same approach, the access view loses its policy to the new variable. This prevents aliasing of authorized policy. Otherwise, if we could copy the policy, it could be violated, e.g., if we had an access view with an authorized policy to call a method only one time, we could create other access views with the same policy as the initial and call the method with each one of them, violating the authorized policy. With our solution, only one of the new access views would have the authorized policy.

A method's code is assumed to be always executed with "administrator" privileges (full access policy), having unrestricted access to the object's fields and methods through the self reference. As explained before, both method parameters and results of method calls will have empty policies associated with them. So, when calling a method, [R - Method Call - Base], the method's parameter will be substituted by a new access view ($u_3$) to the same location ($l_u$) as the argument's but with an empty policy. On the other hand, we substitute the self reference with a new access view ($u_t$) with the same properties as the self reference. Finally, as a consequence of calling the method, the current policy of the object's access view ($u_1$) takes a step with the method's name ($\pi \xrightarrow{m} \pi'$).

Creating an authorization has no effect in any policy, by rule [R - Authorization]. The condition $\pi <: \pi_u$ ensures that the new policy $\pi$ is a sub-policy of the current policy $\pi_u$. One can only create authorizations with equal or less privileges than his own. When applying an authorization, a verification is performed to validate the pair (location, policy) with the authorization (definition 2). If the pair is valid, then rule [R - Authorize OK] is applied and the access view's policy is changed. Otherwise, rule [R - Authorize KO] is applied, leaving the access view unchanged. In either case, when the authorize block ends, the policy of access view $u$ is permanently altered if the object is used, according to the typing rule [T - Authorize].

**Definition 2 (Authorization Applicability).** *We define authorization applicability, written* $a \vdash p$*, to validate a pair* $p = [l_p,\ \pi_p]$ *with an authorization* $a = [l_a,\ \pi_a]$*, as follows:*

$$[l_a,\ \pi_a] \vdash [l_p,\ \pi_p] \stackrel{def}{=} l_p = l_a \wedge \pi_p <: \pi_a \quad .$$

[R - Object Creation]

$$\frac{l, u \notin Dom(S) \qquad c \rightarrow \{F_s \;\; M_s \;\; \pi\} \in S}{< S \; ; \; new \; c \; > \longrightarrow < S' \; ; \; u >}$$

$$S' = S \uplus \{l \rightarrow \{F_s \;\; M_s\}, u \rightarrow (l, \; \pi)\}$$

[R - Field Access]

$$\frac{\begin{array}{ll} u \rightarrow (l, \; \pi_t) \in S & l \rightarrow \{F_s \;\; M_s\} \in S \\ u' \notin Dom(S) & fd \rightarrow (l', \; \pi) \in F_s \end{array}}{< S \; ; \; u.fd > \longrightarrow < S' \; ; \; u' >}$$

$$S' = S[u.fd \leftarrow (l', \; \emptyset)] \uplus \{u' \rightarrow (l', \; \pi)\}$$

[R - Field Update]

$$\frac{< S \; ; \; e > \longrightarrow < S' \; ; \; e' >}{< S \; ; \; u.fd = e > \longrightarrow < S' \; ; \; u.fd = e' >}$$

[R - Field Update - Base]

$$\frac{\begin{array}{ll} u \rightarrow (l, \; \pi) \in S & l \rightarrow \{F_s \;\; M_s\} \in S \\ u' \rightarrow (l', \; \pi') \in S & fd \in Dom(F_s) \end{array}}{< S \; ; \; u.fd = u' > \longrightarrow < S' \; ; \; u' >}$$

$$S' = S[u.fd \leftarrow (l', \; \pi'), u' \leftarrow (l', \; \emptyset)]$$

[R - Variable Binding]

$$\frac{< S \; ; \; e_1 > \longrightarrow < S' \; ; \; e_1' >}{< S \; ; \begin{array}{l} let \; x \; = e_1 \\ in \; e_2 \end{array} > \longrightarrow < S' \; ; \begin{array}{l} let \; x \; = e_1' \\ in \; e_2 \end{array} >}$$

[R - Variable Binding - Base]

$$\frac{u \rightarrow (l, \; \pi) \in S \qquad u_2 \notin Dom(S)}{< S \; ; \begin{array}{l} let \; x \; = u \\ in \; e_2 \end{array} > \longrightarrow < S' \; ; \; e_2\{^{u_2}/_{x}\} >}$$

$$S' = S[u \leftarrow (l, \; \emptyset)] \uplus \{u_2 \rightarrow (l, \; \pi)\}$$

[R - Authorize OK]

$$\frac{u \rightarrow (l, \; \pi_u) \in S \qquad S(a) \vdash [l, \; \pi]}{< S \; ; \begin{array}{l} authorize \; u : a \\ case \; \pi \; : \{e_1\} \\ case \; error\text{:} \; \{e_2\} \end{array} > \longrightarrow < S' \; ; \; e_1 >}$$

$$S' = S[u \leftarrow (l, \; \pi)]$$

[R - Authorize KO]

$$\frac{u \rightarrow (l, \; \pi_u) \in S \qquad S(a) \nvdash [l, \; \pi]}{< S \; ; \begin{array}{l} authorize \; u : a \\ case \; \pi \; : \{e_1\} \\ case \; error\text{:} \; \{e_2\} \end{array} > \longrightarrow < S \; ; \; e_2 >}$$

[R - Method Call]

$$\frac{< S \; ; \; e > \longrightarrow < S' \; ; \; e' >}{< S \; ; \; u.m(e) > \longrightarrow < S' \; ; \; u.m(e') >}$$

[R - Authorization]

$$\frac{\begin{array}{ll} u \rightarrow (l, \; \pi_u) \in S & \\ \pi <: \pi_u & a \notin Dom(S) \end{array}}{< S \; ; \; authorization(u, \pi) > \longrightarrow < S' \; ; \; a >}$$

$$S' = S \uplus \{a \rightarrow [l, \; \pi]\}$$

[R - Method Call - Base]

$$\frac{\begin{array}{ll} u_1 \rightarrow (l, \; \pi) \in S & l \rightarrow \{F_s \;\; M_s\} \in S \\ u_2 \rightarrow (l_u, \; \pi_u) \in S & m(x) = e \in M_s \\ u_3, u_t \notin Dom(S) & \pi \xrightarrow{m} \pi' \end{array}}{< S \; ; \; u_1.m(u_2) > \longrightarrow < S' \; ; \; e\{^{u_3}/_{x}\}\{^{u_t}/_{this}\} >}$$

$$S' = S[u_1 \leftarrow (l, \; \pi')] \uplus \{u_3 \rightarrow (l_u, \; \emptyset), u_t \rightarrow (l, \; *)\}$$

**Fig. 4.** Reduction Rules

# 3 Type System

In this section, we present and discuss our type system. The types are given by:

$$
\begin{array}{llcll}
T, V & ::= & O\{\pi\} & \mid & Auth \mid int & (Types) \\
O & ::= & M & \mid & [F \;\; M] & (Object\ Types) \\
F & ::= & \emptyset & \mid & F, fd : T & (Fields) \\
M, N & ::= & \emptyset & \mid & M, m : T(V) & (Methods)
\end{array}
$$

Object references are typed by *access types*. An access type $O\{\pi\}$ is composed by an *object type* $O$ and the current policy $\pi$ for the object. The types $Auth$ and $int$ are associated with authorizations and integer values, respectively. An object type may be either *external*, to type variables and access views where field types are not visible ($M$), or *internal*, to type variables and access views alias of the self reference "this", where fields are visible ($[F \;\; M]$). Method types have the form $T(V)$, where $T$ is the return type and $V$ is the parameter type.

Types are assigned to variables, access views and authorizations by typing environments defined as follows:

$$
\begin{array}{lll}
\Delta ::= & & (Typing\ Environment) \\
\mid & \emptyset & (empty\ environment) \\
\mid & \Delta, c : [F \;\; M \;\; \pi] & (class) \\
\mid & \Delta, x : T & (variable) \\
\mid & \Delta, this : [F \;\; M]\{*\} & (self\ reference) \\
\mid & \Delta, a : Auth & (authorization) \\
\mid & \Delta, u : O\{\pi\} & (access\ view)
\end{array}
$$

Operations over typing environments are defined as usual. We write $Dom(\Delta)$ to denote the domain of $\Delta$, $\Delta(x)$ to denote the type of $x$ in $\Delta$, and $\Delta[id \leftarrow \pi]$ to denote the policy modification of access view or variable $id$ to the policy $\pi$. We also use the standard subset relation ($\subseteq$) and we define a special subset relation we call $\pi$-subset ($\subseteq^{\pi}$), that ignores access view policies, since we need to compare environments from different points of the program, where the policies of the same access views may vary.

– ($\pi$-*subset*). Let $\Delta_1$ and $\Delta_2$ be typing environments.

$$
\begin{aligned}
\Delta_1 \subseteq^{\pi} \Delta_2 \triangleq\ & (\forall\, u : O\{\pi_1\} \in \Delta_1 \Rightarrow u : O\{\pi_2\} \in \Delta_2) \wedge \\
& \wedge\ (\forall\ (x : T) \in \Delta_1 \ .\ x \ \textit{is not an access view} \ \Rightarrow (x : T) \in \Delta_2)
\end{aligned}
$$

An expression $e$ is closed in a typing environment $\Delta$ if all free identifiers (variables, access views and authorizations) of $e$ are declared in $\Delta$.

## 3.1 Typing Rules

The typing rules are defined in Figure 5, following the structure of a type and effect system. A typing judgement takes the form $\Delta \vdash e : T \mapsto \Delta'$, asserting that expression $e$ is typed with type $T$ in the typing environment $\Delta$, with some

[T - Object Creation]

$$\frac{c : [F \;\; M \;\; \pi] \in \Delta}{\Delta \vdash new\ c : M\{\pi\} \mapsto \Delta}$$

[T - Authorization Value]

$$\frac{a : Auth \in \Delta}{\Delta \vdash a : Auth \mapsto \Delta}$$

[T - id - 1]

$$\frac{id : M\{\pi\} \in \Delta}{\Delta \vdash id : M\{\emptyset\} \mapsto \Delta}$$

[T - id - 2]

$$\frac{id : M\{\pi\} \in \Delta}{\Delta \vdash id : M\{\pi\} \mapsto \Delta[id \leftarrow \emptyset]}$$

[T - This - 1]

$$\frac{this : [F \;\; M]\{*\} \in \Delta}{\Delta \vdash this : [F \;\; M]\{\emptyset\} \mapsto \Delta}$$

[T - This - 2]

$$\frac{this : [F \;\; M]\{*\} \in \Delta}{\Delta \vdash this : [F \;\; M]\{*\} \mapsto \Delta}$$

[T - Field Access]

$$\frac{\begin{array}{c} id : [F \;\; M]\{\pi\} \in \Delta \\ fd : M'\{\pi'\} \in F \end{array}}{\Delta \vdash id.fd : M'\{\emptyset\} \mapsto \Delta}$$

[T - Variable Binding]

$$\frac{\begin{array}{c} \Delta_1 \vdash e_1 : M_1\{\pi_1\} \mapsto \Delta_2 \\ \Delta_2, x : M_1\{\pi_1\} \vdash e_2 : M_2\{\pi_2\} \mapsto \Delta_3, x : M_1\{\pi_3\} \end{array}}{\Delta_1 \vdash let\ x = e_1\ in\ e_2 : M_2\{\pi_2\} \mapsto \Delta_3}$$

[T - Field Update]

$$\frac{\begin{array}{c} id : [F \;\; M]\{\pi\} \in \Delta \\ fd : M'\{\pi'\} \in F \\ \Delta \vdash e : M'\{\pi_e\} \mapsto \Delta' \end{array}}{\Delta \vdash id.fd = e : M'\{\emptyset\} \mapsto \Delta'[id.fd \leftarrow \pi_e]}$$

[T - Method Call]

$$\frac{\begin{array}{ll} \Delta \vdash e : M_2\{\emptyset\} \mapsto \Delta' & m : M_1(M_2) \in M \\ id : M\{\pi_a\} \in \Delta & \pi_b \xrightarrow{m} \pi \\ id : M\{\pi_b\} \in \Delta' & \end{array}}{\Delta \vdash id.m(e) : M_1\{\emptyset\} \mapsto \Delta'[id \leftarrow \pi]}$$

[T - Authorization]

$$\frac{id : M\{\pi_{id}\} \in \Delta \qquad \begin{array}{c} \pi <: \pi_{id} \\ M \vdash \pi \end{array}}{\Delta \vdash authorization(id, \pi) : Auth \mapsto \Delta}$$

[T - Authorize]

$$\frac{\begin{array}{l} id : M\{\pi_{id}\} \in \Delta \\ a : Auth \in \Delta \\ M \vdash \pi \end{array} \qquad \begin{array}{r} \Delta[id \leftarrow \pi] \vdash e_1 : T \mapsto \Delta' \\ \Delta \vdash e_2 : T \mapsto \Delta' \end{array}}{\Delta \vdash \begin{array}{l} authorize\ id : a \\ case\ \pi : \{e_1\} \\ case\ error\text{:}\ \{e_2\} \end{array} : T \mapsto \Delta'}$$

[T - Class]

$$\frac{\begin{array}{c} \forall i \in \{1..n\}.\ \Delta \vdash e_i : T_i\{\pi_i\} \mapsto \Delta \\ F_t = \{fd_i : T_i\{\pi_i\} \mid i \in \{1..n\}\} \\ M_t = \{m_i : M_i(V_i) \mid i \in \{1..k\}\} \\ \forall j \in \{1..k\}.\ \Delta_j = \Delta, this : [F_t \;\; M_t]\{*\}, x_j : N_j\{\emptyset\} \\ \Delta_j \vdash e'_j : M_j\{\emptyset\} \mapsto \Delta_j \end{array}}{\begin{array}{l} \Delta \vdash_c class\ cn : \pi\{ \\ \quad T_1\ fd_1 = e_1\ ...\ T_n\ fd_n = e_n \\ \quad M_1\ m_1(N_1\ x_1)\{e'_1\}\ ...\ M_k\ m_k(N_k\ x_k)\{e'_k\} \\ \} \end{array}}$$

**Fig. 5.** Typing Rules

effects that originate the typing environment $\Delta'$. As such, we can say that $\Delta$ is a $\pi$-subset of $\Delta'$, $\Delta \subseteq^{\pi} \Delta'$, since effects only target policies.

Notice that, for presentation purposes, we consider that expressions and variables are only typed by access types, allowing us to focus on policies evolution. However, authorization types are also considered when expected.

For typing accesses to views we need two rules: one rule to apply when the access policy is returned along with the value, and other when the policy is kept in the environment (registered in the effect). We illustrate the subtlety with the following example:

$$\dfrac{\dfrac{u : M_1\{\pi_1\} \in \Delta_1}{\Delta_1 \vdash u : M_1\{\pi_1\} \mapsto \Delta_1[u \leftarrow \emptyset]}\,(b) \qquad \begin{array}{c}\Delta_1[u \leftarrow \emptyset], x : M_1\{\pi_1\} \vdash \\ x.m(0) : T \mapsto \Delta_2, x : M_1\{\pi_2\}\end{array}}{\Delta_1 \vdash \mathit{let}\ x = u\ \mathit{in}\ x.m(0) : T \mapsto \Delta_2}\,(a)$$

By rule [T - Variable Binding] (a), access view $u$ needs to be well-typed with $M_1\{\pi_1\}$, which means that it loses its policy, by applying rule [T - id - 2] (b). On the other hand, in the following example, rule [T - id - 1] (d) is applied, since rule [T - Method Call] (c) does not need to change the access view's policy.

$$\dfrac{\dfrac{u : M_2\{\pi_u\} \in \Delta}{\Delta \vdash u : M_2\{\emptyset\} \mapsto \Delta}\,(d) \qquad \begin{array}{c}x : M\{\pi_x\} \in \Delta \\ m : M_1(M_2) \in M\end{array} \qquad \pi_x \xrightarrow{m} \pi}{\Delta \vdash x.m(u) : M_1\{\emptyset\} \mapsto \Delta[x \leftarrow \pi]}\,(c)$$

Rule [T - Method Call] is the most interesting rule. When typing an access view's method call, its policy changes, taking a step ($\pi_x \xrightarrow{m} \pi$). If this step is not possible, the method call was not authorized, and the method call is not typable. Also, notice that a returned value is always assigned an empty policy.

A different judgement ($\Delta \vdash_c \mathit{defn}$) is used to type classes, since they produce no effect. So, a class is well-typed if all field's initial expressions are well-typed and if all methods are well-typed. Note methods cannot change the typing environment, i.e., field's policies are invariant, as explained in Section 4.

### 3.2 Type Safety

We now state and prove our main technical result of this work: the type soundness theorem. To that end, we prove type safety by combining a type preservation theorem and a progress theorem (along the lines of [22]). If a program is well-typed, then its evaluation does not get stuck; it will not reach an error configuration, particularly unauthorized method calls.

In the substitution lemma, we have to take into account the access views. As such, variables (or access views) can only be substituted by access views with the same object type and policy. Otherwise, the effects could not be the same. Furthermore, the access view cannot already exist in the environment or its policy could be violated (aliasing problem). Weakening is defined as usual.

**Lemma 1 (Substitution).** *Let* $\Delta, x : M\{\pi\} \vdash e : T \mapsto \Delta', x : M\{\pi'\}$ *and* $u \notin Dom(\Delta)$. *Then* $\Delta, u : M\{\pi\} \vdash e\{^u/_x\} : T \mapsto \Delta', u : M\{\pi'\}$.

*Proof.* By induction on the derivation of $\Delta, x : M\{\pi\} \vdash e : T \mapsto \Delta', x : M\{\pi'\}$ .

**Lemma 2 (Weakening).** *Let* $\Delta \vdash e : T \mapsto \Delta'$ *and* $x \notin Dom(\Delta)$. *Then* $\Delta, x : T' \vdash e : T \mapsto \Delta', x : T'$.

*Proof.* Follows by induction on the derivation of $\Delta \vdash e : T \mapsto \Delta'$.

We say that we have a store type conformance between a typing environment $\Delta$ and a store $S$, written $\Delta \vdash S$, if all elements of $dom(S)$ are well-typed in $\Delta$.

We can now state and prove the subject reduction and progress theorems.

**Theorem 1 (Subject Reduction).** *Let* $\Delta$ *and* $\Delta''$ *be typing environments, e an expression such that e is closed in* $\Delta$, *and* $T$ *a type.*

$$\begin{array}{ll} \text{if} & \Delta \vdash e : T \mapsto \Delta'' \quad \text{and} \quad \exists\, S \,.\, \Delta \vdash S \wedge < S \,;\, e > \longrightarrow < S' \,;\, e' > \\ \text{then} & \exists\, \Delta', \Delta''' \,.\, \Delta' \vdash S',\ \Delta \subseteq^{\pi} \Delta',\ \Delta'' \subseteq \Delta''' \quad \text{and} \quad \Delta' \vdash e' : T \mapsto \Delta'''. \end{array}$$

*Proof.* By induction on the derivation of $< S \,;\, e > \longrightarrow < S' \,;\, e' >$ (see [17]).

**Theorem 2 (Progress).** *Let* $\Delta$ *and* $\Delta'$ *be typing environments, e an expression such that e is closed in* $\Delta$, *and* $T$ *a type.*

$$\begin{array}{ll} \text{if} & \Delta \vdash e : T \mapsto \Delta' \\ \text{then} & \exists\, S \,.\, \Delta \vdash S \wedge < S \,;\, e > \longrightarrow < S' \,;\, e' > \quad \text{or} \quad e \text{ is a value.} \end{array}$$

*Proof.* By induction on the typing derivation $\Delta \vdash e : T \mapsto \Delta'$ (see [17]).

We need to define the set of error configurations - the errors that the typechecker is able to capture; an expression where the operational semantics get stuck. For the sake of brevity, we will omit traditional error configurations, such as class not found, field not found, etc. The two we show in Figure 6 are the unauthorized method call and the creation of an authorization with an invalid policy, which follow from this work. Preventing the first kind of error is a main motivation for this work: the ability to detect an unauthorized method call statically. As we can see, if the access view's policy does not have a step with the method's name ($\pi \stackrel{m}{\nrightarrow}$ ), then the method call is considered a typing error. Therefore, a well-typed program will only perform authorized method calls. The second error shows how it is possible to detect invalid creations of authorizations. If the new policy is not a sub-policy of the current access view's policy ($\pi \not<: \pi_u$), then the authorization creation is considered a typing error. This prevents unauthorized clients to create authorizations to a protected object.

So, we define the type soundness theorem as follows:

**Theorem 3 (Type Soundness).** *Let* $\Delta$ *and* $\Delta''$ *be typing environments, e an expression such that e is closed in* $\Delta$, $T$ *a type, and* $S$ *a store such that* $\Delta \vdash S$.

$$\begin{array}{l} \text{if } \Delta \vdash e : T \mapsto \Delta'' \\ \text{then } \forall\, e' \,.\ < S \,;\, e > \longrightarrow^{*} < S' \,;\, e' > \\ \Rightarrow < S' \,;\, e' > \textit{ is not an error configuration.} \end{array}$$

$$\left[\begin{array}{c}\text{F - Method Call}\\ \text{security policy violation}\\ \text{unauthorized access}\end{array}\right] \qquad \left[\begin{array}{c}\text{F - Authorization}\\ \text{invalid policy}\end{array}\right]$$

$$\frac{\begin{array}{ll} u \rightarrow (l,\ \pi) \in S & m(x) = e \in M_s \\ l \rightarrow \{F_s\ \ M_s\} \in S & \pi \overset{m}{\not\rightarrow} \end{array}}{< S\ ;\ u.m(e) >} \qquad \frac{u \rightarrow (l,\ \pi_u) \in S \qquad \pi \not<: \pi_u}{< S\ ;\ authorization(u, \pi) >}$$

**Fig. 6.** Selected error configurations

*Proof.* Applying the progress theorem (2) and subject reduction theorem (1) we get the desired type soundness property.

## 4 Further Discussion

In this section we discuss the main challenges that arise from our approach and present the solutions for them.

**Fields.** Fields can hold access views. Therefore, their policies must be followed for every possible object usage. Figure 7 demonstrates the problem. Class `B` and `C` have a field with initial policy $\{(\mathtt{f};\mathtt{g})*\}$ and a method `m`() that uses the field. The problem resides in class `B`, where there is only one call to a field's method. If we called method `m`() two times, the field's policy would be violated. To solve this problem, field's policies are invariant. Therefore, methods are well-typed only if all fields' policies remain the same at the end of each method. So the method `m`() of class `B` is not well-typed and method `m`() of class `C` is well-typed.

This conservative solution has some practical consequences: fields' policies must be cyclic; they must be able to reach the same state at some point. As such, policy languages must take that into consideration in order to be properly used. Another consequence are `set` methods. In Figure 9, we have two possible implementations for a `set` method for class `C`. The first is not well-typed, since we are assigning an access view (`other`) with an empty policy to the field, changing its policy to an empty policy also, breaking the invariant. To correctly modify the value of a field, one must apply an authorization to change the new access view's policy to the same as the field's, as in the second `set`. This reflects an intuitive argument: if we have fixed privileges over some data and it is updated to another data, we must have the same privileges over the new data to be able to perform the same actions. On the other hand, if the initial policy of a field is empty, a set method can be quite simple, but when using the field, one must apply an authorization to gain access to it, as we can see in Figure 8.

**Self reference `this`.** The self reference is considered to be a special access view; it has full access ($\{*\}$) to the object. A perfect analogy is the difference between user space and administrator space. While in user space there are operations that cannot be performed, in administrator space one can do anything.

```
class A : { (f ; g)* } {
  int f() { 0 }
  int g() { 0 }
}

class B : { m* } {
  A a = new A;
  // a: A{ (f;g)* }
  int m()
  { this.a.f() }
}

class C : { m* } {
  A a = new A;
  // a: A{ (f;g)* }
  int m()
  { this.a.f(); this.a.g() }
}
```

**Fig. 7.** Field's policies problem

```
class D { (set+m)* } {
  A a = null ; // a: A{ }
  void set (A other) {
    this.a = other;
    // a:A{ } --> OK
  }

  int m(Auth auth) {
    this.a.g(); // --> ERROR
    authorize this.a : auth
    case { g;g } :
    // --> a : A{ g;g }
     {this.a.g(); this.a.g()}
     // --> a : A{ }
    case error : { 0 }
    // --> a : A{ }
    // a : A{ } --> INV. OK
  }
}
```

**Fig. 8.** Field with empty policy

```
int set (A other) {
  this.a = other; 0
  // a:A{} --> ERROR
}
int set(A other, Auth auth){
  authorize other : auth
  case { (f+g)* } :
    { this.a = other; 0 }
    // a: A{ (f+g)* } --> OK
  case error: { 0 }
  // a: A{ (f+g)* } --> OK
}
```

**Fig. 9.** Set method implementations

```
class E : { (f ; g)* } {
  int f() { this.g() }
  int g() { this.h() } // OK
  int h() { 0 }
}
{
  E e = new E; // e:E{(f;g)*}
  e.f(); e.g() // ALL OK
}
```

**Fig. 10.** Self reference usage

```
class F : { m* } {
  int m(A a1, A a2,
        Auth auth){
    authorize a1 : auth
    case { f;g } : { //(1)
      authorize a2 : auth
      case { f;g } : { //(2)
        a1.f(); a2.f();
        a2.g(); a1.g() //(3)
      }
      case error { 0 } }
    case error { 0 }
  }
}

{
  A a = new A;  F f = new F;
  Auth auth =
    authorization(a, {f;g});
  f.m(a, a, auth); // (4)
}
```

**Fig. 11.** Aliasing example

In our case, normal access views are protected with a policy, restricting which methods can be called. The access view `this` does not have that restriction - it can call any method, any time. As we can see in Figure 10, in method `g()` we call method `h()` with the self reference. Also, notice that the maximal class policy of `E` does not allow method `h()` to be called. So, only the self reference has access to it, just as a private method. Finally, method calls performed by the self reference, as in method `f()`, do not interfere with any method caller's policy.

**Aliasing.** In this work, access view aliasing is not a problem with respect to policies, since each access view has its own policy. Consider Figure 11. When we call method `m()` in (4) with the same access view, we are introducing aliasing inside the method. However, the access views `a1` and `a2` are considered different by the type system. After instruction (1), the access view `a1` has policy {`f`; `g`} and only after instruction (2), access view `a2` will also have policy {`f`; `g`}. Though they are *equal*, they are not the *same*. So, the sequence of calls in (3) is well-typed and safe to execute. Fields, representing the object state, could be the source of aliasing problems. However, since we consider fields' policies to be invariant, after any method call the object's type state does not change.

Therefore, our solution has the benefit of being a statically verified dynamic access control mechanism that does not have aliasing problems.

## 5 Related Work

Researchers have explored access control in many different environments, from logics for access control [7,2], to process calculus with access control [3,1] and programming languages with native access control support [10,21,13]. A common technique used to ensure access control is the development of a type system.

Bengtson et al. developed a language with refinement types [6], where types are extended with access formulas that need to hold to use the respective value. Fournet et al. [10] developed a type system for a process calculus where a special message is typed with a logical expression that needs to be previously assumed for the channel to be well-typed. Both works use primitives to create and verify access conditions (assume/assert, statements/expectations), as we do with authorizations, but our authorizations are first class values, and we develop the multiple view approach. It would be interesting to investigate how our policy language could be defined as a more expressive authorization logic.

Fable [21] is a programming language by Swamy et al. where programmers create labels to protect data and attach them to individual value types. So, each variable has a label restricting its usage, much like our policies can control methods calls. However, we use first class authorizations capable of changing policies, whereas they define functions to change the labels of values.

Jia et al. [13] developed the AURA language with a type system that contains a logic to create authorizations. These authorizations are also values of the language, though they are context dependent and, consequently, are not first class values. Our authorizations, on the other hand, can be stored on data structures, used as an argument to a method call or as a return value.

Skalka and Smith [20] and Bartoletti et al. [4,5] combine type and effect systems with model-checking techniques, where the type systems infer a sequence of events, called history, and use model-checking over the history to verify the desired access policies. However, these policies need to be followed by all users of a resource, while in our work, users have their own policy to follow.

With session types introduced in [12,8,9], interfaces are typed with a sequence of events describing the *behavior* or *protocol* for that interface, i.e., the order by which messages are transmitted with that interface, including the type of each message. Policies held by access views in our approach could considered as the behavior of the respective object, but while a session type is assign to an interface and all users *must* follow (and share) the same protocol, with access views each user has its own policy, describing the privileges they *might* use. Additionally, access view's policies can be modified to a completely different one, whereas session types fix the usage protocol once for all.

In user-based access control (UCON [16]) each component of an access control system is categorized by how and when the usage decisions should be performed to authorize the access to objects by subjects depending on their rights. In our framework, an access policy is both a mutable subject attribute and a right. The decision process defined by the UCON model can be seen as our authorize command, which verifies if a given authorization (another subject attribute, in UCON) is applicable to an object (definition 2). Hence, this is a pre-decision process. Authorizations in UCON are function predicates that decide if a subject can perform the requested rights on the object. This is analogue to our subset relation between policies ($\pi <: \pi'$), which validates the requested policy with an authorized one. Finally, our step relation ($\pi \xrightarrow{m} \pi'$) is a post-update in the UCON model, changing the corresponding access view's policy ($S[u \leftarrow \pi]$).

## 6 Concluding Remarks

We have presented a provably correct type and effect system which guarantees an authorized usage of objects with respect to policies. The system supports dynamic modification of policies using first class authorizations, and keeps track of different policies for a same object by means of access views. Access views allow different users to exercise different authorized usages for the same object, unlike in other approaches in which a policy is attached to the protected object, and not to the user-object relationship. Additionally, our type system is generic and can be instantiated with different access control policy definition languages.

As future work, we need to analyze how access views and authorizations can be efficiently implemented in a distributed run-time environment. In particular, authorization values must be manipulated using cryptographic operations. Additionally, as we are dealing with an object-oriented language, we need to analyze the impact that the maximal class policy has over inheritance, since it is the only class-depended property we have introduced. Exception handling and other extensions to the core language should also be considered to determine the practical applicability of our solution. Finally, we could consider the delegation of authorizations as an authorized capability and design richer policy languages. An implementation of our typechecking algorithm is publicly available in [18].

*Acknowledgments.* We acknowledge the Certified Interfaces research project by CMU-Portugal. We also would like to thank Bernardo Toninho and Francisco Martins for interesting insights on some version of this work, and the anonymous referees for their comments.

## References

1. Abadi, M.: Secrecy by typing in security protocols. J. ACM 46(5), 749–786 (1999)
2. Abadi, M.: Logic in access control. In: Proceedings of LICS 2003, pp. 228–233. IEEE Computer Society, Los Alamitos (2003)
3. Abadi, M., Burrows, M., Lampson, B., Plotkin, G.: A calculus for access control in distributed systems. ACM Trans. Program. Lang. Syst. 15(4), 706–734 (1993)
4. Bartoletti, M., Degano, P., Ferrari, G.: History-based access control with local policies. In: Proc. of Foundations of Software Science and Computation Structure 2005, pp. 316–332. Springer, Heidelberg (2005)
5. Bartoletti, M., Degano, P., Ferrari, G., Zunino, R.: Types and effects for resource usage analysis. In: Proc. of Foundations of Software Science and Computation Structure 2007. LNCS, pp. 32–47. Springer, Heidelberg (2007)
6. Bengtson, J., Bhargavan, K., Fournet, C., Gordon, A.D., Maffeis, S.: Refinement types for secure implementations. In: CSF 2008: Proceedings of the 2008 21st IEEE Computer Security Foundations Symposium, pp. 17–32. IEEE Computer Society Press, Los Alamitos (2008)
7. Crampton, J., Loizou, G.: A logic of access control. The Computer Journal 44, 54–66 (2001)
8. Dezani-Ciancaglini, M., Mostrous, D., Yoshida, N., Drossopoulou, S.: Session types for object-oriented languages. In: Thomas, D. (ed.) ECOOP 2006. LNCS, vol. 4067, pp. 328–352. Springer, Heidelberg (2006)
9. Dezani-Ciancaglini, M., Drossopoulou, S., Mostrous, D., Yoshida, N.: Objects and session types. Inf. Comput. 207(5), 595–641 (2009)
10. Fournet, C., Gordon, A.D., Maffeis, S.: A type discipline for authorization policies. In: Sagiv, M. (ed.) ESOP 2005. LNCS, vol. 3444, pp. 141–156. Springer, Heidelberg (2005)
11. Gosling, J., Joy, B., Steele, G., Bracha, G.: Java(TM) Language Specification, 3rd edn. (Java (Addison-Wesley)) Addison-Wesley Professional, Reading (2005)
12. Honda, K.: Types for dyadic interaction. In: Best, E. (ed.) CONCUR 1993. LNCS, vol. 715, pp. 509–523. Springer, Heidelberg (1993)
13. Jia, L., Vaughan, J.A., Mazurak, K., Zhao, J., Zarko, L., Schorr, J., Zdancewic, S.: Aura: a programming language for authorization and audit. In: ICFP 2008: Proceeding of the 13th ACM SIGPLAN international conference on Functional programming, pp. 27–38. ACM Press, New York (2008)
14. Kozen, D.: Language-based security. In: Mathematical Foundations of Computer Science, pp. 284–298. Springer, Heidelberg (1999)
15. Nielson, F., Nielson, H.R.: Type and effect systems. ACM Computing Surveys, 114–136 (1999)
16. Park, J., Sandhu, R.: The UCONABC usage control model. ACM Trans. Inf. Syst. Secur. 7(1), 128–174 (2004)

17. Pires, M.: A type system for access control in an object-oriented language. Master's thesis, Faculdade de Ciências e Tecnologia, Universidade Nova de Lisboa (2009)
18. PLASTIC. Plastic homepage (2009), `http://ctp.di.fct.unl.pt/PLASTIC/`
19. Schneider, F.B., Morrisett, G., Harper, R.: A language-based approach to security. In: Informatics: 10 Years Back, 10 Years Ahead, pp. 86–101. Springer, Heidelberg (2000)
20. Skalka, C., Smith, S.: History effects and verification. In: The 2nd Asian Symp on Programming Languages and Systems, pp. 107–128. Springer, Heidelberg (2004)
21. Swamy, N., Corcoran, B.J., Hicks, M.: Fable: A language for enforcing user-defined security policies. IEEE Symp. on Security and Privacy (2008)
22. Wright, A.K., Felleisen, M.: A syntactic approach to type soundness. Information and Computation 115, 38–94 (1994)

# Formal Analysis of Key Integrity in PKCS#11*

Andrea Falcone and Riccardo Focardi

Università Ca' Foscari di Venezia, Italy
andrea.falcone@tin.it, focardi@dsi.unive.it

**Abstract.** PKCS#11 is a standard API to cryptographic devices such as smarcards, hardware security modules and usb crypto-tokens. Though widely adopted, this API has been shown to be prone to attacks in which a malicious user gains access to the sensitive keys stored in the devices. In 2008, Delaune, Kremer and Steel proposed a model to formally reason on this kind of attacks. We extend this model to also describe flaws that are based on integrity violations of the stored keys. In particular, we consider scenarios in which a malicious overwriting of keys might fool honest users into using attacker's own keys, while performing sensitive operations. We further enrich the model with a *trusted key* mechanism ensuring that only controlled, non-tampered keys are used in cryptographic operations, and we show how this modified API prevents the above mentioned key-replacement attacks.

## 1 Introduction

PKCS#11 [9] defines an API to cryptographic devices, such as smartcards, hardware security modules and usb crypto-tokens. Apart from providing access to the functionalities offered by devices as, e.g., data encryption, the API is specifically developed to carefully manipulate cryptographic keys. As an example, keys marked as *sensitive* should never be accessible as plaintext outside the device: an application requiring the encryption of confidential data with a sensitive key stored in the device, will refer to the key via a *handle* pointing to the location where the key is stored; the cryptographic operation will then happen inside the device without exposing the key to the external, untrusted world. Access to devices is regulated via a PIN-based authentication check but RSA Security clearly states that PIN leakage, foreseeable, e.g., if the device is used on an untrusted machine, should not ruin the security of PKCS#11 devices.

Following this consideration, the attacker is assumed to execute any possible sequence of legal API calls. Even under this fairly strong attacker model, the secrecy of *sensitive* keys should still be preserved. Unfortunately, in [4] Clulow showed that this is not the case: there exist rather simple API call sequences that enable to recover the value of a sensitive key. The simplest example is the *wrap-decrypt* attack in which a sensitive key is wrapped, i.e. encrypted, with another key which has been generated with the double role of *wrapping* (sensitive) keys

* Work partially supported by Miur'07 Project SOFT: "*Security Oriented Formal Techniques*".

A. Armando and G. Lowe (Eds.): ARSPA-WITS 2010, LNCS 6186, pp. 77–94, 2010.

and *decrypting* data. These roles are, indeed, conflicting. It is clear, in fact, that once the sensitive key has been wrapped and exported, encrypted, out of the device it is sufficient to ask for decryption to obtain the key as plaintext.

In [5], Delaune, Kremer and Steel (DKS) proposed a model of PKCS#11 for formally reasoning on Clulow's attacks. We propose an extension of the DKS-model, in order to reason on how both an attacker and a regular user act on a cryptographic device. The model can therefore explore how the users' actions would influence each other's, accounting for some new capabilities we give to the attacker:

1. overwriting of keys in the device;
2. interception of messages sent on the network by the regular user;
3. disconnection from the system, interrupting the session with the device.

The first capability takes advantage of a vulnerability we found in the API, which may fool the regular user into using some untrusted key. The second capability is typical of attacker models for protocol analysis but is not considered in the DKS-model where there is no distinction between the API calls performed by the honest user and the ones performed by the attacker. For example, in DKS, the result of an encryption call is directly available to the attacker. In our model, this is true only if the call has been performed by the attacker, otherwise the ciphertext has to be explicitly intercepted. The third capability is useful to distinguish attacks where the opponent is always connected to the device, like the ones described in [5], from attacks requiring only a temporary connection. In this way we can describe rather convenient scenarios for the attacker who does not need to constantly break into the user's system in order to stay connected to the device.

Disconnection might also be caused by an external event. Suppose, for example, that the attacker is be able to break the integrity of a key in a token only when it is used on a specific compromised machine, at some public access point. Any subsequent use of that key will be potentially compromised, even when the user connects from her highly secure workstation, inaccessible to any attacker. Our extended model is able to capture this behaviour. In fact, we detail a scenario in which the attacker exploits the loss of one key integrity and manages to violate the secrecy of some sensitive data subsequently sent on the network, encrypted using the tampered key. The second part of the attack does not require the attacker to be connected to the device and is independent of *where* the token is used next.

It is worth noticing that dropping the explicit disconnect event would still find the same attack sequences, as disconnecting simply reduces the actions that the attacker can perform. However, discovering that an attack can be performed, even partially, in a disconnected state is interesting, as it enables the new scenarios described above and points out a dangerous flaw in the API enabling future exploits even when the token becomes inaccessible to the attacker.

We conclude by studying a modified API with a simple mechanism to ensure that only controlled, non-tampered keys are used in sensitive operations, and then show how this countermeasure impedes the previously described attack. The mechanism is based on the *trusted key* attribute of PKCS#11 used to prevent exporting keys in an insecure way, and is extended to any key involved in sensitive operations, i.e., any such key is required to be trusted. As trusted keys cannot be set by regular users, this prevents the key integrity problems discussed above. It is quite surprising that a similar mechanism is not mandatory in the API. As a matter of fact, in all the experiments we have performed on real crypto-tokens and smartcard, we have ascertained that no one supports the trusted key attribute.

The paper is organized as follows. In Section 2 we introduce the DKS-model [5]. In Section 3 we present the vulnerability we found concerning the integrity of keys, we introduce our model and we illustrate its adequacy through a detailed example of attack; in Section 4 we refine this first model, tweaking a small but significant detail and giving birth to a variation of the model; we then formally compare the relative expressive power of the two proposals. Finally, in Section 5 we study a modified API preventing the previously described attack. Section 6 gives some concluding remarks.

## 2 Background: The DKS-Model of PKCS#11

In [5], Delaune, Kremer and Steel (DKS) proposed a model of PKCS#11 for formally reasoning on API-level attacks. This model is the starting point of our work and we describe it in the following.

**Terms.** Let $\mathcal{N}$ be a possibly infinite set of *names*, representing keys, data values, nonces, etc., and $\mathcal{X}$ a possibly infinite set of *variables*. Let also $\Sigma$ be a finite set of *function symbols*, with arity $ar : \Sigma \to \mathbb{N}$, representing, e.g., handles to keys and cryptographic primitives. The set of *plain terms* $\mathcal{PT}$ is defined by the following grammar:

$$\begin{array}{lll} t, t_i := & x & x \in \mathcal{X} \\ & \mid\; n & n \in \mathcal{N} \\ & \mid\; f(t_1, \ldots, t_n) & f \in \Sigma \text{ and } ar(f) = n \end{array}$$

PKCS#11 specifies a number of different attributes for keys and data stored in the devices, dictating their respective usage. For example, a *sensitive* key should never be exported from the device as plaintext. Let now $\mathcal{A}$ be a set of unary function symbols disjoint from $\Sigma$, called *attributes*. The set of *attribute terms* $\mathcal{AT}$ is built by applying these attributes to plain terms, i.e., $\mathcal{AT} = \{att(t) \mid att \in \mathcal{A},\, t \in \mathcal{PT}\}$. Attribute terms are interpreted as propositions, meaning that there will be a truth value associated with them, representing the value of a given attribute of some plain term. A *literal* is an expression $a$ or $\neg a$ where $a \in \mathcal{AT}$. The set of all terms is $\mathcal{T} = \mathcal{PT} \cup \mathcal{AT}$. Finally, we denote as $\sigma$ substitutions of variables into terms and we write $t\sigma$ to note the application of $\sigma$ to all variables of $t$.

*Example 1.* Term $senc(k_2, k_1) \in \mathcal{PT}$, with $k_1, k_2 \in \mathcal{N}$, represents the symmetric encryption of key $k_2$ under key $k_1$. Terms $h(n_1, k_1)$ and $h(n_2, k_2)$ specify two handles $n_1, n_2$ to the respective keys $k_1, k_2$. Attributes $sensitive(n_2)$, $extract(n_2)$ and $wrap(n_1)$ specifies that $k_2$ is sensitive and extractable and $k_1$ is a key for wrapping, i.e., encrypting other extractable, possibly sensitive keys. Wrapping keys, such as $k_1$, is useful to export sensitive and extractable keys in a secure, encrypted form.

**Syntax.** Rules for modelling APIs are expressed in the form

$$T; L \xrightarrow{\text{new } \tilde{n}} T'; L'$$

where $T, T' \subseteq \mathcal{PT}$ are plain terms, $L$ and $L'$ are sets of literals, $\tilde{n} \in \mathcal{N}$ is a set of names. $T$ and $L$ specify the conditions under which the rule is applicable, whereas $T'$ and $L'$ specify what will be the result of this rule, if applied. Intuitively, the rule can be executed if all the terms in $T$ are present and all the literals in $L$ are evaluated to true in the current state. We will see, in fact, that a *state* is a pair of two elements: a set of ground plain terms $S$, which represents data in the attacker knowledge, and a partial valuation function $V$, which maintains the values of the key attributes. The effect of the rule is that the terms in $T'$ are added to the state and the valuation of the attributes is updated according to $L'$. Label 'new $\tilde{n}$' binds names $\tilde{n}$ in $T'$ and $L'$, forcing them to be different from all the other names in the state. This mechanism, named *fresh renaming*, allows for modelling nonce or key generation.

*Example 2.* Symmetric encryption is modelled as follows.

$$h(x_1, y_1), y_2; \; encrypt(x_1) \; \rightarrow \; senc(y_2, y_1)$$

Intuitively, if the attacker knows some data $y_2$ that he wants to encrypt and he also has a reference, represented by the *handle* term $h(x_1, y_1)$, to some internally stored key $y_1$ with the *encrypt* attribute set, then the attacker may perform an API call and obtain the ciphertext resulting from the encryption of $y_2$ under key $y_1$, i.e., $senc(y_2, y_1)$.

The DKS-model rules for more PKCS#11 functionalities are reported in Appendix A.

**Semantics.** As previously mentioned, A *state* $(S, V)$ is a pair of two elements: a set of ground plain terms $S$, which represents data in the attacker knowledge, and a partial valuation function $V$, which maintains the boolean values of the key attributes. $V$ is extended to literals and to sets of literals as expected, i.e., $V(\neg a) = \neg V(a)$ and $V(L) = \bigwedge_{l \in L} V(l)$ when $V(l)$ is defined for all $l \in L$.

Given a rule[1] $T; L \rightarrow T'; L'$ transition $(S, V) \rightsquigarrow (S', V')$ may take place if there exists a grounding substitution $\theta$ for the rule such that:

- $T\theta \subseteq S$, i.e., terms in $T$ are in the enemy knowledge;
- $V(L\theta) = true$, i.e., all literals in $L$ are evaluated to *true*.

[1] We omit here the formalization of rule fresh renaming, consisting of removing label 'new $\tilde{n}$' from the arrow after having renamed names $\tilde{n}$ so that they differ from all the other names in the rule and in the state. For more detail see [5].

Then, $S' = S \cup T'\theta$, and function $V'$ is defined as follows:

$$dom\,(V') = dom\,(V) \cup \{a \mid (a \in L'\theta) \vee (\neg a \in L'\theta)\}$$

and $\forall a \in dom\,(V')$:

$$V'\,(a) = \begin{cases} true & \text{if } a \in L'\theta \\ false & \text{if } \neg a \in L'\theta \\ V\,(a) & \text{otherwise} \end{cases}$$

Intuitively, literals in $L'$ override the evaluation function for their attributes. All the other attributes are untouched.

*Example 3 (The wrap-decrypt attack, single key variant).* We show how the models work by illustrating a variant of the wrap-decrypt attack of [4] with one single key. The DKS-rules for wrap and decrypt are as follows:

$$h\,(x_1, y_1)\,, h\,(x_2, y_2)\,; wrap\,(x_1)\,, extract\,(x_2) \rightarrow senc\,(y_2, y_1)$$
$$h\,(x_1, y_1)\,, senc\,(y_2, y_1)\,; decrypt\,(x_1) \rightarrow y_2$$

It now sufficient to consider an initial state $(S_0, V_0)$ with $S_0 = \{h(n,k)\}$ and $V_0(wrap(n)) = V_0(extract(n)) = V_0(decrypt(n)) = V_0(sensitive(n)) = true.$ Intuitively, we consider a single key $k$ with handle $n$, with the attributes *wrap*, *extract*, *decrypt* and *sensitive* set. Notice that, being it sensitive, $k$ should never be extracted from the device as plaintext. Intuitively, being $k$ both a wrapping and extractable key, it can be wrapped under itself. To see this, formally, consider the first rule above (wrap) and the substitution $\theta = \{n/x_1, n/x_2, k/y_1, k/y_2\}$. We have:

$$\begin{aligned} T\theta &= \{h\,(x_1, y_1)\,, h\,(x_2, y_2)\}\theta \\ &= \{h(n,k)\} \subseteq S_0 \end{aligned}$$

$$\begin{aligned} V_0(L\theta) &= V_0(\{wrap\,(x_1)\,, extract\,(x_2)\}\theta) \\ &= V_0(\{wrap\,(n)\,, extract\,(n)\}) \\ &= V_0(wrap\,(n)) \wedge V_0(extract\,(n)) = true \end{aligned}$$

Thus $(S_0, V_0) \rightsquigarrow (S_0 \cup \{senc(k,k)\}, V_0)$, with term $senc(k,k)$ representing the wrapping of $k$ under itself and obtained as $T'\theta = senc\,(y_2, y_1)\,\theta = senc(k,k)$. Now, being $k$ also a decryption key it can be used to decrypt term $senc(k,k)$ giving the sensitive key $k$ as a plaintext. We leave as an exercise the formal application of the decrypt rule using substitution $\theta' = \{n/x_1, k/y_1, k/y_2\}$ and giving transition $(S_0 \cup \{senc(k,k)\}, V_0) \rightsquigarrow (S_0 \cup \{senc(k,k), k\}, V_0)$. This attack shows that *wrap* and *decrypt* are conflicting attributes for keys: they should never be both set on the same key.

The decision procedure arising from the model has been automated via model checking, leading to a series of experiments reproducing the attacks already shown by Clulow in [4], and also finding new ones [11]. The authors also proposed 'patches' on the API preventing the attacks in the model.

## 3 Extending the Model: Key Integrity

We shift the focus of the analysis by taking into account a new vulnerability we observed on real tokens: the attacker is able to overwrite keys stored on the token, in such a way that the user application will refer the new substitute key as it was its own. Assume one application refers to keys by means of their *label* attribute, a short textual description, managed by the applications themselves, on which no security policy is enforced by the API. Thus, an attacker logged into the token can overwrite one of the regular user's keys, say $k_1$, with another key of his choice, $k_2$, by simply copying $k_1$'s label onto $k_2$ and then deleting $k_1$ from the token. As a result, the next time a honest user will refer the target key $k_1$ by means of its label, he will be given access to the attacker's key $k_2$, in a transparent way. We have tested this attack on different USB crypto-tokens we possess.

We now extend the DKS-model of previous section so to also represent the above mentioned scenario. In particular, we describe the actions of two users: together with the enemy $E$ we take into consideration a regular, trusted user $T$. Their sessions on the device may run concurrently, thus each step of the system represents an API call performed by one of them. States are enlarged to provide both users with their own sets of known terms, namely $S_E$ and $S_T$. The states also maintain the attribute values for token keys and the *connection status* of the users. The state of the system may be altered as a result of the users' actions: for instance an encryption operation would generate in the model a new term, representing the resulting ciphertext, to be added to the knowledge set of the user requesting this operation.

Having both an attacker and a regular user acting at the same time on the token, this model can describe scenarios in which the two affect each other's actions. Based on this idea, we give the enemy new capabilities: the ability to intercept information sent on the network by the trusted user and the ability to indirectly affect the actions of the regular user, by modifying keys stored on the token. In fact, in our model the attacker has the ability to overwrite keys stored on the device, as discussed above.

Furthermore, the enemy has the ability to disconnect himself from the system, ceasing the session with the device. Disconnecting from the token means losing all the references to the keys stored on it and also losing the ability to require cryptographic operations from the device. Note that nonetheless, even if disconnected, the attacker can still perform cryptographic operations implemented in software libraries. As discussed in the Introduction, this allows for more practical and convenient attacks, in which a compromised key also compromises subsequent cryptographic operations based on such a key. The enemy, for example, does not need to be connected to the device to decrypt any sensitive data encrypted under a previously tampered key he possesses. For the sake of simplicity we omit modelling a complementary 'reconnect' action but this could easily accounted for in the model.

We formalize the above ideas by extending the DKS-model of section 2.

**Table 1.** Rules for key overwriting and disconnected users

Key overwriting

$$h(x_1, y_2), senc(y_1, y_2); unwrap(x_1) \xrightarrow{\text{used } n} h(n, y_1); extract(n), L$$

$$h(x_1, priv(z)), aenc(y_1, pub(z)); unwrap(x_1) \xrightarrow{\text{used } n} h(n, y_1); extract(n), L$$

$$h(x_1, y_2), senc(priv(z), y_2); unwrap(x_1) \xrightarrow{\text{used } n} h(n, priv(z)); extract(n), L$$

where, $L = \neg wrap(n), \neg unwrap(n), \neg encrypt(n), \neg decrypt(n), \neg sensitive(n)$.

Disconnected

$$x, y \longrightarrow senc(x, y)$$

$$senc(x, y), y \longrightarrow x$$

$$pub(z), x \longrightarrow aenc(x, pub(z))$$

$$aenc(x, pub(z)), priv(z) \longrightarrow x$$

**Syntax.** We extend rule syntax as follows:

$$T; L \xrightarrow{\text{new } \tilde{n}, \text{ used } \tilde{m}} T'; L'$$

The only difference is the new label 'used $\tilde{m}$' forcing the usage of names occurring in some handle already known by the user: when the rule is fired, all the occurrences in $T'$ and $L'$ of names in $\tilde{m}$ must be replaced by names already in use as the first element $m$ of a handle term $h(m, k)$ in the actual user's knowledge set. This mechanism, named *used renaming*, allows us to model the key overwriting operation, because it pinpoints handle names already in use, thus selecting the handle to be replaced.

**Key overwrite rules.** Based on the extended syntax, we give new rules for modelling key overwrite. As an example:

$$h(x_1, y_2), senc(y_1, y_2); unwrap(x_1) \xrightarrow{\text{used } n} h(n, y_1); extract(n), \mathcal{L}$$

with $\mathcal{L} = \neg wrap(n), \neg unwrap(n), \neg encrypt(n), \neg decrypt(n), \neg sensitive(n)$, models an unwrap operation overwriting key referred by handle $n$. Knowing the handle $h(x_1, y_2)$ and the wrapped key $senc(y_1, y_2)$, and assuming $x_1$ refers to an unwrapping key, we can unwrap $y_1$ giving a used handle $n$ to refer to it, thus overwriting a key already stored in the device. The appropriate attributes are set to the unwrapped key. Notice that this rule corresponds to the first unwrap DKS-rule of appendix A with 'new $n$' replaced by 'used $n$'.

The other rules to model key overwriting for asymmetric cryptography are given in table 1. In the same table we also give rules for operations implemented in software and called 'Disconnected', being them executable even when users are not connected to the token. These rules are not described in [5] but they are implicitly part of the DKS-model too, as they correspond to standard Dolev-Yao attackers.

**Semantics.** A state is now represented by a tuple $(S_T, S_E, V, C_T, C_E)$, where

- $S_T, S_E \subseteq \mathcal{PT}$ represent the knowledge of the trusted user and the enemy;
- $V$, as before, is a partial boolean function evaluating attributes $\mathcal{AT}$;
- $C_T, C_E \in \{true, false\}$ are two booleans indicating the connection status of the two users.

We define the following operations on set of ground plain terms:

$$H(S) = \{h(n,k) \in S \mid n \in \mathcal{N}\}$$
$$\hat{H}(S_1, S_2) = \{h(n,k) \in S_1 \mid n \in \mathcal{N} \text{ and } \exists k' \text{ such that } h(n,k') \in S_2\}$$

$H(S)$ returns the set of all the handles in a given set $S$ of ground plain terms. $\hat{H}(S_1, S_2)$ returns all the handles in $S_1$ also referring to keys in $S_2$.

*Example 4.* Let $S_E = \{k_1, h(n_1, k_2), h(n_2, k_3)\}$ and $S_T = \{k_1, h(n_1, k_4)\}$, then $H(S_E) = \{h(n_1, k_2), h(n_2, k_3)\}$, $H(S_T) = \{h(n_1, k_4)\}$ give the handles in $S_E$ and $S_T$. Moreover, $\hat{H}(S_E, S_T) = \{h(n_1, k_2)\}$ since $n_1$ refers to a key also in $S_T$. Similarly, $\hat{H}(S_T, S_E) = \{h(n_1, k_4)\}$.

In the following we will use $\sigma \in \{T, E\}$ to select one of the users, with the complement $\bar{\sigma}$ defined as expected, i.e. $\bar{T} = E$ and $\bar{E} = T$. The system can evolve through one of the following transitions:

- **$\sigma$-call:** user $\sigma$ performs a call to the API or an operation in software, the former only possible if she is connected;
- **Send:** one or more terms of the trusted user's knowledge become part of the attacker's knowledge. This mimics the attacker intercepting data sent over the network by the regular user;
- **Disconnect:** the attacker closes his session with the token and loses all his handles.

We describe the three kinds of transition in detail.

*The $\sigma$-call transition.* This transition extends the execution of a rule in the DKS-model: first, if the rule is not one of the 'Disconnected' (table 1), i.e. if the rule uses handles referring to keys stored in the device, the user must be connected. Second, the premises of the rule must be in the knowledge of user $\sigma$ and the non-handle terms generated by the rule-firing are visible only to such user, i.e. the one performing the call, while new handles are visible to both. As for DKS-model, we assume rules have been renamed so that new names are different from any other name around (fresh renaming). Moreover, for each label 'used $m$', we rename $m$ so that there exists $h(m,k) \in H(S_T) \cup H(S_E)$, i.e., $m$ is the handle of some key in one of the knowledge sets (used renaming).

Given $T; L \rightarrow T'; L'$ transition $(S_T, S_E, V, C_T, C_E) \rightsquigarrow (S'_T, S'_E, V', C_T, C_E)$ takes place if there exists a grounding substitution $\theta$ for the rule such that

- $C_\sigma \vee H(T\theta) = L\theta = H(T'\theta) = L'\theta = \emptyset$, i.e., either the user is connected or the rule does not refer to any handles and attributes (it is a 'Disconnected');

- $T\theta \subseteq S_\sigma$, i.e., terms in $T\theta$ are in the knowledge of user $\sigma$;
- $\mathrm{V}(L\theta) = true$, i.e., all literals in $L$ are evaluated to $true$.

Then $S'_\sigma = S_\sigma \setminus \hat{H}\left(S_\sigma, T'\theta\right) \cup T'\theta$ and

$$S'_{\bar\sigma} = \begin{cases} S_{\bar\sigma} \setminus \hat{H}\left(S_{\bar\sigma}, T'\theta\right) \cup H\left(T'\theta\right) & \text{if } C_{\bar\sigma} \\ S_{\bar\sigma} & \text{if } \neg C_{\bar\sigma} \end{cases}$$

Intuitively, the terms in the rule consequence are added to the knowledge set of the $\sigma$-user; terms that represent homonym handles, i.e. key handles that share their first argument with some handle in the rule consequence, must be subtracted from the system, since they are going to be overwritten. The manipulation of token keys is immediately visible to all the sessions on the token, thus the other user's knowledge set (i.e. $S_{\bar\sigma}$) must be updated accordingly: only handle terms in the rule consequence are added to it and homonym handles are subtracted; of course, if instead $\bar\sigma$ is disconnected, there will be no change on user's knowledge.

Function $V'$ is defined as follows

$$dom\left(V'\right) = dom\left(V\right) \setminus \hat{A} \cup \left\{a \mid \left(a \in L'\theta\right) \vee \left(\neg a \in L'\theta\right)\right\}$$

where $\hat{A} = \left\{att\left(n\right) \mid \exists h\left(n,k\right) \in \hat{H}\left(S_\sigma, T'\theta\right),\ att \in \mathcal{A},\ n \in \mathcal{N}\right\}$ is the set of the attribute-terms in the $V$ function domain that will be "forgotten" due to their respective handles being overwritten in this transition. Also, attribute terms in the rule consequence are added to the function domain. $V'$ values then are defined as in DKS-model (section 2). Finally, notice that $C_T$ and $C_E$ are unchanged since no disconnection can happen within this transition.

*Example 5 ($\sigma$-call transition).* We illustrate how a symmetric encryption operation performed by the attacker is represented in the model. Consider the names set $\mathcal{N} = \{m, n, k_1, k_2\}$. Assume, also, that at step number $i$ the state is $q_i = (S_{T,i}, S_{E,i}, V_i, true, true)$ with $S_{E,i} = \{h\left(n, k_1\right), k_2\}$, $V_i\left(encrypt\left(n\right)\right) = true$. In state $q_i$ the attacker has thus access to key $k_1$ through the handle named $n$, which is entitled for encryption, and he knows the value of key $k_2$; also, both the users are connected to the token. The values of the other state elements are irrelevant here.

To carry out the next step in computation, an applicable transition must be looked for, on behalf of either the regular user or the attacker. Of all the applicable transitions in this state, an *E-call* for the symmetric encryption is chosen. We report the corresponding rule here for convenience:

$$h\left(x_1, y_1\right), y_2; encrypt\left(x_1\right) \rightarrow senc\left(y_2, y_1\right)$$

There is no need for a renaming operation on this rule before execution, and it is applicable in the current state $q_i$ with the substitution $\theta_i = \{n/x_1, k_1/y_1, k_2/y_2\}$: in fact, we have that $\{h\left(x_1, y_1\right), y_2\}\,\theta_1 \subseteq S_{E,i}$ and $V_i\left(\{encrypt\left(x_1\right)\}\,\theta_1\right) = true$. Therefore, $q_i \rightsquigarrow q_{i+1} = (S_{T,i+1}, S_{E,i+1}, V_{i+1}, true, true)$ such that:

- $S_{T,i+1} = S_{T,i}$
- $S_{E,i+1} = S_{E,i} \cup \{senc(y_2, y_1)\}\theta_i = S_{E,i} \cup \{senc(k_2, k_1)\}$
- $V_{i+1}$ is such that
  - $dom(V_{i+1}) = dom(V_i)$
  - $V_{i+1}(encrypt(x_1)) = true$, thus $V_{i+1} = V_i$

*Example 6 (overwriting a key).* We now illustrate what happens when firing the previously described key overwriting rule:

$$h(x_1, y_2), senc(y_1, y_2); unwrap(x_1) \xrightarrow{\text{used } n} h(n, y_1); extract(n), L$$

We give a synthetic representation of the scenario, detailing only the knowledge set of the attacker, who is executing the rule.

| step | $S_E$ |
|---|---|
| i | $h(n_1, k_1), senc(k_3, k_2), h(n_2, k_2)$ |
| i+1 | $h(n_1, \mathbf{k_3}), senc(k_3, k_2), h(n_2, k_2)$ |

We see that key $k_3$ is unwrapped and *overwrites* key $k_1$. Formally, to fire the overwriting rule we first have to perform the 'used renaming' operation obtaining:

$$h(x_1, y_2), senc(y_1, y_2); unwrap(x_1) \to h(n_1, y_1); extract(n_1), L\{n_1/n\}$$

We have removed the 'used $n$' label by renaming $n$ in a way it matches an existing handle, in this case $h(n_1, k_1)$. Now we can fire the rule using the substitution $\theta_i = \{n_2/x_1, k_2/y_2, k_3/y_1\}$. We obtain that

$$\begin{aligned} S_{E,i+1} &= S_{E,i} \setminus \hat{H}(S_{E,i}, T'\theta) \cup T'\theta = \\ &= S_{E,i} \setminus \hat{H}(S_{E,i}, \{h(n_1, k_3)\}) \cup \{h(n_1, k_3)\} = \\ &= S_{E,i} \setminus \{h(n_1, k_1)\} \cup \{h(n_1, k_3)\} = \\ &= \{h(n_1, k_3), senc(k_3, k_2), h(n_2, k_2)\} \end{aligned}$$

Notice that the existing conflicting handle $h(n_1, k_1)$ is correctly removed before the new overwriting key $h(n_1, k_3)$ is added to the knowledge.

*The Send transition.* When a user asks a device for generating a ciphertext it is plausible that she is going to send it on the network or store it in a place she does not completely trust. This transition models exactly the attacker intercepting such an encrypted data.

Given a subset $I \subseteq S_T$ of the trusted user's knowledge set, the system can perform a Send transition $(S_T, S_E, V, C_T, C_E) \rightsquigarrow (S_T, S_E \cup I, V, C_T, C_E)$.

*Example 7 (Send transition).* Suppose that the trusted user has to send a ciphertext on the network and that this will be intercepted by the attacker. Consider the state is $q = (S_T, S_E, V, C_T, C_E)$, where $S_T = \{h(n_1, k_1), senc(d, k_1)\}$, meaning that the trusted user has access to the key $k_1$ through the handle named $n_1$ and he also knows the ciphertext resulting from the encryption of some data $d$ under key $k_1$. Furthermore, $S_E = \{h(n_1, k_1)\}$. The values of the other state elements are irrilevant here. In this state the Send transition is applicable, considering $I \subseteq S_T$, $I = \{senc(d, k_1)\}$. Thus, we have $q \rightsquigarrow q' = (S_T, S_E \cup \{senc(d, k_1)\}, V, C_T, C_E)$.

*The Disconnect transition.* Since this transition models the disconnection of the attacker from the device with the consequence of losing access to all the token keys, key handles must be deleted from the attacker's knowledge set in the process.

The system may evolve by a Disconnect transition $(S_T, S_E, V, C_T, C_E) \rightsquigarrow (S_T, S_E \setminus H(S_E), V, C_T, false)$.

*Example 8 (Disconnect transition).* Let $q = (S_T, S_E, V, true, true)$, where $S_E = \{h(n_1, k_1), h(n_2, k_2)\}$, meaning that the attacker has access to two keys through their respective handles. A disconnect operation is issued and reflected in the model as $q_i \rightsquigarrow q_{i+1} = (S_T, \emptyset, V, true, false)$.

**A complete key overwriting attack.** The features introduced in our model make it possible to describe a scenario in which a key integrity violation is exploited by the attacker to illegally obtain secret data. The regular user possesses some secret data $d$, which he needs to send on the net, after having encrypted it to protect its secrecy. Also, recall that the attacker knows the regular user's PIN code for the token and he is also able to send commands to the token. Furthermore, the attacker knows which key will be used for the encryption operation and has access to the corresponding handle (but not to the key value).

In Table 2 we give a summary of the attack sequence, detailing only the knowledge sets; in bold font we emphasize what is new at each step. In the initial state the device holds two keys and both users have handles to them: $k_t$ is the trusted user's key and $k_i$ is a wrap/unwrap key that will be exploited by the attacker to import in the device his own key $k_e$ (initially not stored on the device); the trusted user knows the sensitive data $d$.

During steps 1 and 2 the attacker illegally imports his key in the device, through a process already shown in [5, section 5.3, experiment 2]: he encodes key $k_e$ in the same format used for wrap operations and makes the device encrypt it under $k_i$. This yields the same result as $k_e$ was regularly wrapped by the token. Then, the attacker calls an unwrap of this piece of data, creating as a result a copy of $k_e$ in the device and obtaining a new handle for it. We adapted this process to model the key overwriting operation: while unwrapping key $k_e$, the trusted user's key is deleted after having copied its label onto $k_e$. Note that having key $k_i$ is not mandatory, it's just for clarity: key $k_t$ itself could be used to import $k_e$, in case its *unwrap* attribute is set to *true*.

Having done this, at step 3 the attacker can disconnect himself from the system: the user key $k_t$ as been replaced and any subsequent encryption (apparently) based on such a key will be compromised, as show below.

At step 4 the trusted user encrypts $d$: she (unconsciously) refers to $k_e$ because her reference is now pointing to it. At step 5 the trusted user sends the ciphertext resulting from encryption on the net; the attacker intercepts it. Finally, at

**Table 2.** Key overwriting attack

| step | transition | $\sigma$ | $S_T$ | $S_E$ |
|---|---|---|---|---|
| 0 | - | - | $d, h(t, k_t), h(i, k_i)$ | $h(t, k_t), h(i, k_i), k_e$ |
| 1 | encrypt | E | $d, h(t, k_t), h(i, k_i)$ | $h(t, k_t), h(i, k_i), k_e, \mathbf{senc}(\mathbf{k_e}, \mathbf{k_i})$ |
| 2 | overwrite | E | $d, h(t, \mathbf{k_e}), h(i, k_i)$ | $h(t, \mathbf{k_e}), h(i, k_i), k_e, senc(k_e k_i)$ |
| 3 | Disconnect | - | $d, h(t, k_e), h(i, k_i)$ | $k_e, senc(k_e k_i)$ |
| 4 | encryption | T | $d, h(t, k_e), h(i, k_i),$ $\mathbf{senc}(\mathbf{d}, \mathbf{k_e})$ | $k_e, senc(k_e k_i)$ |
| 5 | Send | - | $d, h(t, k_e), h(i, k_i),$ $senc(d, k_e)$ | $k_e, senc(k_e k_i), \mathbf{senc}(\mathbf{d}, \mathbf{k_e})$ |
| 6 | decryption (disconn.) | E | $d, h(t, k_e), h(i, k_i),$ $senc(d, k_e)$ | $k_e, senc(k_e k_i), senc(d, k_e), \mathbf{d}$ |

step 6 the attacker can decrypt the data $d$. Notice that this last operation is performed off-line, possibly using some software implementation of the decryption algorithm.

## 4 The $\mathcal{H}$-Transition System

We give another formalization of the transition system, aiming at making it more rational in the way it manages the handle terms: as can be seen in examples of previous section the key handles are often redundantly maintained in both the knowledge sets. In the new transition system, the handle terms are made explicit from the knowledge sets and uniquely maintained in a new element in the state vector, named $\mathcal{H}$. The state becomes thus $(\mathcal{H}, S_T, S_E, V, C_T, C_E)$ and we note the new transition as $\rightsquigarrow_{\mathcal{H}}$. We now describe how **$\sigma$-call**, **Send** and **Disconnect** are modified to accommodate the new separate information on handles.

**The $\mathcal{H}$ $\sigma$-call transition.** The $\sigma$-call transition requires the same conditions as in the previous transition system to be met in order to execute a rule from $\mathcal{R}$ (recall that a call to the API is only possible for connected users). The only difference is that the handle terms are to be found in the $\mathcal{H}$ element of the state vector. More specifically, in place of condition $T\theta \subseteq S_\sigma$, requiring that terms in $T\theta$ are in the knowledge of user $\sigma$, we require:

- $H(T\theta) \subseteq \mathcal{H}$, i.e., all the required handles are in $\mathcal{H}$;
- $T\theta \setminus H(T\theta) \subseteq S_\sigma$, i.e., all the required terms that are not handles are in the knowledge of user $\sigma$.

If these conditions are met, then the system can evolve with the transition $(\mathcal{H}, S_T, S_E, V, C_T, C_E) \rightsquigarrow (\mathcal{H}', S'_T, S'_E, V', C_T, C_E)$, where:

$$\mathcal{H}' = \mathcal{H} \setminus \hat{H}(\mathcal{H}, T'\theta) \cup H(T'\theta)$$
$$K'_\sigma = K_\sigma \cup T'\theta \setminus H(T'\theta)$$
$$K'_{\overline{\sigma}} = K_{\overline{\sigma}}$$

Handle terms in the rule's consequence are added to the handle set, accounting for overwriting operations if needed. The non-handle terms in the rule's consequence are added to the knowledge set of the $\sigma$-user. Notice that for $\bar{\sigma}$-user nothing is done, since handles are stored in the 'centralized' set $\mathcal{H}$.

The attribute valuation function $V$ is updated as before, carefully removing all the attributes of overwritten keys.

**The $\mathcal{H}$ Send transition.** The $\mathcal{H}$ Send transition is analogous to the Send. Given a subset $I \subseteq S_T$ of terms in the trusted user's knowledge set, the system can perform $(\mathcal{H}, S_T, S_E, V, C_T, C_E) \rightsquigarrow_{\mathcal{H}} (\mathcal{H}, S_T, S_E \cup I, V, C_T, C_E)$.

**The $\mathcal{H}$ Disconnect transition.** The $\mathcal{H}$ Disconnect transition differs from the Disconnect in that no handle terms are deleted from the state vector; just the connection flag is updated: $(\mathcal{H}, S_T, S_E, V, C_T, C_E) \rightsquigarrow_{\mathcal{H}} (\mathcal{H}, S_T, S_E, V, C_T, false)$.

**Expressiveness results.** We now show that the two presented models are equivalent regarding their ability to describe evolutions of the token-users system. We formalize and prove a theorem stating that, given a $\rightsquigarrow$ transition there exists a correspondent $\rightsquigarrow_{\mathcal{H}}$ transition, and vice-versa. First we give some preliminary definitions.

Let $\bar{H}(S) = \{S \setminus H(S)\}$ be the set of all the non-handle terms in a set S.. We let also $Q$ and $Q_{\mathcal{H}}$ denote the set of states in the two models.

**Definition 1 (State encoding).** *The state encoding function* $[\![\cdot]\!] : Q \longrightarrow Q_{\mathcal{H}}$ *is defined as* $[\![(S_T, S_E, V, C_T, C_E)]\!] \triangleq \left(H(S_T), \bar{H}(S_T), \bar{H}(S_E), V, C_T, C_E\right)$.

This definition of state encoding is based on the observation that the trusted user never disconnects from the token: the $\mathcal{H}$ element of $Q_{\mathcal{H}}$ is filled with handles taken explicitly from the trusted user's knowledge set $S_T$.

**Definition 2 (Inverse state encoding).** *The inverse state encoding function* $[\![\cdot]\!]^{-1} : Q_{\mathcal{H}} \longrightarrow Q$ *is defined as*

$$[\![(\mathcal{H}, S_T, S_E, V, C_T, C_E)]\!]^{-1} \triangleq \left([\![S_T]\!]^{-1}, [\![S_E]\!]^{-1}, V, C_T, C_E\right)$$

*where* $[\![S_\sigma]\!]^{-1} = \begin{cases} S_\sigma \cup \mathcal{H}, & \text{if } C_\sigma \\ S_\sigma & \text{if } \neg C_\sigma \end{cases}$

Next lemma states that $[\![\cdot]\!]^{-1}$ is the inverse of $[\![\cdot]\!]$. Proof is given in Appendix B.

**Lemma 1.** $\forall q \in Q$ we have $[\![[\![q]\!]]\!]^{-1} = q$.

Relying on these encodings, we formalize our main result.

**Theorem 1 (models equivalence).** *Let* $q_i, q_f \in Q$

$$q_i \rightsquigarrow q_f \quad \Longleftrightarrow \quad [\![q_i]\!] \rightsquigarrow_{\mathcal{H}} [\![q_f]\!]$$

The proof for this theorem is long, but rather mechanical; we give a sketch of it in Appendix B.

## 5 Adding Trusted Keys

In this section, we propose a way to remedy the PKCS#11 API vulnerability that lets an attacker break a key integrity, discussed above. The idea is based on the use of one of the cryptographic key attributes, already part of the API: the *trusted* attribute. As the name suggests, this attribute is used to discriminate between trusted and untrusted keys. It is designed to be part of a mechanism by which the API can prevent exporting keys in an insecure way, by forbidding the usage of untrusted keys for wrapping sensitive keys. The *trusted* attribute can only be set by the Security Officer in charge of the token. Since the Securiy Officer's PIN code is different from that of the normal user and is never used on untrusted hosts, the enemy cannot manipulate the *trusted* attribute.

Key integrity can be thus checked by just reading the value of its *trusted* attribute: if the *trusted* attribute value is found to be *false*, it means the key has possibly been tampered. Note that this check can be done either explicitly by the user application, or implicitly by the API or the device itself.

In order to model this new mechanism, we simply check the *trusted* attribute of every key appearing in a rule, before its application. To this aim, we need to update all the rules for the $\sigma$-call transition which yield new key handles and have them explicitly set the *trusted* attribute of the newly created handles to *false*, as a default value. The rules affected by this update are all the key generation rules and all the unwrap rules. To this aim it is sufficient to extend $\mathcal{L}$ with $\neg trusted(n)$.

**$\mathcal{T}$ $\sigma$-call semantics.** We let $Tr\left(S\right) = \left\{trusted\left(n\right) \mid \exists h\left(n,k\right) \in S \text{ with } n \in \mathcal{N}\right\}$ be the set of *trusted* attribute terms relative to all the handle terms in $S$. We add to the rule applicability conditions a check for the *trusted* attribute value for all the key handle terms in rule premises $T$. This new condition will only allow the execution of a rule if each of the required key handles has the *trusted* attribute set to *true*. Formally, this is achieved by asking $V\left(Tr\left(T\right)\right) = true$.

Note that this new behavior does not directly forbid the key overwriting operation but it makes it possible to detect it in a simple way, as shown below.

**Key overwriting attack and trusted keys.** Given the above modifications to the semantics, the example attack showed in Example 3 on page 87 is prevented. In Table 3 on the next page we show how the attack sequence is revealed and blocked. Suppose that initially the trusted attribute on the handle for $k_t$ is set to *true*. After step 2 the attacker has successfully overwritten $k_t$ with $k_e$, $h(t, k_t)$ being replaced by $h(t, k_e)$; nonetheless, the new handle $h(t, k_e)$ does not possess the *trusted* attribute. Thus, at step 4 the normal user's request for a symmetric encryption is refused, because the supplied key, referenced by the name $t$, fails the *trusted* attribute check. Therefore, the same attack will not be possible. Note that the key still gets overwritten, but the loss of integrity is disclosed.

**Table 3.** Key overwriting attack

| st. | transition | $\sigma$ | $S_T$ | $S_E$ | $trusted\,(t)$ |
|---|---|---|---|---|---|
| 0 | - | - | $d, h\,(t, k_t)\,, h\,(i, k_i)$ | $h\,(t, k_t)\,, h\,(i, k_i)\,, k_e$ | *true* |
| 1 | encryption | E | $d, h\,(t, k_t)\,, h\,(i, k_i)$ | $h\,(t, k_t)\,, h\,(i, k_i)\,, k_e,$ $\mathbf{senc}\,(\mathbf{k_e}, \mathbf{k_i})$ | *true* |
| 2 | unwrap | E | $d, h\,(t, \mathbf{k_e})\,, h\,(i, k_i)$ | $h\,(t, \mathbf{k_e})\,, h\,(i, k_i)\,, k_e,$ $senc\,(k_e k_i)$ | **false** |
| 3 | Disconnect | | $d, h\,(t, k_e)\,, h\,(i, k_i)$ | $k_e, senc\,(k_e k_i)$ | *false* |
| 4 | encryption (**not exec**) | T | - | - | - |

## 6 Conclusions

We have proposed an extension to an existent model for the PKCS#11 API, in order to broaden its descriptive capabilities, taking into account the integrity of cryptographic keys. We have granted the attacker some new capabilities, among which the overwriting of keys on the token. We have given a result reasoning on the expressiveness of two variations of the model semantics. Finally, we have proposed a simple mechanism to ensure in the model that only non-tampered keys are used in cryptographic operations.

The PKCS#11 API does not provide a way to satisfactorily manage the integrity of keys stored on a device, in a transparent manner for the user applications. We believe this is a major flaw of the standard. As discussed in the introduction, a user might need to perform some critical operation connecting a crypto-token to an untrusted host and she would expect no one is allowed to tamper with her crypto-device in a way that might compromise *any* further usage of it. Connecting a crypto-device to an untrusted host should not, in fact, compromise what is done/stored inside the device. We have shown that, apart from known attacks where sensitive keys are extracted, an enemy might also substitute a user key with one he knows and learn any data subsequently encrypted with such compromised key. This is, in our opinion, a rather irritating behaviour for what is expected to be a 'secure' crypto-device.

Alternative ways to check key integrity, other than the proposed use of the *trusted* attribute, could be: the use of cryptographic functions to validate key values (e.g. digital signatures or MACs), of course having computational costs; the introduction of a new attribute to specify that a key cannot be deleted, making a key impossible to be overwritten.

The use of the *trusted* attribute we suggest as a countermeasure to the integrity issue has an advantage in that it is simple and fast. Also, it can be implemented at several levels: at user application level, without the need to alter the API or the devices, or at API or device level, gaining transparency for the applications. A main disadvantage is that, since only keys with the *trusted* attribute set to *true* are authorized for any operation, to be of use, a key needs to be "promoted" right after its generation by the Security Officer in charge of the token. This might become quite restrictive especially in applications that need to establish new session-keys. We intend to explore alternative, less-restrictive, solutions.

We are glad that the automated DKS framework of [11] has been extended by Graham Steel so to include our model and analysis. In [12] it is possible to find the result of the performed experiments. First, a device patched to prevent confidentiality attack is modelled and analysed in the standard DKS-model. As expected no attacks are found. Then, the model is extended so to capture key overwriting and the same patched device is found to be vulnerable. The attack sequence pointed out by the SATMC model checker is essentially the same as the one presented in Table 2. It only differs on what is encrypted with the tampered key and then disclosed by the attacker: a freshly generated sensitive key `ks1` instead of generic sensitive data *d*.

## References


1. Armando, A., Compagna, L.: SAT-based model-checking for security protocols. International Journal of Information Security 7(1) (January 2008)
2. Bond, M., Anderson, R.: API-Level Attacks on Embedded Systems. IEEE Computer Magazine, 67–75 (2001)
3. Cimatti, et al.: NuSMV version 2: an OpenSource Tool for Symbolic Model Checking. In: Brinksma, E., Larsen, K.G. (eds.) CAV 2002. LNCS, vol. 2404, pp. 359–364. Springer, Heidelberg (2002)
4. Clulow, J.: On the security of PKCS#11. In: Walter, C.D., Koç, Ç.K., Paar, C. (eds.) CHES 2003. LNCS, vol. 2779, pp. 411–425. Springer, Heidelberg (2003)
5. Delaune, S., Kremer, S., Steel, G.: Formal analysis of PKCS#11. In: Proceedings of the 21st IEEE Computer Security Foundations Symposium (CSF 2008), Pittsburgh, PA, USA, June 2008, pp. 331–344. IEEE Computer Society Press, Los Alamitos (2008)
6. Dolev, D., Yao, A.: On the security of public key protocols. IEEE Transactions in Information Theory, 198–208 (1983)
7. International Telecommunication Union: X.690 - Abstract Syntax Notation One, ASN.1 (2002)
8. RSA Laboratories: PKCS#8: Private-Key Information Syntax Standard (1993)
9. RSA Security Inc: PKCS #11 v.2.20: Cryptographic Token Interface Standard (June 2004)
10. Steel, G.: Analysis of Security APIs FAQ, `http://www.lsv.ens-cachan.fr/~steel/security_APIs_FAQ.html`
11. Steel, G.: Experiments: Secure Configuration of PKCS11, `http://www.lsv.ens-cachan.fr/~steel/pkcs11/`
12. Steel, G.: Experiments: Key Integrity in PKCS#11, `http://www.lsv.ens-cachan.fr/~steel/pkcs11/replacement.php`

# A DKS-Rules Modelling Cryptographic Operations

Wrap

$$h(x_1, y_1), h(x_2, y_2); wrap(x_1), extract(x_2) \to senc(y_2, y_1)$$
$$h(x_1, priv(z)), h(x_2, y_2); wrap(x_1), extract(x_2) \to aenc(y_2, pub(z))$$
$$h(x_1, y_1), h(x_2, priv(z)); wrap(x_1), extract(x_2) \to senc(priv(z), y_1)$$

Unwrap

$$h(x_1, y_2), senc(y_1, y_2); unwrap(x_1) \xrightarrow{\text{new } n} h(n, y_1); extract(n), \mathcal{L}$$
$$h(x_1, priv(z)), aenc(y_1, pub(z)); unwrap(x_1) \xrightarrow{\text{new } n} h(n, y_1); extract(n), \mathcal{L}$$
$$h(x_1, y_2), senc(priv(z), y_2); unwrap(x_1) \xrightarrow{\text{new } n} h(n, priv(z)); extract(n), \mathcal{L}$$

Key generation

$$\xrightarrow{\text{new } n, k_1} h(n, k_1); \neg extract(n), \mathcal{L}$$
$$\xrightarrow{\text{new } n, s} h(n, priv(s)), pub(s); \neg extract(n), \mathcal{L}$$

Encryption

$$h(x_1, y_1), y_2; encrypt(x_1) \to senc(y_2, y_1)$$
$$h(x_1, priv(z)), y_1; encrypt(x_1) \to aenc(y_1, pub(z))$$

Decryption

$$h(x_1, y_1), senc(y_2, y_1); decrypt(x_1) \to y_2$$
$$h(x_1, priv(z)), aenc(y_2, pub(z)); decrypt(x_1) \to y_2$$

Attribute set

$$h(x_1, y_1); \neg wrap(x_1) \to wrap(x_1)$$

$$\vdots$$

Attribute unset

$$h(x_1, y_1); wrap(x_1) \to \neg wrap(x_1)$$

$$\vdots$$

where $\mathcal{L} = \neg wrap(n), \neg unwrap(n), \neg encrypt(n), \neg decrypt(n), \neg sensitive(n)$. The ellipsis in the attribute set and unset rules indicates that similar rules exist for other attributes.

# B Proofs from Section 4

To prove Lemma 1 we need the following simple lemma, stating that equality of the handles in $S_T$ and $S_E$ is preserved by transitions as long as the attacker stays connected. When he disconnects, the handles in $S_E$ are permanently removed. This allows us to implicitly assume $H(S_T) = H(S_E)$ if $C_E$ and $H(S_E) = \emptyset$ otherwise, for all states $(S_T, S_E, V, C_T, C_E)$ in $Q$.

**Lemma 2.** *Let* $(S_T, S_E, V, true, true)$ *be such that* $H(S_T) = H(S_E)$. *Then,* $(S_T, S_E, V, true, true) \rightsquigarrow^* (S'_T, S'_E, V', C'_T, C'_E)$ *implies* $H(S'_T) = H(S'_E)$ *if* $C'_E$ *and* $H(S'_E) = \emptyset$*, otherwise.*

*Proof. Lemma 1.* Let $q \in Q$, $q = (S_T, S_E, V, C_T, C_E)$. By definition of encoding, $[\![q]\!] = \left(H(S_T), \overline{H}(S_T), \overline{H}(S_E), V, C_T, C_E\right)$. To this we apply the inverse encoding; we have to distinguish whether the attacker is connected or disconnected from the device.

If the attacker is connected:

$$\begin{aligned}
&[\![(H(S_T), \overline{H}(S_T), \overline{H}(S_E), V, C_T, C_E)]\!]^{-1} = \\
&= \left([\![\overline{H}(S_T)]\!]^{-1}, [\![\overline{H}(S_E)]\!]^{-1}, V, C_T, C_E\right) \\
&= \left(\overline{H}(S_T) \cup H(S_T), \overline{H}(S_E) \cup H(S_T), V, C_T, C_E\right) \\
&= (S_T, S_E, V, C_T, C_E) \text{ because } H(S_E) = H(S_T) \\
&= q
\end{aligned}$$

If the attacker is disconnected:

$$\begin{aligned}
&[\![(H(S_T), \overline{H}(S_T), \overline{H}(S_E), V, C_T, C_E)]\!]^{-1} = \\
&= \left([\![\overline{H}(S_T)]\!]^{-1}, [\![\overline{H}(S_E)]\!]^{-1}, V, C_T, C_E\right) \\
&= \left(\overline{H}(S_T) \cup H(S_T), \overline{H}(S_E), V, C_T, C_E\right) \\
&= (S_T, S_E, V, C_T, C_E) \text{ because } H(S_E) = \emptyset \\
&= q
\end{aligned}$$

□

*Proof sketch. Theorem 1.*
($\Longrightarrow$) Let $q_i \rightsquigarrow q_f$. We explore case by case, for each kind of derivation applied. We express $q_f$ as a function of $q_i$ by the applied transition and we express $q_i'$ as a function of $q_i$ by the definition of state encoding. Then, given the applicability conditions of the assumed derivation, we verify that analogous conditions, required to apply the same transition in the $\mathcal{H}$ system, hold in state $q_i'$. Thus, we can apply the same transition to state $q_i'$, which by hypothesis is the encoding of $q_i$, yielding state $q_f'$. Finally, we show that $q_f'$ obtained in this way is the encoding of $q_f$: this is done checking the vector state elements one at a time, to show that the state encoding definition is complied with.

($\Longleftarrow$) This part of the proof is symmetric to the first part and it relies on the inverse state encoding.

# Secure Upgrade of Hardware Security Modules in Bank Networks*

Riccardo Focardi and Flaminia L. Luccio

Università Ca' Foscari Venezia
{focardi,luccio}@dsi.unive.it

**Abstract.** We study the secure upgrade of critical components in wide networked systems, focussing on the case study of PIN processing Hardware Security Modules (HSMs). These tamper-resistant devices, used by banks to securely transmit and verify the PIN typed at the ATMs, have been shown to suffer from API level attacks that allow an insider to recover user PINs and, consequently, clone cards. Proposed fixes require to reduce and modify the HSM functionality by, e.g., sticking on a single format of the transmitted PIN or adding MACs for the integrity of user data. Upgrading HSMs worldwide is, of course, unaffordable. We thus propose strategies to incrementally upgrade the network so to obtain upgraded, secure subnets, while preserving the compatibility towards the legacy system. Our strategies aim at finding tradeoffs between the cost for special "guardian" HSMs used on the borderline between secure and insecure nodes, and the size of the team working in the upgrade process, representing the maximum number of nodes that can be simultaneously upgraded.

**Keywords:** Security APIs, PIN processing, Hardware Security Modules, Upgrade strategies.

## 1 Introduction

Automated Teller Machines (ATMs) verify the user's Personal Identification Number (PIN) by sending it to the issuing bank on an international bank network. During their journey, PINs are decrypted and re-encrypted on the traversed network switches by special tamper-resistant devices called Hardware Security Modules (HSMs). As shown in figure 1, the keypad itself is an HSM that performs the first PIN encryption with a symmetric key $k_1$ shared with the neighbour acquiring bank. Before the encrypted PIN is routed to the next network node, it is passed to the HSM in the switch that decrypts and re-encrypts it with another key $k_2$, shared with the destination node, and so on.

In the last years, several API-level attacks have been discovered on these HSMs [5,6,9]. The attacker is assumed to be an insider gaining access to the HSM at some bank switch. Then, by performing subtle sequences of API calls he is able

* Work partially supported by Miur'07 Project SOFT: "*Security Oriented Formal Techniques*".

A. Armando and G. Lowe (Eds.): ARSPA-WITS 2010, LNCS 6186, pp. 95–110, 2010.

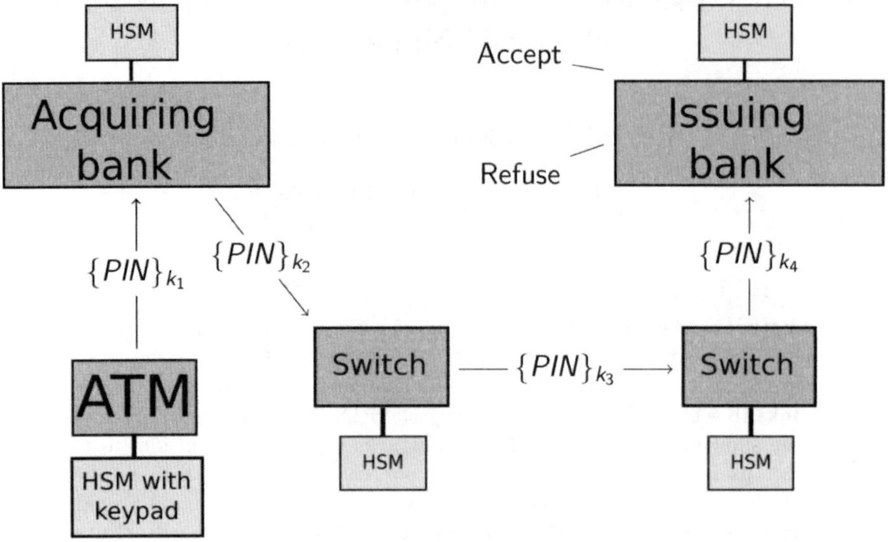


**Fig. 1.** PIN processing infrastructure

to deduce the value of the PIN. As an example, the so-called *dectab attack* is based on manipulating public user data given as input to the PIN verification API at the issuing bank HSM. One of these data is a decimalization table that maps an intermediate hexadecimal representation of the user PIN into a decimal number. By modifying the way numbers are decimalized and by observing if this affects the result of the verification, the attacker can deduce which are the actual PIN digits: if the original dectab maps, e.g., A into 0 and the attacker modifies it so to map A into 1 causing a failure in the PIN verification API, then he is guaranteed that a 0 digit was occurring in the decimalized user PIN. If it were not the case, PIN verification result would be unaffected by the change in the *dectab*. The attack goes on using another public parameter, the *offset*, to reconstruct the whole PIN code. The interested reader is referred to, e.g., [8,9,12,20], for more detail.

The interest in these API-level attacks has recently increased [1,2] and it becomes more an more plausible that some of them have been really exploited by malicious insiders to steal thousands of user PINs. This has motivated research on formal methods for analysing PIN recovery attacks and API-level attacks in general [20]. In particular, in [8] we have proposed a language-based setting for analysing PIN processing API via a type-system. We have formally modelled existing attacks, proposed some fixes and proved them correct via type-checking. These fixes typically require to reduce and modify the HSM functionality by, e.g., sticking on a single format of the transmitted PIN or adding MACs for the integrity of user data. Notice, in fact, that the above mentioned attack is based on the absence of integrity on public user data such as the *dectab* and the *offset*.

There are crucial difficulties when trying to implement these fixes on a real bank network: first of all, upgrading the bank network HSMs worldwide is complex and very expensive; moreover, adding improved APIs in the HSMs is not enough: we also need to remove old flawed APIs if we want to stop the attacks. This typically makes upgraded HSMs incompatible with the old ones, for example when one switch expects a MAC and the previous non-upgraded one cannot provide it. These difficulties can be circumvented at the price of loosing some security: in [11] we have proposed a low-impact, easily implementable fix requiring no hardware upgrade which makes attacks 50000 times slower, but yet not impossible.

**Our contribution.** We propose a novel way of upgrading critical components in wide networked system that mitigates the above discussed difficulties. In particular, we propose strategies to incrementally upgrade the network so to obtain upgraded, secure subnets while preserving the compatibility towards the legacy system. This should make the upgrading process more appealing to banks, as they might decide to invest money for upgrading part of the system still maintaining the interoperability with the non-upgraded part. Of course, PINs travelling through non-upgraded subnets would be exposed to the same attacks as before, but PINs traversing secured subnets would be robust against API-level attacks.

To guarantee the compatibility with the old system we propose the adoption of special *borderline* HSMs translating from/to the old protocol. These HSMs are temporarily placed on the borderline between upgraded and non-upgraded nodes and can be thought as the 'union' of the old and the new HSMs, thus supporting the functionalities of both and being able to translate from/to the old protocol. Of course, this hardware is far from being secure but it can be used to temporarily keep the network working while the upgrade is performed. Our strategies aim at finding tradeoffs between the cost for borderline HSMs and the size of the team working in the upgrade process, representing the maximum number of nodes that can be simultaneously upgraded: since HSMs are quite expensive, it might make sense to have bigger teams of technicians able to upgrade a whole subtree in one shot, with no need of placing many borderline HSMs around.

We formally state the HSM upgrading problem and we prove that, when only one technician is present, it is strictly related to the Connected Monotone Decontamination (CMD) problem [3], where a team of agents aims at decontaminating a graph and capturing an intruder. The analogy is that decontaminated nodes should never be directly in contact with contaminated ones to avoid the intruder re-contaminating them, thus some agents must stay on the borderlines to 'guard' the decontaminated subnetwork. This is similar to what happens when placing a borderline HSM between upgraded and non-upgraded nodes. We then generalize the optimum algorithm for the CMD problem to our setting, also considering many technicians. We prove the new algorithm correct and we show how it can be applied to estimate upgrading cost for a real bank (sub)network.

**Paper structure.** The paper is organized as follows: in section 2 we formalize the HSM upgrading problem and we prove it equivalent to the CMD problem, up to one borderline HSM; in section 3, we give an algorithm for upgrading HSMs which is parametrized by the size of the technician team; in section 4 we give an example of application of the algorithm to estimate the upgrading cost on a network; finally, in section 5 we give some concluding remarks and we discuss future work.

## 2 The HSM Upgrading Problem

Given a bank network, we want to study strategies for incrementally upgrading HSMs while keeping the network functionality up, apart from the lapse of time in which HSMs are physically substituted. While applying an upgrading technique, only part of the HSMs will be upgraded. As we have mentioned in the introduction, in this upgraded hardware we certainly want to remove old flawed functionalities, thus it will not be able, in general, to support the old protocol and communicate with non-upgraded HSMs. To this aim, the technicians performing the upgrade can place special *borderline* HSMs translating from/to the old protocol.

We briefly discuss two possible settings, depending on whether these special HSMs are placed on *links* as in figure 2, or on *switches*, as in figure 3. The former setting makes all the paths in the upgraded network secure, but in case we have many links towards the non-upgraded network it would require to install many borderline HSMs thus becoming more complicated and expensive. The latter setting is cheaper and more flexible: once an HSM becomes borderline all the neighbouring switches can be indifferently upgraded or not. Notice, however, that the paths passing through borderline HSMs in the upgraded network are still subject to the attacks. This is because borderline nodes still support old,

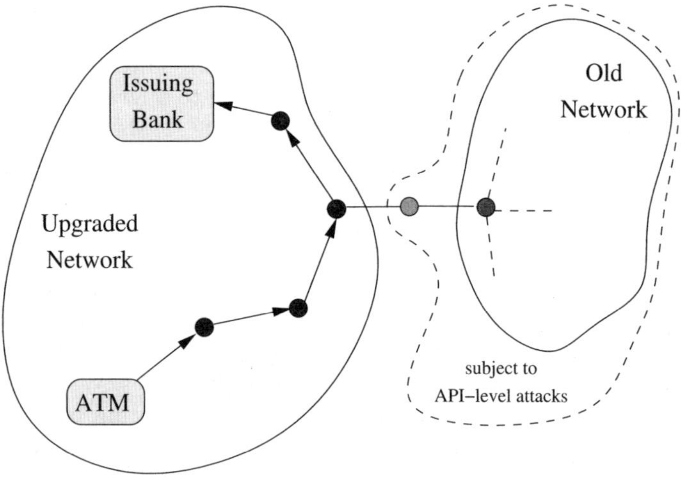


**Fig. 2.** Borderline HSM on a link

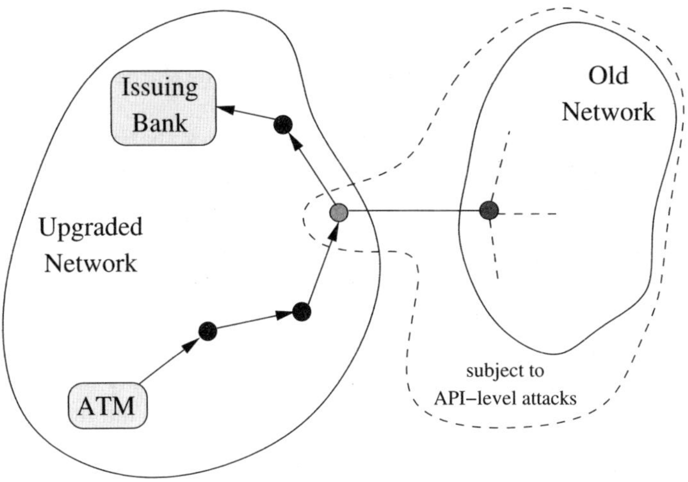


**Fig. 3.** Borderline HSM on a node

flawed functionalities. This setting is cheaper than the former, but the same degree of security is only achieved later on, when more nodes will be upgraded. Given that we believe the cost is likely to be the major issue we prefer to analyse this latter setting and leave the former as a future work.

Another issue to be considered is which network *topology* we can expect to be faced with, when starting an upgrade. In the USA, real systems are composed of regional networks shared by different banks and are hierarchically connected through switches of one of the existing national networks [13]. In our opinion, a reasonable assumption to make is that the updates start inside regional networks which will be composed of different trees, each representing a different bank network, rooted at the issuing bank. It seems plausible that different banks will upgrade their hardware independently, thus we imagine they will first install a sufficient number of borderline switches to 'separate' their network from the other bank networks in the same region. We assume this preliminary separation as done and we focus on single trees representing single bank networks, rooted at the issuing bank node and having all the ATMs as leaves.

We can now formally state the HSM upgrading problem as an algorithmic problem on trees.

**The HSM upgrading problem.** We consider an initially *non-upgraded* tree network that has to be *upgraded* by a set of *technicians* arbitrarily moving inside the network and possibly placing *borderline HSMs*. All technicians and borderline HSMs are placed in one initial node. A technician can move only in a *connected* way, i.e., from a node to another along an edge, in doing so she upgrades the traversed nodes. Borderline HSMs can only be moved by one technician; in that case the HSM and the technician move together along edges. The technician moves such special hardware when all the neighbouring nodes, except the destination one, have been upgraded. In this case, in fact, the borderline HSM is not any more needed. We implicitly assume that this hardware, in the presence of one technician and with all neighbouring nodes upgraded is switched off, making the node upgraded. At the end of the computation all the nodes are upgraded.

An *HSM upgrading strategy* is a sequence of moves that will upgrade an initially non-upgraded network. While devising efficient updating techniques we consider different parameters that we would like to optimize:

1. The number $B$ of available borderline HSMs: each of them has a cost which may be very high, typically around 10000$, thus $B$ has to be minimized;
2. The number $U$ of technicians in the upgrading team: each technician can upgrade one HSM in one node, so having many technicians allows for simultaneous upgrading of subsets of nodes; the salary we pay to the technicians is proportional to this parameter, thus even $U$ should me minimized;

**Definition 1 (HSM upgrading number).** *It is the minimal number of borderline HSMs needed to solve the HSM upgrading problem on a given tree $T$ and with a given number $U$ of technicians. We note it $uhn(T, U)$.*

## 2.1 Upgrading vs. Decontaminating

We now show that the HSM upgrading problem with a single technician is very strictly related to the *Connected Monotone Decontamination* (CMD) problem, formalized below.

**The CMD problem [3].** We consider an initially *contaminated* network that has to be *decontaminated* by a set of agents (or *searchers*) arbitrarily moving inside the network. All nodes and edges are initially *contaminated*, except for the initial node where all the agents are located, which is *guarded*. An agent can move only in a *connected* way, i.e., from a node to another along an edge. The network contains an intruder that contaminates the nodes and edges it traverses. The intruder cannot traverse guarded nodes, otherwise it would be captured by the agents, but we assume that he will immediately recontaminate nodes or edges that are left unguarded. In the *node decontamination problem* a node is guarded when it contains at least one agent, clean when an agent has been on the node and all the neighbouring nodes are clean or guarded, and contaminated otherwise. At the end of the computation all the nodes of the network are simultaneously clean. In the *edge decontamination problem* an edge becomes *clean* whenever an agent passes through it, and its starting node is either clean or guarded. At the end of the computation all the nodes and edges of the network are simultaneously clean.

A *decontamination (or search) strategy* is a sequence of moves that will clear an initially contaminated network. A strategy is *monotone*, if a decontaminated node or edge is never recontaminated. Finally, the strategy has to be efficient, where efficiency is measured in terms of the size of the agent team. A strategy is optimal if the size of the team is minimal.

**Definition 2 (Connected search number).** *It is the minimal team size needed to solve the edge CMD problem on a given network $G$, and is noted $csn(G)$.*

The problem of finding an optimal strategy has been studied in some specific topologies such as trees [3]. In the same work it is also proved that, for trees, a non-monotone solution, i.e., allowing re-contamination of nodes, would not reduce the optimal number of required agents.

Originally, the decontamination problem has been introduced in [7,17] and has been extensively studied in the literature under the term *graph search* (e.g., see [10,14,15,16,18]). The difference with the *CMD* problem is that searchers do not necessarily move in a connected way, i.e., may 'jump' from one node to another. In the HSM upgrading problem technicians do not travel via the network they repair, but via lorries or cars. In an ideal setting we would thus have to think our scenario as a composition of two networks: the bank network overlapped with a geographical network where technicians physically move. Another approach could consist of considering only the bank network where the travelling cost is added by assigning weights to the edges (where weights represent physical distances), and by letting searchers jump from one node to the other. It is interesting to note that for any non-weighted tree $T$ with $n$ nodes the ratio between the connected search number $csn(T)$ and the regular search number $sn(T)$ (i.e., for agents that may jump) is bounded by, $csn(T)/sn(T) \leq 2$ (see [4]), i.e., any optimal connected strategy will require at most twice the number of agents than a non-connected one (at least in the non-weighted case). We thus leave the two above mentioned extensions as a future work and for simplicity, in this work we concentrate on the scenario in which we do not consider the technician motion as a parameter to optimize.

**Equivalence of HSM upgrading and CMD.** We now prove that the HSM upgrading problem solved using the minimal number of borderline HSMs and a single technician is equivalent, up to one extra agent, to the problem of finding a connected monotone technique for the edge decontamination of the tree network using the smallest number of agents.

**Theorem 1.** *Given a tree $T$, we have $uhn(T,1) \leq csn(T) \leq uhn(T,1)+1$.*

*Proof.* Let us first assume we have solved the HSM upgrading problem in a tree using the minimal number $uhn(T,1)$ of borderline HSM and a single technician. We show that the adopted strategy can be mapped into a valid strategy for the CMD problem with a number of agents equal to $uhn(T,1)+1$. We can see upgraded and non-upgraded HSMs respectively as decontaminated and contaminated nodes. Moreover, we see each borderline HSM and the (single) technician as agents. We now show that moves of the technician and of borderline HSMs (that are anyway transported by the technician) are correctly mapped into agent moves.

We first consider the technician moving alone, bringing no HSM. The only crucial case is when the node where she moves from has no borderline HSM on it meaning, in the other problem, that she is the only agent on the node. In this case we are guaranteed that all the neighbouring nodes are either upgraded or borderline HSMs, as an upgraded node (the one where the technician is moving from) can never be directly connected to a non-upgraded one. The corresponding move in the CMD problem can be safely performed.

We now consider the technician moving with some borderline HSMs. If at least one HSM is left on the node the move can be safely simulated in the CMD problem, as at least one agent will stay on the originating node, guarding it. If all the borderline HSMs are moved by the technician we are in a situation similar to the one where the technician alone is moving: all the neighbouring nodes need to be either upgraded or borderline HSMs, except the destination node which, if needed, will be protected by one of the incoming borderline HSMs. This is perfectly safe in the CMD problem, as the moving agents will guard the destination node. The important thing is that the node left alone is protected by the upgraded/guarded neighbouring nodes.

When all the nodes are upgraded in the HSM upgrading problem they will correspondingly be decontaminated in the CMD problem, thus the strategy in the former problem is also a strategy in the latter, with a number of agents equal to $uhn(T, 1) + 1$. This implies $csn(T) \leq uhn(T, 1) + 1$.

Similarly, let us now assume we have solved the CMD problem with $csn(T)$ agents. We show that the adopted strategy can be mapped into a valid strategy for the HSM upgrading problem with one technician and with a number of borderline HSMs equal to $csn(T)$. We can see decontaminated and contaminated nodes as upgraded and non-upgraded HSMs, respectively. Moreover, we see each agent as a borderline HSM. We now show that moves of the agents are correctly mapped into borderline HSM moves, via the technician. Notice that no agent is mapped into the technician, so the position of the technician on the tree is immaterial. Notice also that, at any point of the computation, all upgraded/borderline HSMs are on a connected subtree of the network, given that agents start from a single initial node, they move in a connected way and HSMs can never be downgraded. Thus, we can freely move the technician on this upgraded/borderline nodes reaching all the borderline HSMs.

Now, any agent move is simulated by the technician reaching the corresponding borderline HSM and moving it in the destination node. The only crucial case is when the node which is left has no other agents guarding it. In this case, however, we are guaranteed that all of the neighbouring nodes, except the destination one, are upgraded or guarded, since an agent cannot allow a decontaminated node to be recontaminated. Thus, the corresponding borderline HSM can be safely removed from the node.

When all the nodes are decontaminated in the CMD problem they will correspondingly be upgraded or borderline in the HSM upgrading problem. At this point the technician can go around an collect all the borderline HSMs 'deactivating' them. Thus the strategy in the former problem is also a strategy in the latter, with a number of borderline HSMs equal to $csn(T)$. This implies $uhn(T, 1) \leq csn(T)$. ∎

## 3 Upgrading Strategies

In this section we show different techniques to solve the HSM upgrading problem. We first provide strategies which aim at minimizing $B$, i.e., the number of borderline switches used, and then present trade-offs between $B$ and $U$, i.e., the number of nodes $U$ that can be simultaneously upgraded by a team of technicians.

**Case U = 1.** Nodes are sequentially updated by a unique technician. As we have proved in the previous section, in this case this problem is equivalent to the CMD problem where agents are seen as borderline HSMs. We thus slightly modify the algorithm presented in [3] in order to solve our problem.

The main idea is to first compute, from every possible starting point, i.e., every node of the tree $T$, the minimal number of borderline switches required for the solution of the upgrading problem. Then, one of the nodes with minimal value is chosen as starting point and the actual upgrading algorithm is applied. In order to compute this minimal value two different rules (similar to the ones of [3]) need to be applied. For each edge $\{x, y\}$, we first compute $\lambda_x(x, y)$, i.e., the minimal number of borderline HSMs necessary for the upgrade of the tree rooted at $y$ while arriving from $x$.

**Rule 1 for computing minimal number of borderline HSMs on an edge**

1. An edge $e = \{x, y\}$ leading from a node $x$ to a leaf $y$ requires only the technician moving from $x$ to $y$ to upgrade the HSM on $y$, thus $\lambda_x(x, y) = 0$;
2. An edge $e = \{x, y\}$ leading from a node $x$ to a node $y$ that has other $k$ out-going edges requiring $l_1, \ldots, l_k$ borderline HSMs, with $l_1 \geq l_2 \geq, \ldots, \geq l_k$, requires $\lambda_x(x, y) = \max\{l_1, l_2 + 1, 1\}$ borderline HSMs.

From this value we can then compute the minimal number of borderline HSMs which are necessary for the upgrade of the tree starting from any node. The two rules are:

**Rule 2 for computing minimal number of borderline HSMs on a node**

1. A leaf $y$ requires a number of borderline HSMs defined by $\lambda_y(y, x)$ to move to node $x$; in fact, being a leaf we do not need to leave any borderline HSM on $y$;
2. A node $x$ that has $h$ out-going edges each respectively requiring $l_1, \ldots, l_h$ borderline HSMs, with $l_1 \geq l_2 \geq, \ldots, \geq l_h$, needs $\max\{l_1, l_2 + 1\}$ borderline HSMs.

We now apply Rules 1 and 2 and then choose one of the nodes, say $z$, requiring a minimal number $B$ of borderline HSMs. Similarly to the algorithm of [3], consider $T_z$, the tree rooted at $z$ and, for each node $y$ of $T_z$, order its children by increasing values assigned by $\lambda_z$ to the related links. Apply then the following:

**Algorithm** UPGRADE
1. Start at $z$ with $B$ borderline HSMs and a technician;
2. Traverse $T_z$ in pre-order (by increasing values of $\lambda_z$). While moving from a node $x$ to a node $y$ use $\lambda_x(x, y)$ borderline HSMs and a technician, while returning to $x$ bring back $\lambda_x(x, y)$ borderline HSMs and a technician.

*Example 1.* Let us now show how to apply Rules 1, 2 and Algorithm UPGRADE on a small example. Assume we have a tree $T$ of 6 nodes called $a, b, c, d, e, f$ (see figure 4). We first compute the values associated to the edges, i.e., we apply Rule 1. E.g., consider node $d$. As $d$ is a leaf by Rule 1.1 we have $\lambda_b(b, d) = 0$, that is there is just a technician moving from $b$ to $d$. The same holds for the other leaves $e$ and $f$, thus $\lambda_c(c, e) = 0$, and $\lambda_c(c, f) = 0$. Consider now node $a$ and edge $\{a, b\}$ and apply Rule 1.2. Node $b$ has only one other out-going edge, i.e., $\{b, d\}$ that requires $l_1 = \lambda_b(b, d) = 0$ borderline HSMs. Thus, edge $\{a, b\}$ requires $\lambda_a(a, b) = \max\{l_1 = 0, 1\} = 1$ borderline HSM. That is, path $\{a, b, d\}$ is a chain thus we need at least one borderline HSM to upgrade it. On the other hand, if we consider edge $\{a, c\}$ and apply Rule 1.2 we have that node $c$ has two other out-going edges, i.e., $\{c, e\}$ and $\{c, f\}$ that respectively require $l_1 = \lambda_c(c, e) = 0$ and $l_2 = \lambda_c(c, f) = 0$ borderline HSMs. Thus, edge $\{a, c\}$ requires $\lambda_a(a, c) = \max\{l_1 = 0, l_2 = 0 + 1 = 1, 1\} = 1$ borderline HSM. To compute the minimal number of borderline HSMs on a node we apply Rule 2. E.g., consider a leaf $d$. It requires a number of borderline HSMs defined by $\lambda_d(d, b) = 1$ to move to node $b$, thus we write 1 inside node $d$. Consider now node $c$ that has 3 out-going edges each respectively requiring $l_1 = 1, l_2 = 0, l_3 = 0$ borderline HSMs, thus $c$ needs $\max\{l_1 = 1, l_2 + 1 = 0 + 1 = 1\} = 1$ borderline HSM.

After having applied Rules 1 and 2 to all the nodes, we choose one of them requiring a minimal number of borderline HSMs, e.g., $c$ requiring 1 HSM. We consider $T_c$, the tree rooted at $c$ and order its children by increasing values assigned by $\lambda_c$ to the related links, e.g., we consider node $e$, then $f$, then $a$, and finally apply Algorithm UPGRADE starting from $c$ with 1 borderline HSMs and a technician.

Figure 5 shows an application of Algorithm UPGRADE starting from node $c$. Black nodes represent updated HSMs. Nodes surrounded by squares represent borderline HSMs, the lady represents the technician. At the end the technician goes back to $c$.

We now prove the correctness and the optimality of algorithm UPGRADE.

**Theorem 2.** *Algorithm* UPGRADE *together with Rule 1 and Rule 2 correctly and optimally solve the HSM upgrading problem in a bank tree network $T$.*

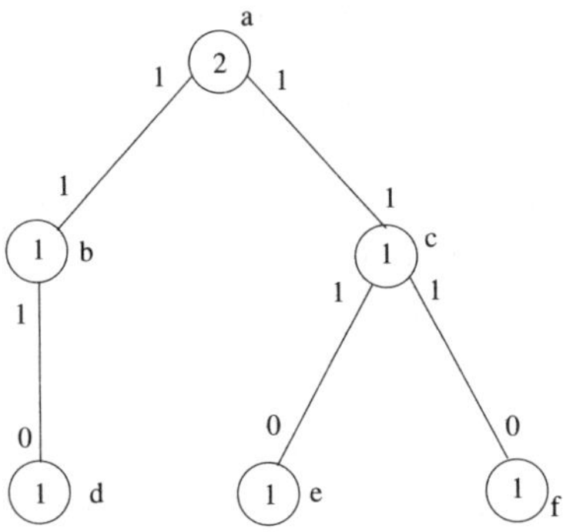


**Fig. 4.** Application of Rule 1 and 2

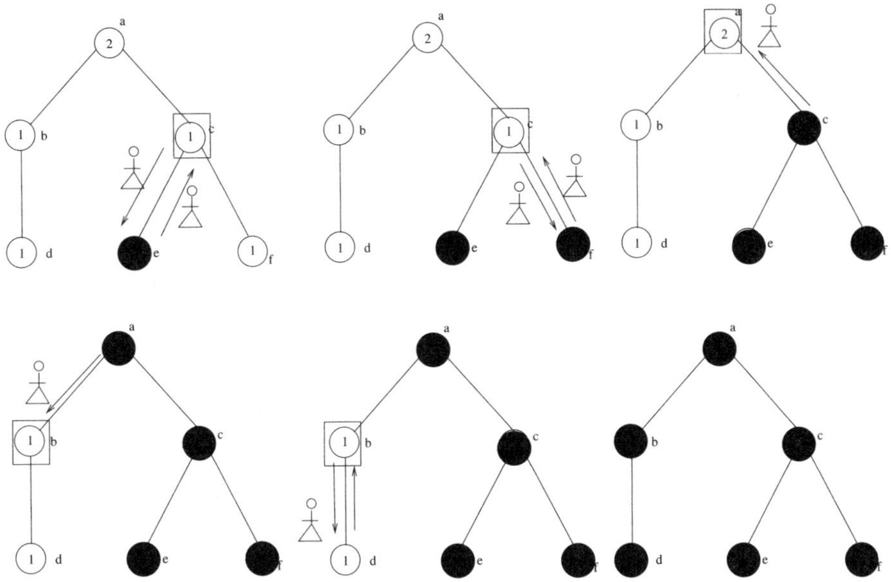


**Fig. 5.** Algorithm UPGRADE starting from $c$

*Proof.* The general correctness directly derives from the one of the rules and the algorithm presented in [3]. In particular, we first have to prove that an optimal monotone strategy for HSM upgrading with a single starting point on any tree $T$ exists. Then, we choose the entry point that minimizes the number of required HSMs. Another key point for the correctness of the strategy is the property that the minimal number of required HSMs from a node $x$ is given by the minimal number between the biggest minimal value of a son of $x$ and the second biggest minimal value plus one. These values will correspond to the edge labels and will imply a specific ordering in the strategy visit. Finally, we prove that using the minimal number of HSMs, we can upgrade the system as moving back and forth with such number of HSMs does not leave parts of the network unprotected.

The existence of an optimal monotone strategy for CMD on any tree $T$ has been proved in [3] using a variation of the proof of [15] for the non-monotone setting with the addition of the single starting point (i.e., the initially guarded node). The main idea that we borrow is that it is possible to build a progressive connected crusade (i.e., a sequence of moves where a new single un-traversed edge is added at each step, leading to the visit of the whole network and using only connected sub-networks) using at most $uhn(T, 1)$ HSMs on the borderline between the non-upgraded and upgraded sub-networks.

The correctness of the optimal strategy for the HSM upgrading problem also derives from the one of [3]. In particular, from what is stated above we can limit the upgrading to strategies having a single entry point, thus one of the starting point requiring the smallest number of HSMs will be chosen. Another key point is the fact that, given a tree $T$ rooted at $r$ (call it $T_r$) and considering a sub-tree of $T_r$ rooted at $x$ ($T_r[x]$) with $k$ children $x_1, \ldots, x_k$ such that $uhn(T_r[x_i], 1) \geq uhn(T_r[x_{i+1}], 1)$ for all $i = 1, \ldots, k$, then $uhn(T_r[x], 1) = \max\{uhn(T_r[x_1], 1), uhn(T_r[x_2], 1)+1\}$. Obviously $uhn(T_r[x], 1) \geq uhn(T_r[x_1], 1)$ otherwise $T_r[x_1]$ cannot be upgraded. We now have two possible cases:

1. $uhn(T_r[x_1], 1) \geq uhn(T_r[x_2], 1)+1$. Then $T_r[x]$ is upgraded by visiting $T_r[x_1]$ as the last subtree, after having placed an HSM on $x$ and cleaned all the other children;
2. $uhn(T_r[x_1], 1) = uhn(T_r[x_2], 1)$. Assume $S$ is a strategy that upgrades $T_r[x]$ using $uhn(T_r[x_2], 1)$ HSMs. If $T_r[x_2]$ is upgraded before $T_r[x_1]$ no HSM may be left on $x$, thus an untraversed edge (towards $x_1$) remains unprotected. The same holds if $T_r[x_2]$ is upgraded after $T_r[x_1]$. Thus more than $uhn(T_r[x_2], 1)$ HSMs have to be used. In fact, $uhn(T_r[x_2], 1)+1$ HSMs are sufficient by first visiting $T_r[x_2]$ and then $T_r[x_1]$ with one HSM on $x$.

Label now each edge $\{a, b\}$ of the network with a function $\lambda_a(a, b)$ that is 0 if $b$ is a leaf and $max\{l_1, l_2+1, 1\}$ if $b$ has $h$ out-going edges each respectively requiring $l_1, \ldots, l_h$ HSMs, with $l_1 \geq l_2 \geq, \ldots, \geq l_h$. The next step borrowed from [3] is to prove that $\lambda_a(a, b) = uhn(T_a[b], 1)$ and this is done by induction on the height of $T_a[b]$.

All the proofs of [3] can thus be directly mapped to our problem. There are some differences on the rules which we report below. Rule 1.1 for the HSM upgrading problem avoids the placement of a borderline switch (i.e., the agent in the other problem) on $y$, i.e., at the end of the chain, but, by the recursive construction, a borderline switch will however be placed on $x$ while upgrading $y$, with the only exception being a tree composed of a single edge $\{x, y\}$, that we do not treat (it could be treated via an ad-hoc rule but we prefer not to complicate the algorithm for a trivial case). Now, if $x$ has degree at least 2, by Rule 2 node $x$ will require at least one borderline HSM (used on $x$) and one technician (the two edges out-going from $x$ have associated 0). Thus, $y$ will be safely upgraded. Moreover, Rule 1.2 states that, if $x$ is the starting point of a chain of HSMs we need at least one borderline HSM to upgrade the system. This is included in the constant 1 of the relation $\lambda_x(x, y) = \max\{l_1, l_2 + 1, 1\}$. This is peculiar of our algorithm and is not present in [3].

Consider now Algorithm UPGRADE. In point 1 we start from the node that requires the minimal number $B = uhn(T, 1)$ of borderline HSMs. $B$ has been correctly computed by Rule 1 and 2. Consider now point 2 of Algorithm UPGRADE. The proof is similar to the one of [3] with the inclusion of the case where a node is a leaf that has to be directly updated by the technician (that is in this case $\lambda_x(x, y) = 0$ no borderline HSMs, only the technician). Very briefly, the main idea is that technician and HSM move may be forward and backward. Backward moves are safe as they leave an upgraded network and move to an already upgraded one. Forward moves upgrade a non-upgraded subtree by increasing number of HSMs. Moreover the relation $\lambda_x(x, y) = \max\{l_1, l_2 + 1, 1\}$ assures that at least one HSM will be left on node $x$, avoiding new attacks and enough HSMs can be moved to $y$.

Finally, observe that Rule 1 and 2 compute the minimal number of borderline switches required on the tree and starting from every possible node, and $B$ is the minimal of such values. ∎

**Case U > 1.** We now assume that our network is a tree $T$, and that $U = k > 1$, i.e., that nodes can be simultaneously upgraded by a team of $k$ technicians. Using this issue we now try to compute what is the related decrease in $B$. To do this we extend Rule 1 and Algorithm UPGRADE 1 basing our changes on the following observation: given $U = k$, and the tree $T$, if we have a subtree $T_z$ of $T$ rooted at $z$ and containing $<= k$ nodes, we can then use the team to upgrade $T_z$ in one shot, one technician sent to each node. That is, the team can collaborate to upgrade a contiguous part of $T$, decreasing the number $B$ of borderline nodes required by Algorithm UPGRADE 1.

In order to do this we have to compute, for each node $z$ of $T$, the number of nodes in each subtree of $T$ rooted in $z$ (i.e., in $T_z$). More precisely, assuming $z$ has $h$ neighbouring nodes $z_1, \ldots, z_h$, we have to compute $s_{z,z_i}$ the size of the subtrees $T_z[z_i]$ of $T_z$ rooted in $z_i$, for $i = 1, \ldots, h$. We can do this recursively as follows:

**Computing the number of nodes of subtrees**

1. An edge $e = \{x, y\}$ leading from a node $x$ to a leaf $y$. We trivially have $s_{x,y} = 1$;
2. Consider an edge $e = \{x, y\}$ leading from a node $x$ to a node $y$ that has other $k$ out-going edges $\{y, z_1\}, \ldots, \{y, z_k\}$ with subtree sizes $s_{y,z_i}$, with $i = 1, \ldots, k$. Then the size of the subtree of $T_x$ rooted at $y$ is $s_{x,y} = s_{y,z_1} + \ldots + s_{y,z_k} + 1$.

Based on this computation we can give a new rules, RULE 1 NEW which substitutes Rule 1:

**Rule 1 new for computing minimal number of borderline HSMs on an edge using $U$ technicians**

1. An edge $e = \{x, y\}$ leading from $x$ to $y$ such that $s_{x,y} \leq U$ requires only the technician team moving from $x$ to $y$ to upgrade the HSM on the whole subtree rooted in $y$, thus $\lambda_x(x, y) = 0$;
2. An edge $e = \{x, y\}$ leading from $x$ to $y$ such that $s_{x,y} > U$ and having other $k$ out-going edges requiring $l_1, \ldots, l_k$ borderline HSMs, with $l_1 \geq l_2 \geq, \ldots, \geq l_k$, requires $\lambda_x(x, y) = \max\{l_1, l_2 + 1, 1\}$ borderline HSMs.

**Theorem 3.** *Algorithm* UPGRADE *together with Rule 1 new and Rule 2 correctly solve the HSM upgrading problem in a bank tree network $T$ where $U$ technicians operate. The number of borderline switches required is value $B$ computed via Rule 1 new and Rule 2.*

*Proof.* Rule 2 and the UPGRADE algorithm are the one previously presented, their correctness thus follows. The correctness of Rule 1 new derives from the one of Rule 1. Moreover, the computation of the sub-tree sizes is based on the standard saturation technique widely used in the field of distributed algorithms (see, e.g., [19]). This technique assumes that the computation of the size of a sub-tree is started at the leaves (which in this case count one) and is propagated on the sub-tree by collecting values from all but one edge and propagating it to through the remaining edge. Finally, given $U$ technicians that may work on a non-upgraded network of $\leq U$ nodes, all these technicians may obviously upgrade this sub-tree in parallel. ∎

## 4 Estimating the Upgrading Cost: An Example

We consider a simple example to show how to compute a trade-off between the number $U$ of technicians and the the number of needed borderline HSMs. The example is depicted in figure 6. We use the same notation adopted in the previous section to label edges and nodes. On the left, we execute the algorithm with $U = 1$: it gives 2 on all nodes, thus the minimal number of needed borderline HSMs is 2. We now want to evaluate the benefits of hiring one more technician. On the right we have executed the algorithm with $U = 2$, pointing out the difference in red, and we see that in 2 nodes just one HSM is needed. Thus, if we start from those nodes with two technicians we only need one borderline HSM to upgrade the whole network. Notice that we cannot do best than this as one HSM is for sure needed.

We can now reason as follows: let $C_H$ be the cost for one HSM and $C_U$ the cost for one technician. In the first case the overall upgrade cost is estimated as $2C_H + C_U$ while in the second case we estimate as $C_H + 2C_U$. It is now clear that depending on how $C_H$ and $C_U$ are related we will go one direction or the other. For example, if a technician costs around 5000$ and an HSM around 10000$, we will opt for the second solution spending 20000$ instead of 25000$.

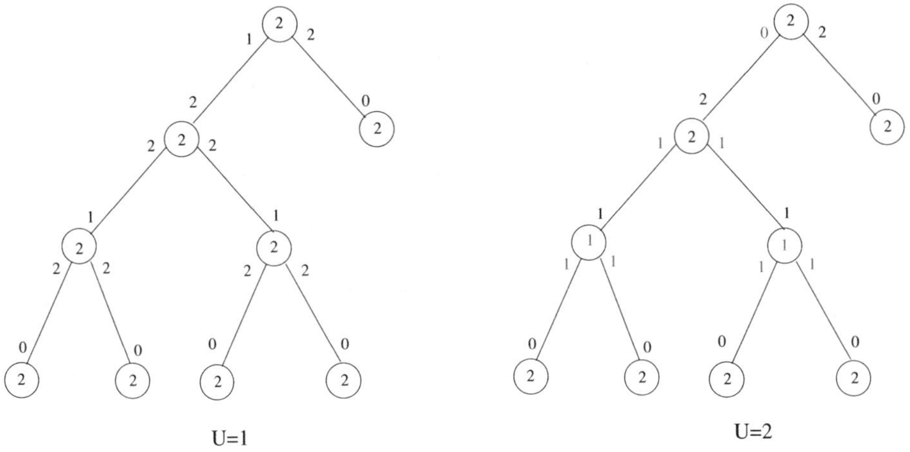


**Fig. 6.** An example of cost estimation

## 5 Conclusion

We have proposed a novel way of upgrading critical components in wide networked system which are incremental and aim at finding a trade-off between the extra hardware needed to maintain the functionality of the network, and the size of the technician teams simultaneously operating on the bank network switches. The presented techniques are not specific for HSMs and PIN managing but could be reused in any networked system requiring the upgrade of some security-critical component.

There are some aspects that we have not treated in this paper and might be interesting to investigate. We have mentioned in section 2 that borderline HSMs might be placed on edges instead of nodes. This increases the number of secured paths but, intuitively, requires more hardware to isolate secure subnetworks from insecure ones. To understand the benefits of this approach it would be useful to measure the degree of security of the network, i.e., the size of the secure subgraph from the ATMs to the related issuing bank or, in other words, the number of secured, upgraded paths in a network. Having this measure, we could compare the present strategies with ones placing borderline HSMs on edges, also comparing the degree of security provided by the new approach. The trade-off, thus, might be between the cost and the degree of security.

Finally, another interesting issue, we have previously mentioned, is the optimization of a new parameter, i.e., the technician motion either inside a weighted network or on a new independent physical network overlapped to the bank network. In this case, time complexity would probably become an issue as in the traveling salesman problem. Depending on the size of the analyzed trees, the solution might thus require heuristic approaches.

## References


1. Hackers crack cash machine PIN codes to steal millions. The Times online, http://www.timesonline.co.uk/tol/money/consumer_affairs/article4259009.ece
2. PIN Crackers Nab Holy Grail of Bank Card Security. Wired Magazine Blog Threat Level, http://blog.wired.com/27bstroke6/2009/04/pins.html
3. Barrière, L., Flocchini, P., Fraigniaud, P., Santoro, N.: Capture of an intruder by mobile agents. In: Proceedings of the 14th ACM Symposium on Parallel Algorithms and Architectures (SPAA),Winnipeg, Manitoba, Canada, pp. 200–209 (2002)
4. Barrière, L., Fraigniaud, P., Santoro, N., Thilikos, D.M.: Searching is not jumping. In: Bodlaender, H.L. (ed.) WG 2003. LNCS, vol. 2880, pp. 34–45. Springer, Heidelberg (2003)
5. Berkman, O., Ostrovsky, O.M.: The unbearable lightness of PIN cracking. In: Dietrich, S., Dhamija, R. (eds.) FC 2007 and USEC 2007. LNCS, vol. 4886, pp. 224–238. Springer, Heidelberg (2007)
6. Bond, M., Zielinski, P.: Decimalization table attacks for pin cracking. Technical Report UCAM-CL-TR-560, University of Cambridge, Computer Laboratory (2003), http://www.cl.cam.ac.uk/TechReports/UCAM-CL-TR-560.pdf
7. Breish, R.: An intuitive approach to speleotopology. Southwestern cavers VI(5), 72–82 (1967)
8. Centenaro, M., Focardi, R., Luccio, F., Steel, G.: Type-based analysis of PIN processing APIs. In: Backes, M., Ning, P. (eds.) ESORICS 2009. LNCS, vol. 5789, pp. 53–68. Springer, Heidelberg (2009)
9. Clulow, J.: The design and analysis of cryptographic APIs for security devices. Master's thesis, University of Natal, Durban (2003)
10. Ellis, J.A., Sudborough, I.H., Turner, J.S.: The vertex separation and search number of a graph. Information and Computation 113, 50–79 (1994)
11. Focardi, R., Luccio, F., Steel, G.: Blunting differential attacks on PIN processing APIs. In: Knapskog knapskog@q2s.ntnu.no, S.J. (ed.) NordSec 2009. LNCS, vol. 5838, pp. 88–103. Springer, Heidelberg (2009)
12. Focardi, R., Luccio, F.L.: Cracking bank PINs by playing Mastermind. In: Proceedings of the Fifth International Conference on Fun with algorithms (FUN 2010). LNCS, Springer, Heidelberg (2010)
13. Hayashi, F., Sullivan, R., Weiner, S.E.: A Guide to the ATM and Debit Card Industry. Federal Reserve Bank of Kansas City (2003)
14. Kirousis, L.M., Papadimitriou, C.H.: Searching and pebbling. Theoretical Computer Science 47, 205–218 (1986)
15. Lapaugh, A.: Recontamination does not help to search a graph. Journal of the ACM 40(2), 224–245 (1993)
16. Megiddo, N., Hakimi, S., Garey, M., Johnson, D., Papadimitriou, C.: The complexity of searching a graph. Journal of the ACM 35(1), 18–44 (1988)
17. Parson, T.: Pursuit-evasion problem on a graph. Theory and applications of graphs, 426–441 (1976)
18. Peng, S., Ko, M., Ho, C., Hsu, T., Tang, C.: Graph searching on chordal graphs. Algorithmica 27, 395–426 (2002)
19. Santoro, N.: Design and Analysis of Distributed Algorithms. John Wiley & Sons, Chichester (2006)
20. Steel, G.: Formal Analysis of PIN Block Attacks. Theoretical Computer Science 367(1-2), 257–270 (2006)

# Interactive Information Flow
## (Invited Talk)

Catuscia Palamidessi[1], Mário S. Alvim[1], and Miguel E. Andrés[2]

[1] INRIA and LIX, École Polytechnique Palaiseau, France
[2] Institute for Computing and Information Sciences, The Netherlands

**Abstract.** In recent years, there has been a growing interest in considering the quantitative aspects of Information Flow, partly because often the a priori knowledge of the secret information can be represented by a probability distribution, and partly because the mechanisms to protect the information may use randomization to obfuscate the relation between the secrets and the observables.

We consider the problem of defining a measure of information leakage in interactive systems. We show that the information-theoretic approach which interprets such systems as (simple) noisy channels is not valid anymore when the secrets and the observables can alternate during the computation, and influence each other. However, the principle can be retrieved if we consider more complicated types of channels, that in Information Theory are known as channels with memory and feedback. We show that there is a complete correspondence between interactive systems and such kind of channels. Furthermore, the proposed framework has good topological properties which allow to reason compositionally about the worst-case leakage in these systems.

## References

1. Andrés, M.E., Palamidessi, C., van Rossum, P., Smith, G.: Computing the leakage of information-hiding systems. In: Proc. of TACAS (2010) (to appear)
2. Chatzikokolakis, K., Palamidessi, C., Panangaden, P.: Anonymity protocols as noisy channels. Inf. and Comp. 206(2-4), 378–401 (2008)
3. Clark, D., Hunt, S., Malacaria, P.: Quantified interference for a while language. In: Proc. of QAPL 2004. ENTCS, vol. 112, pp. 149–166. Elsevier, Amsterdam (2005)
4. Desharnais, J., Jagadeesan, R., Gupta, V., Panangaden, P.: The metric analogue of weak bisimulation for probabilistic processes. In: Proc. of LICS, pp. 413–422 (2002)
5. Malacaria, P.: Assessing security threats of looping constructs. In: Proc. of POPL, pp. 225–235. ACM, New York (2007)
6. James, M.: Causality, feedback and directed information. In: Proc. of the International Symposium on Information Theory and its Applications, Honolulu (1990)
7. Smith, G.: On the foundations of quantitative information flow. In: de Alfaro, L. (ed.) FOSSACS 2009. LNCS, vol. 5504, pp. 288–302. Springer, Heidelberg (2009)
8. Tatikonda, S., Mitter, S.K.: The capacity of channels with feedback. IEEE Transactions on Information Theory 55(1), 323–349 (2009)

A. Armando and G. Lowe (Eds.): ARSPA-WITS 2010, LNCS 6186, p. 111, 2010.

# Portunes: Representing Attack Scenarios Spanning through the Physical, Digital and Social Domain

Trajce Dimkov, Wolter Pieters, and Pieter Hartel

Distributed and Embedded Security Group
University of Twente, The Netherlands
{trajce.dimkov,wolter.pieters,pieter.hartel}@utwente.nl

**Abstract.** The security goals of an organization are realized through security policies, which concern physical security, digital security and security awareness. An insider is aware of these security policies, and might be able to thwart the security goals by combining physical, digital and social means. A systematic analysis of such attacks requires the whole environment where the insider operates to be formally represented. This paper presents Portunes, a framework which integrates all three security domains in a single environment. Portunes consists of a high-level abstraction model focusing on the relations between the three security domains and a lower abstraction level language able to represent the model and describe attacks which span the three security domains.

Using the Portunes framework, we are able to represent a whole new family of attacks where the insider is not assumed to use purely digital actions to achieve a malicious goal.

**Keywords:** insider threat, physical security, security awareness, security model.

## 1 Introduction

Malicious insiders are a serious threat to organizations. Motivated by greed or malice, insiders can disrupt services, modify or steal data, or cause physical damage to the organization. Protecting assets from an insider is challenging [1] since insiders have knowledge of the security policies in place, have certain privileges on the systems and are trusted by colleagues. An insider may use the knowledge of the security policies to avoid detection and use personal credentials or social engineer colleagues to carry out an attack. Thus, the environment in the organization where the insider operates spans all three security domains, physical security, digital security and security awareness of the employees. If the environment is represented formally, it is possible to analyze potential insider attacks systematically.

The three security domains presented in the environment focus on different elements of security. Physical security restricts access to buildings, rooms and

A. Armando and G. Lowe (Eds.): ARSPA-WITS 2010, LNCS 6186, pp. 112–129, 2010.

objects. Digital security is concerned with access control on information systems. Finally, security awareness of employees focuses on resistance to social engineering, and is achieved through education of the employees.

The majority of formal models for the insider threat assume the insider uses only digital means to achieve an attack. Therefore an essential part of the environment of interest is not captured. Indeed, a study performed by the National Threat Assessment Center in the US (NTAC) [2] shows that 87% of the attacks performed by insiders required no technical knowledge and 26% used physical means or the account of another employee as part of the attack. Thus, a whole family of attacks, digitally-enabled physical attacks and physically-enabled digital attacks [3], in which the insider uses physical, digital and social means to compromise the asset cannot be presented nor analyzed. An example of a physically-enabled digital attack is the road apple attack [4], where an insider tricks an employee into plugging a malicious dongle into a server located in a physically restricted area. The road apple attack will be used as the main example in the paper.

Representing all three security domains in a single formalism is challenging. Firstly, the appropriate abstraction level needs to be found. A too low level of abstraction for each domain (down to the individual atoms, bits or conversation dynamics) makes the representation complicated and unusable. However, abstracting away from physical spaces, data and relations between people might omit details that contribute to an attack. Secondly, the domains have different properties making them hard to integrate. For example, mobility of digital data is not restricted by its locality as it is the case with objects in the physical domain. Likewise, physical objects cannot be reproduced as easily as digital data.

The contribution of this paper is the Portunes framework[1], a framework which integrates all three security domains in a single environment. Portunes consists of a model and a language. The model is a high-level abstraction of the environment focusing on the relations between the three security domains. It provides a conceptual overview of the environment easy to understand by the user. The language is at a relatively low level of abstraction, close to the enforcement mechanisms. The language is able to describe attacks which span the three security domains.

The rest of the paper is structured as follows. Section 2 gives an overview of related work which contributed to the design of Portunes. Section 3 formalizes the Portunes model and Portunes language. We use the road apple attack as an example of the scenarios Portunes is designed to represent. The final section concludes and identifies future work.

## 2 Related Work

The design of the Portunes model and Portunes language is influenced by several research directions, such as insider threat modeling, physical modeling and

[1] After Portunes, the Roman god of keys.

process calculi. This section lists several papers which influenced the design of Portunes and describes how Portunes extends or deviates from them.

Dragovic et al. [5] are concerned with modeling the physical and digital domain to determine data exposure. Their model defines a containment relation between layers of protection. Data security is determined not by access control policies, but by the number of layers of protection above the data and the confidentiality provided by each layer. The Portunes model uses a similar relation to present the location of elements, but uses access control policies to describe security mechanisms. Scott [6] focuses on mobility of software-agents in a spatial area and usage policies that define the behavior of the agents depending on the locality of the hosting device. The mobility of the agents is restricted through edges on a graph. The Portunes model adds semantics on the graph structure by giving meaning to the nodes and edges and defines invariants enforced directly into the semantics of the language.

KLAIM [7] is a process calculus for agent interaction and mobility, consisting of three layers: nodes, processes and actions. There are several KLAIM dialects, including $\mu$Klaim [8], OpenKlaim [9] and acKlaim [10]. The goal of the acKlaim language is to present insider threats by combining the physical and digital security domain. Mobility is presented by remote evaluation of processes. The Portunes language builds upon these KLAIM dialects. Firstly, the actions for mobility and embedding of objects (login, logout) are similar to OpenKlaim. Secondly, the security policies expressed in Portunes language are similar to acKlaim and $\mu$Klaim. However, in the Portunes language mobility is represented by moving nodes rather than evaluating processes. Additionally, the Portunes language introduces delegation, whereby a node can delegate a task to another node.

# 3 Portunes

This section presents the Portunes framework. We first present the requirements which Portunes needs to satisfy and the motivation behind some of the design decisions. Based on the requirements, we formally define the Portunes model and the Portunes language. To show the expressiveness of the framework, we use an instance of the road apple attack as an example.

## 3.1 Requirements and Motivation

A model integrating multiple security domains needs to be expressive enough to present the details of an attack in each security domain. In a previous work [11], we provided the basic requirements for an integrated security model to be expressive enough to present detailed attacks. Briefly, an integrated security model should be able to present the data of interest, the physical objects in which the data resides, the people that manipulate the objects and the interaction between data, physical objects and people.

An additional requirement for Portunes is to restrict interactions and states which are not possible in reality. For example, it is possible to put a laptop in a room, however, putting a room in a laptop is impossible; a person can move

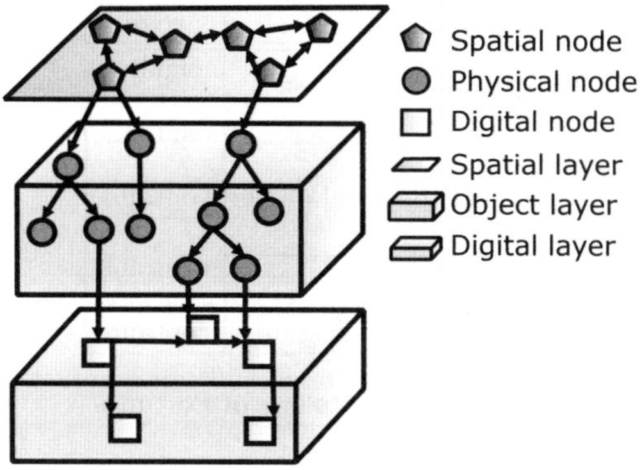


**Fig. 1.** Graphic presentation of Portunes

only to a neighboring location, while data can move to any location; data can be easily copied, while the reproduction of a computer requires assembling of other objects or materials.

### 3.2 The Portunes Model

To present the different properties and behavior of elements from physical and digital security, the Portunes model stratifies the environment of interest in three layers: spatial, object and digital. The spatial layer presents the facility of the organization, including rooms, halls and elevators. The object layer consists of objects located in the facility of the organization, such as people, computers and keys. The digital layer presents the data of interest. Stratification of the environment in three distinct layers allows specification of actions that are possible only in a single layer (copying can only happen for digital entities) or between specific layers (a person can move data, but data cannot move a person).

The Portunes model abstracts the environment of an organization in a graph. The model stratifies the nodes of the graph in three layers and restricts the edges between layers to reflect reality. A node abstracting a location, such as an elevator or a room, belongs to the spatial layer $L$ and it is termed a spatial node. A node abstracting a physical object, such as a laptop or a person, belongs to the object layer $O$ and it is termed an object node. A node abstracting data, such as an operating system or a file, belongs to the digital layer $D$. The edges between spatial nodes denote a neighbor relation and all other edges in the model denote a containment relation. The ontology used in Portunes is given in Figure 2. An edge $(n, m)$ between two spatial nodes means $n$ *is a neighbor of* $m$. This is a symmetric relation where the direction of the edge is not important. For all other nodes, an edge $(n, m)$ means that node $n$ *contains* node $m$; this is an asymmetric relation.

The above statements are illustrated in Figure 1 and formalized in the following definition.

| layer | node | edge |
| --- | --- | --- |
| spatial | location | neighbors |
| | | contains |
| object | physical object | contains |
| | | contains |
| digital | data | contains |

**Fig. 2.** The ontology of Portunes

**Definition 1.** *Let $G = (Node, Edge)$ be a directed graph and $\mathcal{D} : Node \to Layer$ a function mapping a node to the $Layer = \{L, O, D\}$. A tuple $(G, \mathcal{D})$ is a Portunes model if it satisfies the following invariants $C(G, \mathcal{D})$:*

1. *Every object node can have only one parent.*
   $\forall n \in Node : \mathcal{D}(n) = O \to indegree(n) = 1$
2. *One of the predecessors of an object node must be a spatial node.*
   $\forall n \in Node : \mathcal{D}(n) = O \to \exists m \in Node : \mathcal{D}(m) = L \wedge \exists \langle m, ...., n \rangle$; *where* $\langle m, ...., n \rangle$ *denotes a finite path from* $m$ *to* $n$.
3. *There is no edge from an object to a spatial node.*
   $\nexists (n, m) \in Edge : \mathcal{D}(n) = O \wedge \mathcal{D}(m) = L$
4. *There is no edge from a digital to an object node.*
   $\nexists (n, m) \in Edge : \mathcal{D}(n) = D \wedge \mathcal{D}(m) = O$
5. *A spatial and a digital node cannot be connected.*
   $\nexists (n, m) \in Edge : (\mathcal{D}(n) = D \wedge \mathcal{D}(m) = L) \vee (\mathcal{D}(n) = L \wedge \mathcal{D}(m) = D)$
6. *The edges between digital nodes do not generate cycles.*
   $\nexists \langle n, ..., m \rangle : \mathcal{D}(n) = ... = \mathcal{D}(m) = D \wedge n = m$

The intuition behind the invariants is as follows. An object node cannot be at more than one place, thus an object node can have only one parent (1). An object node is contained in a known location (2). An object node cannot contain any spatial objects (3) (for example, a laptop cannot contain a room) nor can a digital node contain an object node (4) (for example, a file cannot contain a laptop). A spatial node cannot contain a digital node and vice versa (5), and a digital node cannot contain itself (6).

**Theorem 1.** *A graph $G = (Node, Edge)$ in a Portunes model $(G, \mathcal{D})$ can have cycles only in the spatial layer:*
$\exists \langle n, ..., m \rangle : n = m \to \mathcal{D}(n) = ... = \mathcal{D}(m) = L$

*Proof.* The proof is presented in the appendix.

**Example: Road apple attack.** To show how Portunes can be used for representing insider threats across domains, we will use the example of the road

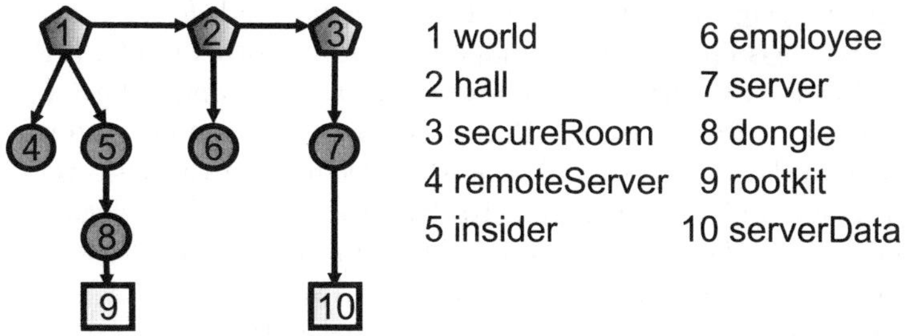


**Fig. 3.** Graph of the road apple attack environment

$$\mathcal{D}(hall) = \mathcal{D}(secureRoom) = \mathcal{D}(world) = L$$
$$\mathcal{D}(remoteServer) = \mathcal{D}(insider) = \mathcal{D}(employee) = \mathcal{D}(server) = \mathcal{D}(dongle) = O$$
$$\mathcal{D}(serverData) = \mathcal{D}(rootkit) = D$$

**Fig. 4.** The function $\mathcal{D}$ for the road apple attack environment

apple attack [4]. In this attack, an insider uses the trust of an employee (social domain) to steal sensitive data (digital domain) from a a server in a restricted area (physical domain).

To describe the attack, the environment in which the attack takes place needs to include information from all three security domains. Concerning physical security, the organization has a restricted area where a server with sensitive data resides. Additionally there is a public area where employees can socialize. Regarding the digital domain, the sensitive data on the server is isolated from the rest of the network, making the data accessible only locally. The security awareness of the employees is such that they trust each other enough to share office material (for example: CDs and dongles).

An abstraction of the environment is represented as a Portunes model in Figure 3 and 4. The nodes *hall*, *secureRoom* and *world* are spatial nodes, *serverData* and *rootkit* are digital nodes. All other nodes are object nodes. In Section 3.4 we will revisit the example and show how the road apple attack takes place.

### 3.3 The Portunes Language

In the previous section, we defined a graph-based model to present the facilities of an organization, the objects in a facility and the data of interest. This model is on a conceptual level, and it simplifies the presentation of the environment to the user. In this section we introduce the Portunes language, which is closer to the enforcement mechanisms. The language consists of nodes, processes and actions, where a node in the Portunes model represents a node in the Portunes language. The main goal of the language is to model the interaction between the nodes in the Portunes model.

The language captures two interactions, *mobility* and *delegation*. By making all nodes first class citizens, every node can move. For example, a node representing an insider can move through the organization and collect keys, which increase his initial privileges. The Portunes language lets a delegator node delegate a task to a delegatee node. During the execution of the task, the delegatee uses the privileges of the delegator. To delegate a task, the delegatee needs to trust the delegator. For example, an insider can delegate a task to a colleague. The colleague will execute the task only if he trusts the insider.

The above two interactions, mobility and delegation, are restricted by the invariants from Definition 1 and by the security policies associated with each node. Policies on nodes from the spatial and object layer represent the physical security. These policies restrict the physical access to spatial areas in the facility and the objects inside the spatial areas. Policies on nodes from the digital layer represent the digital security of the organization and focus on access control on the data of interest. In the Portunes language people can interact with other people. Policies on people give the social aspect of the model, or more precisely, they define under which circumstances a person *trusts* another person.

**Syntax.** As with other members of the KLAIM family, the syntax of the Portunes language consists of nodes, processes and actions. The Portunes language lacks the tuple spaces and the actions associated with tuple spaces, which are present in the KLAIM family of languages, and focuses on the connections between nodes. This is because connectivity is the main interest from the perspective of security modeling.

The syntax of the Portunes language is shown in Figure 5. A single *node* $l ::_s^\delta P$ consists of a name $l \in \mathcal{L}$, where $\mathcal{L}$ is a finite set of names, a set of node names $s \in \mathcal{P}(\mathcal{L})$, representing nodes that are connected to node $l$ , an access control policy $\delta$ and a process $P$. The relation between the graph of the Portunes model and the expressions in the Portunes language is intuitive: a node $l$ in the graph represents a node with name $l$ in the language, an edge $(l, l')$ in the graph

| | | |
|---|---|---|
| $N ::=$ | | Node |
| $\mid$ | $l ::_s^\delta P$ | Single node |
| $\mid$ | $N_1 \parallel N_2$ | Net composition |
| $P ::=$ | | Process |
| $\mid$ | $nil$ | Null process |
| $\mid$ | $P_1 \mid P_2$ | Process composition |
| $\mid$ | $a^l.P$ | Action prefixing |
| $a ::=$ | | Action |
| $\mid$ | $login(l)$ | Login |
| $\mid$ | $logout(l)$ | Logout |
| $\mid$ | $eval(P)@l$ | Spawning |

**Fig. 5.** Syntax of the Portunes language

connects $l$ to a node name $l'$ in the set $s$ of the node $l ::_s^\delta P$. Thus, the node name uniquely identifies the node in the model, while the set $s$ defines which other nodes the node *contains* or *is a neighbor of*. These two relations identify the relative location of each element in the environment. A net is a composition of nodes.

A *process* $P$ is a composition of actions. Namely, $nil$ stands for a process that cannot execute any action and $a^l.P$ for the process that executes action $a$ using privileges from node $l \in \mathcal{L}$ and then behaves as $P$. The label $l$ identifies a node from where the privileges originate, and it is termed the origin node. The structure $P_1|P_2$ is for parallel composition of processes $P_1$ and $P_2$. A process $P$ represents a task. A node can perform a task by itself or delegate the task to another node.

An *action* $a$ is a primitive which manipulates the nodes in the language. There are three primitives, $login(l)$, $logout(l)$ and $eval(P)@l$. The actions $login(l)$ and $logout(l)$ provide the mobility of a node, by manipulating the set $s$. The action $eval(P)@l$ delegates a task $P$ to a node $l$ by spawning a process in the node.

*Example:* For a node representing a room, $room ::_s^\delta nil$, the access control policy $\delta$ defines the conditions under which other entities can enter or leave the room. The set $s$ contains the names of all nodes that are located in the room or connected to the room. Let a supervisor and a person be in a hall $hall ::_{\{person,\ supervisor\}}^\delta nil$ which is neighboring the room. An example of a supervisor delegating a task to a person is: $supervisor ::_s^\delta eval(P)@person^{supervisor}$ where $P$ is a process denoting the task, $person$ is the target node and the label $supervisor$ is the origin node. A person entering the room as part of the task delegated from $supervisor$ is presented through $person ::_s^\delta login(room)^{supervisor}.P'$, while a person leaving the room $person ::_s^\delta logout(room)^{supervisor}.P''$.

Depending on the privileges of the origin node which depend on its identity, location and credentials, a node can grant a set of capabilities $C = \{ln, lt, e\}$, where $ln$ is a capability to execute the action $login$, $lt$ to execute the action $logout$ and $e$ to execute the action $eval$. The access control policy $\delta$ is a function $\delta : (\mathcal{L} \cup \{\bot\}) \times (\mathcal{L} \cup \{\bot\}) \times \mathcal{P}(\mathcal{L}) \rightarrow \mathcal{P}(C)$. The first and the second parameter denote identity based access control and location based access control respectively. If the identity or the location does not influence the policy, it is replaced by $\bot$. The third parameter denotes credential based access control, which requires a set of credentials to allow an action. If a policy is not affected by credentials, the third parameter is an empty set. A security policy can present a situation where: 1) only credentials are needed, such as a door that requires a key $(\bot, \bot, \{key\}) \mapsto \{ln\}$, 2) only the identity is required, such as a door that requires biometrics information $(John, \bot, \emptyset) \mapsto \{ln\}$ or 3) only the location is required, such as data that can be reached only locally $(\bot, office, \emptyset) \mapsto \{ln\}$. The policy supports combinations of these attributes, such as a door requiring biometrics and a key $(John, \bot, \{key\}) \mapsto \{ln\}$. The least restrictive policy that can be used is: $(\bot, \bot, \emptyset) \mapsto \{ln, lt, e\}$.

$$grant(l_o, \delta_t, a) = \exists k_1, k_2 \in \mathcal{L} \cup \{\bot\}, \exists K \in \mathcal{P}(\mathcal{L}) : a \in \delta_t(k_1, k_2, K) \wedge$$
$$\underbrace{(k_1 = l_o \vee k_1 = \bot)}_{(1)} \wedge \underbrace{(k_2 \in parents(l_o) \vee k_2 = \bot)}_{(2)} \wedge \underbrace{(K \subseteq children(l_o))}_{(3)},$$
$$\text{where } parents(l_o) = \{\, l_{po} |\, l_{po} ::_{s_{po}}^{\delta_{po}} R \in N \wedge l_o \in s_{po}\} \text{ and}$$
$$children(l_o) = \{\, s_o |\, l_o ::_{s_o}^{\delta_o} R \in N\}$$

$$l_t \succ_{ln} l = \begin{cases} true & \textit{iff} \;\; (\mathcal{D}(l_t) = L \wedge \mathcal{D}(l) = O) \vee (\mathcal{D}(l_t) = O \wedge \mathcal{D}(l) = D) \\ l_t \succ\succ_{ln} l & \textit{iff} \;\; \mathcal{D}(l_t) = \mathcal{D}(l) \\ false & otherwise \end{cases}$$

$$\text{where } l \succ_e l_t =$$
$$\underbrace{(\mathcal{D}(l) \neq L \wedge \mathcal{D}(l_t) \neq L)}_{(4)} \wedge \underbrace{\neg(\mathcal{D}(l) = D \wedge \mathcal{D}(l_t) = O)}_{(5)} \wedge \underbrace{(l_t \in children(l)}_{(6)}$$
$$\vee \underbrace{(\exists l_p ::_{sp}^{\delta_p} R \in N : l \in s_p \wedge l_t \in s_p)}_{(7)} \vee \underbrace{\mathcal{D}(l_t) = D)}_{(8)}$$

**Fig. 6.** Auxiliary function *grant* and $\succ$ relations

**Auxiliary functions.** Having defined the behavior of nodes using three primitive actions, we now look at the context where these actions can be executed. A node $l ::_s^{\delta} a^{l'}.P$ can be restricted in executing an action $a$ from an origin node $l'$ to a target node for three reasons. The origin node might not have sufficient privileges, execution of the action $a$ invalidates the invariants in Definition 1 from the Portunes model, or the target node might not be in proximity of the node $l$. This section defines auxiliary functions for an implicitly given net N, which take care these restrictions. The auxiliary functions are defined in Figure 6 and are used to simplify the operational semantics of the language.

The *grant* function checks if an origin node has sufficient privileges to execute an action to a target node. The first parameter defines the name of the origin node, the second parameter defines the policies on the target node and the third parameter is a label of an action. Intuitively, a node can execute an action depending on the identity $l_o$ of the origin node (1), its location $parents(l_o)$ (2) or the keys $children(l_o)$ it contains (3). Note that the value of *grant* depends solely of the origin node, not the node executing the process.

The relation $l_t \succ_{ln} l$ states that node $l_t$ can contain node $l$. The goal of this relation is to enforce the invariants 3-6 in Definition 1. From the relation, an object node can always interact with spatial nodes and a digital node can always interact with object nodes. The relation $l_t \succ\succ_{ln} l$ provides ordering between nodes from the same layer. The relation is defined by the user because the ordering depends on the elements we want to model in the environment. For example, an operating system usually can contain a file, but not vice versa. Yet, in scenarios where the systems are virtualized, it is possible and desirable to model a file containing an operating system. The only assumption on $l_t \succ\succ_{ln} l$ is that it does not invalidate invariant 7 in Definition 1, or put differently, the relation does not allow generation of cycles between nodes in the digital layer.

The ordering relation $l \succ_e l_t$ states that node $l$ can delegate a task to node $l_t$ by means of spawning a process. The relation restricts delegation of tasks between nodes depending on the layer a node belongs to and the proximity between nodes. An object node can delegate a task to a digital node or another object node, while a digital node can delegate a task only to another digital node. Thus, spatial nodes cannot delegate tasks, nor can a task be delegated to spatial nodes (4), and digital nodes cannot delegate tasks to object nodes (5). Furthermore, a non-digital node can delegate a task only to nodes it contains (6) or nodes that are in the same location (7). In digital nodes the proximity does not play any role in restricting the delegation of a task (8). The decision (8) assumes the world is pervasive and two digital nodes can delegate tasks from any location as long as they have the appropriate privileges.

The expressions from Figure 6 focus on the relation between nodes. The *grant* function provides the security constraints in the language based on the location and identity nodes, while the $\succ_{ln}$, $\succ\succ_{ln}$ and $\succ_e$ relations provide non-security constraints derived from the layer the nodes belong to and their location. In addition, we put a restriction on the processes inside a node, to distinguish tasks originating from a single node. We call such processes simple processes, and define an additional auxiliary function which helps determine if a process is a simple process.

**Definition 1.** *Let $origin(P) \rightarrow \mathcal{P}(\mathcal{L})$ be a function which returns all the action labels of a process $P$. A process $P$, which is either nil or contains actions only from one origin node is a simple process.* $origin(P) \subseteq \{l_0\}$

**Operational semantics.** Similar to Bettini et al. [9], the semantics of the Portunes language is divided into process semantics and net semantics. The process semantics is given in terms of a labeled transition relation $\xrightarrow{a}$ and describes both the intention of a process to perform an action and the availability of resources in the net. The label $a$ contains the name of the node executing the action, the target node, the origin node and a set of node names which identify which nodes are the target node contains. The net semantics given in terms of a transition relation $\Rightarrow$ describes possible net evolutions and relies on the labeled transition $\xrightarrow{a}$ from the process semantics.

The process semantics of the language is defined in Figure 7. A node can login to another node **[login]** if it has sufficient privileges to perform the action (*grant*) if the node can be contained in the target node ($\succ_{ln}$) and if the process is a simple process with origin node $l_o$ (*origin*). As a result of executing the action, node $l$ enters in node $l_t$, or put differently, the target node $l_t$ now contains node $l$. For a node to logout from a target node **[logout]**, the target node must contain the node ($l \in s_t$), the origin node must have proper privileges (*grant*) and the process must be a simple process with origin node $l_o$ (*origin*). The action results in $l$ leaving $l_t$, specified through removing its node name from $s_t$. Spawning a process **[eval]** requires both the node executing the action and the target node to be close to each other or the target node to be digital ($l \succ_e l_t$), the origin node

$$\frac{origin(P) \subseteq \{l_o\} \quad l_t \succ_{ln} l \quad grant(l_o, \delta_t, ln)}{l ::^{\delta}_{s} login(l_t)^{l_o}.P \| \ l_t ::^{\delta_t}_{s_t} Q \xrightarrow{login(l,l_t,l_o,s_t)} l ::^{\delta}_{s} P \| \ l_t ::^{\delta_t}_{s_t \cup l} Q} \quad \textbf{[login]}$$

$$\frac{origin(P) \subseteq \{l_o\} \quad grant(l_o, \delta_t, lt) \quad l \in s_t}{l ::^{\delta}_{s} logout(l_t)^{l_o}.P \| \ l_t ::^{\delta_t}_{s_t} Q \xrightarrow{logout(l,l_t,l_o,s_t)} l ::^{\delta}_{s} P \| \ l_t ::^{\delta_t}_{s_t \setminus \{l\}} Q} \quad \textbf{[logout]}$$

$$\frac{origin(P) \subseteq \{l_o\} \quad origin(Q) \subseteq \{l_o\} \quad l \succ_e l_t \quad grant(l_o, \delta_t, e)}{l ::^{\delta}_{s} eval(Q)@l_t^{l_o}.P \| \ l_t ::^{\delta_t}_{s_t} R \xrightarrow{eval(l,l_t,l_o,s_t)} l ::^{\delta}_{s} P \| \ l_t ::^{\delta_t}_{s_t} R|Q} \quad \textbf{[eval]}$$

$$\frac{l ::^{\delta}_{s} P \xrightarrow{a} l ::^{\delta}_{s} P'}{l ::^{\delta}_{s} P|Q \xrightarrow{a} l ::^{\delta}_{s} P'|Q} \quad \textbf{[pComp]}$$

**Fig. 7.** Process semantics

$$\frac{N \xrightarrow{eval(l,l_t,l_o,s_t)} N_1}{N \Rightarrow N_1} \ \textbf{[neteval]} \qquad \frac{N_1 \Rightarrow N_1'}{N_1 \parallel N_2 \Rightarrow N_1' \parallel N_2} \ \textbf{[nComp]}$$

$$\frac{N \xrightarrow{logout(l,l_{t_1},l_o,s_{t_1})} N_1 \quad N \xrightarrow{login(l,l_{t_2},l_o,s_{t_2})} N_2 \quad \mathcal{D}(l) = D}{N \Rightarrow N_2} \ \textbf{[netcopy]}$$

$$\frac{N \xrightarrow{logout(l,l_{t_1},l_o,s_{t_1})} N_1 \ N_1 \xrightarrow{login(l,l_{t_2},l_o,s_{t_2})} N_2 \ (l_{t_1} \in s_{t_2} \vee l_{t_2} \in s_{t_1} \vee \mathcal{D}(l) = D)}{N \Rightarrow N_2} \ \textbf{[netmove]}$$

**Fig. 8.** Net semantics

should have the proper privileges (*grant*) and both processes $P$ and $Q$ need to be simple processes with origin node $l_o$ (*origin*). The action results in delegating a new task $Q$ to the target node, which contains actions originating from the same origin node as the task $P$.

The net semantics in Figure 8 use the process semantics to define the possible actions in the Portunes language. Spawning a process is limited solely by the process semantics **[neteval]**. To move, a node executes the logout and login actions in sequence **[netmove]**. Both actions should have the same origin node and should be executed by the same node. Furthermore, an object node can move only to a node in its proximity, while digital nodes do not have this restriction ($l_{t_1} \in s_{t_2} \vee l_{t_2} \in s_{t_1} \vee \mathcal{D}(l) = D$). Data can be copied, which is presented by data entering a new node without leaving the previous **[netcopy]**. The standard rules for structural congruence apply and are presented in Figure 9.

**Theorem 1.** *Nodes from the object and spatial layer cannot move to remote locations.*

*Proof. (Sketch) Follows from the netmove premise:* $l_{t_1} \in s_{t_2} \vee l_{t_2} \in s_{t_1}$

**Theorem 2.** *Nodes from the object and spatial layer can influence only child and sibling nodes.*

$$
\begin{array}{ll}
\text{(ProcCom)} & P_1|P_2 \equiv P_2|P_1 \\
\text{(NetCom)} & N_1\|N_2 \equiv N_2\|N_1 \\
\text{(Abs)} & P_1|nil \equiv P_1
\end{array}
$$

**Fig. 9.** Structural congruence of processes and nets

*Proof. (Sketch) The property follows from the premise of the eval action:* $\succ_e$

**Theorem 3.** *Let G be a Portunes graph and N be a network of nodes in Portunes language. Let* $Map(N) \rightarrow G$ *map a Portunes program in a Portunes model, such that* $C(Map(N), \mathcal{D})$ *holds.*

*The transitions generated from the semantics of Portunes language do not invalidate* $C(Map(N), \mathcal{D})$.

*Proof.* The proof is presented in the appendix.

### 3.4 Using the Portunes Framework to Calculate Attack Scenarios

Having defined Portunes in the previous sections, this section shows how the framework can aid in calculating attack scenarios. The Portunes model helps represent the environment graphically and puts constraints on structure. The user needs to define: (1) a net composition that corresponds to the graph with variables instead of processes, (2) the function $\mathcal{D}$, which stratifies the graph, and (3) the relation $\succ\succ_{ln}$ which tells which node can be contained in which other node.

| $l_t$ \ $l$ | 1 | 2 | 3 | 4 | 5 | 6 | 7 | 8 | 9 | 10 |
|---|---|---|---|---|---|---|---|---|---|---|
| 1. world | | | | | | | | | | |
| 2. hall | | | | | | | | | | |
| 3. secureRoom | | | | | | | | | | |
| 4. remoteServer | | | | | | | | 1 | | |
| 5. insider | | | | 1 | | | 1 | 1 | | |
| 6. employee | | | | 1 | | | 1 | 1 | | |
| 7. server | | | | | | | | 1 | | |
| 8. dongle | | | | | | | | | | |
| 9. rootkit | | | | | | | | | | |
| 10. serverData | | | | | | | | | 1 | |

**Fig. 10.** Definition of the auxiliary relation $\succ\succ_{ln}$ for the road apple attack environment

The previous steps provide a representation of the environment of interest. It is now possible to present attack scenarios through process definitions. The last step (4) is to find concrete process expressions (i.e.instantiations of the variables in item (1) that invalidate a goal. An attack scenario can be generated by hand or automatically, by using model checking techniques. Here we use the road apple attack as an example of an attack scenario.

**Example: Road apple attack - continued.** In section 3.2 we introduced the Portunes model of the environment where the road apple takes place. We defined the relation between the elements through a graph and their properties through the function $\mathcal{D}$. Now, we additionally define the $\succ\!\succ_{ln}$ relation and the security policies on each of the nodes.

The relation $\succ\!\succ_{ln}$ is defined in Figure 10 through a boolean table. For example, cell (4,8) is the result of $remoteServer \succ\!\succ_{ln} dongle$ and indicates that the remote server can contain the dongle.

Figure 11 presents the environment as a net composition. This representation does not provide visual information about the relation between elements, as in the Portunes model. However, the representation contains detailed information about the security policies in place, making it suitable for analysis.

Having defined the environment, now it is possible to reason about possible attack scenarios. An attack scenario is defined through generating processes in the nodes. Figure 12 shows the dynamics of the actual road apple attack as four processes, $P_1$, $P_2$, $P_3$ and $P_4$. All actions in the process $P_1$ have an origin node *insider*, in $P_2$ an origin node *employee*, in $P_3$ an origin node *dongle* and in $P_4$ an origin node *rootkit*. For clarity, the labels on the actions representing the

$$
\begin{array}{l}
world ::^{(\bot,\bot,\emptyset) \mapsto \{ln,lt\}}_{\{remoteServer,\ insider,\ hall\}}\ nil \\
\parallel\ hall ::^{(\bot,\bot,\emptyset) \mapsto \{ln,lt\}}_{\{employee,\ secureRoom\}}\ nil \\
\parallel\ secureRoom ::^{(employee,\bot,\emptyset) \mapsto \{ln,lt\}}_{\{server\}}\ nil \\
\parallel\ remoteServer ::^{(\bot,\bot,\emptyset) \mapsto \{ln\}}_{\{\}}\ nil \\
\parallel\ insider ::^{(\bot,\bot,\emptyset) \mapsto \{ln,lt,e\}}_{\{dongle\}}\ P_1 \\
\parallel\ employee ::^{(insider,\bot,\emptyset) \mapsto \{ln\}\ ;\ (employee,\bot,\emptyset) \mapsto \{ln,lt,e\}}_{\{\}}\ P_2 \\
\parallel\ server ::^{(\bot,secureRoom,\emptyset) \mapsto \{ln,lt\}\ ;\ (\bot,server,\emptyset) \mapsto \{ln,lt\}}_{\{serverData\}}\ nil \\
\parallel\ dongle ::^{(\bot,\bot,\emptyset) \mapsto \{e\}\ ;\ (dongle,\bot,\emptyset) \mapsto \{ln,lt\}}_{\{rootkit\}}\ P_3 \\
\parallel\ rootkit ::^{(dongle,\bot,\emptyset) \mapsto \{ln,lt,e\}}_{\{\}}\ P_4 \\
\parallel\ serverData ::^{(\bot,server,\emptyset) \mapsto \{e\}}_{\{\}}\ nil
\end{array}
$$

**Fig. 11.** The road apple attack environment in the Portunes language

$$
\begin{array}{ll}
P_1 = logout(world).login(hall). & \text{(a)} \\
\quad eval(logout(insider).login(hall).logout(hall). & \\
\quad login(employee))@dongle & \text{(b)} \\
P_2 = eval(logout(employee).login(secureRoom). & \\
\quad logout(secureRoom).login(server))@dongle. & \text{(c)} \\
\quad logout(hall).login(secureRoom) & \\
P_3 = eval(logout(dongle).login(server))@rootkit & \\
P_4 = eval(login(remoteServer))@serverData &
\end{array}
$$

**Fig. 12.** The road apple attack in the Portunes language

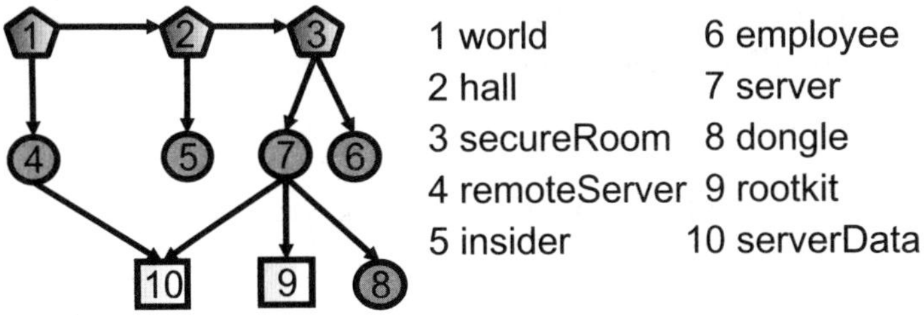


**Fig. 13.** Portunes model of the road apple attack environment after the execution of the attack

origin node are omitted from the process definitions. The insider ($P_1$) goes in the hall and waits for the employee (process $P_1$ until reaches point a). Then, the insider gives the employee the dongle containing the rootkit, which the employee accepts ($P_1$ reaches b). Later, the employee plugs the dongle in the secure server ($P_2$ reaches c) using its own credentials and the server gives the dongle ($P_3$) access to the local data. When the rootkit ($P_4$) reaches the server, it copies all the data to the remote server. The above actions represent the road apple attack with a dongle automatically running when attached to a computer [12]. After executing the processes from Figure 12, the data will reside in the remote server, presented through an edge $(remoteServer, data)$ in the Portunes model in Figure 13.

The process definitions follow the semantics of the language. Thus, no attack defined through processes will violate a security policy. This makes the framework suitable for presenting scenarios where the insider does not violate a policy, but achieves his goal by combining physical access, social engineering and digital actions.

The road apple attack is just one attack scenario. An insider may gain possession of the data by using alternative routes. For example, the employee might be tricked into letting the insider in the secure room, as shown through the process definitions in Figure 14. A proper reasoning about the data exposure requires all attack scenarios to be available to the security professional. The Portunes framework aids in the reasoning of data exposure, by helping answer questions such as:

1. In which locations can an object A end up? For example, show all locations where the server data can reside.
2. Who can reach location A? For example, show all elements who can reach the secure room.
3. What are the scenarios that violate a specific goal? For example, show all attack scenarios where the server data ends up in a remote server.

To answer these questions, we implemented a proof of concept implementation of the framework and used model checking to generate all possible attack scenarios by automatically generating the processes $P_1$ - $P_4$. However, model checking requires heuristics to improve the scalability and we are currently exploring other

$P_1$=*logout(world).login(hall).eval(eval(login(remoteServer)@serverData)@server*
$P_2$=*eval(logout(hall).login(secureRoom))@insider*
$P_3$=*nil*
$P_4$=*nil*

**Fig. 14.** Alternative attack scenario

techniques for the generation of attack scenarios. We will discuss the algorithms in more detail in future work.

## 4 Conclusion and Future Work

This paper presents Portunes, a framework consisting of a high-level model and a language inspired by the KLAIM family of languages. Portunes is capable of representing attacks spanning the digital, physical and social domain. To capture the three domains efficiently, Portunes is able to represent 1) physical properties of elements, 2) mobility of objects and data, 3) identity, credentials and location based access control and 4) trust and delegation between people. The applicability of Portunes is demonstrated using the example of the road apple attack, showing how an insider can attack without violating existing security policies by combining actions from all three domains.

As a future work, we plan to generate attack scenarios automatically from environments presented through the Portunes framework. We are looking at existing model checking techniques and heuristics to generate all possible action traces for each of the processes. Additionally, we are interested in mechanisms to isolate actions which contribute to an attack and automatically generate attack trees.

## References

1. INFOSEC Research Council. Hard problem list (November 2005), `http://www.cyber.st.dhs.gov/docs/IRC_Hard_Problem_List.pdf`
2. Randazzo, M.R., Keeney, M., Kowalski, E., Cappelli, D., Moore, A.: Insider threat study: Illicit cyber activity in the banking and finance sector. U.S. Secret Service and CERT Coordination Center Software Engineering Institute (2004)
3. DePoy, J., Phelan, J., Sholander, P., Smith, B.J., Varnado, G.B., Wyss, G.D., Darby, J., Walter, A.: Critical infrastructure systems of systems assessment methodology. Technical Report SAND2006-6399, Sandia National Laboratories (October 2007)
4. Stasiukonis, S.: Social engineering the usb way (2006), `http://www.darkreading.com/document.asp?doc_id=95556`
5. Dragovic, B., Crowcroft, J.: Containment: from context awareness to contextual effects awareness. In: Proceedings of 2nd Inernational Workshop on Software Aspects of Context. CEUR Workshop Proceedings (2005)
6. Scott, D.J.: Abstracting Application-Level Security Policy for Ubiquitous Computing. PhD thesis, University of Cambridge, Cambridge (2004)

7. De Nicola, R., Ferrari, G.L., Pugliese, R.: KLAIM: A kernel language for agents interaction and mobility. IEEE Transactions on software engineering 24(5), 315–330 (1998)
8. Gorla, D., Pugliese, R.: Resource access and mobility control with dynamic privileges acquisition. In: Baeten, J.C.M., Lenstra, J.K., Parrow, J., Woeginger, G.J. (eds.) ICALP 2003. LNCS, vol. 2719, pp. 119–132. Springer, Heidelberg (2003)
9. Bettini, L., Loreti, M., Pugliese, R.: An infrastructure language for open nets. In: SAC 2002: Proceedings of the 2002 ACM Symposium on Applied Computing, pp. 373–377. ACM, New York (2002)
10. Probst, C.W., Hansen, R.R., Nielson, F.: Where can an insider attack? In: Dimitrakos, T., Martinelli, F., Ryan, P.Y.A., Schneider, S. (eds.) FAST 2006. LNCS, vol. 4691, pp. 127–142. Springer, Heidelberg (2007)
11. Dimkov, T., Tang, Q., Hartel, P.H.: On the inability of existing security models to cope with data mobility in dynamic organizations. In: Proceedings of the Workshop on Modeling Security. CEUR Workshop Proceedings (2008)
12. AlZarouni, M.: The reality of risks from consented use of usb devices. In: Valli, C., Woodward, A. (eds.) Proceedings of the 4th Australian Information Security Conference, pp. 5–15 (2006)

# Appendix

*Proof (of Theorem 1).* The theorem follows from three properties, which we prove in turn:

1. There are no cycles between layers.
2. There are no cycles in the object layer.
3. There are no cycles in the digital layer.

1. There are no cycles between layers
   $\nexists \langle n_0 ... n_i ... n_k \rangle : n_0 = n_k \wedge \mathcal{D}(n_0) \neq \mathcal{D}(n_i)$
   Lets assume that such a cycle exists:
   $\exists \langle n_0 ... n_i ... n_k \rangle : n_0 = n_k \wedge \mathcal{D}(n_0) \neq \mathcal{D}(n_i)$
   Thus, there are at least two edges in the graph which connect nodes from different layers:
   $\exists (n_{j-1}, n_j), (n_l, n_{l+1}) \in Edge : \mathcal{D}(n_{j-1}) \neq \mathcal{D}(n_j) \wedge \mathcal{D}(n_l) \neq \mathcal{D}(n_{l+1}) \wedge \mathcal{D}(n_{j-1}) = \mathcal{D}(n_{l+1}) \wedge \mathcal{D}(n_j) = \mathcal{D}(n_l)$
   From the invariants 3, 4, 5 (tabulated in Table 1) follows that such a pair of edges does not exist.

**Table 1.** Invariants 3,4,5 forbid any cycles between layers

| Layer 1($L_1$) | Layer 2($L_2$) | Edge from $L_1$ to $L_2$ | Edge from $L_2$ to $L_1$ |
|---|---|---|---|
| L | O | + | - (invariant 3) |
| L | D | - (invariant 5) | - (invariant 5) |
| O | D | + | - (invariant 4) |

2. There are no cycles in the object layer.
   $\nexists \langle n, ..., m \rangle : \mathcal{D}(n) = ... = \mathcal{D}(m) = O \wedge n = m$
   Lets assume such a cycle exists:
   $\exists \langle n, ... n_i ..., m \rangle : \mathcal{D}(n) = ... \mathcal{D}(n_i) ... = \mathcal{D}(m) = O \wedge n = m.$
   From invariant 2,
   $\exists m \in Node : \mathcal{D}(m) = L \wedge \exists \langle m, .... n'_{i-1}, n_i \rangle$, follows $\exists (n'_{i-1}, n_i), (n_{i-1}, n_i)$. If $n'_{i-1} \neq n_{i-1}$ there is a contradiction with invariant 1. Otherwise $\mathcal{D}(n'_{i-1}) = O$, and the analysis is repeated for the path $\langle m, .... n'_{i-1} \rangle$. Because $\langle m, .... n'_{i-1} \rangle$ is finite, at one point the path reaches a spatial node, and $n'_{i-1} \neq n_{i-1}$. This again contradicts with invariant 1. Thus, such cycle does not exist.
3. There are no cycles in the digital layer.
   $\nexists \langle n, ..., m \rangle : \mathcal{D}(n) = ... = \mathcal{D}(m) = D \wedge n = m$
   This comes directly from invariant 6.

*Proof (of Theorem 3).* Suppose there is a net $N_1$ which satisfies the invariants $C(Map(N_1), \mathcal{D})$. Suppose exists a net $N_2$ which is a product of a net transformation on $N_1$. $\exists N_2 : N_1 \Rightarrow N_2$. We need to prove that $C(Map(N_2), \mathcal{D})$ also holds.

The relation $\Rightarrow$ is used in the net actions *neteval*, *netcopy* and *netmove*.

1. *neteval* does not cause any changes of the structure of the net. Thus any execution of *neteval* cannot invalidate an invariant.
2. *netmove* removes an edge $(l_{t_1}, l)$ and generates a new one $(l_{t_2}, l)$. We need to show that the $\xrightarrow{login(l, l_{t_2}, l_o, s_{t_2})}$ action does not invalidate any invariant. Suppose the rule invalidates an invariant.
   (a) Let $\mathcal{D}(l) = O$. After $\xrightarrow{logout(l, l_{t_1}, l_o, s_{t_1})}$, $indegree(l) = 0$. Latter, when $\xrightarrow{login(l, l_{t_2}, l_o, s_{t_2})}$ is applied, $indegree(l) = 1$. Thus, invariant 1 is not invalidated.
   (b) Let $\mathcal{D}(l) = O$. After $\xrightarrow{login(l, l_{t_2}, l_o, s_{t_2})}$ is applied, from $\succ_{ln}$, $\mathcal{D}(l_{t_2}) = L$ or $\mathcal{D}(l_{t_2}) = O$. The former case does not invalidate the second invariant by definition. Since $C(Map(N_1), \mathcal{D})$, $\exists m \in Node : \exists \langle m ... l_{t_2} \rangle \wedge \mathcal{D}(m) = S$, the latter case also does not invalidate the second invariant.
   (c) The invariants 3, 4, 5 are not invalidated by the definition of $\succ_{ln}$.
   (d) The last invariant is not invalidated because of the assumption in $\succ\!\succ$.
3. The effect of *netcopy* is an additional edge in the graph edge $(l_t, l)$ generated by the relation $\xrightarrow{login(l, l_t, l_o, s_t)}$. The premise of *netcopy* enforces a restriction $\mathcal{D}(l_t) = D$. Additional restriction comes from the relation $\succ_{ln}$, which allows an edge to be generated only between a node from the object and digital layer $\mathcal{D}(l) = D \wedge \mathcal{D}(l_t) = O$ or between two nodes from the digital layer $\mathcal{D}(l) = D \wedge \mathcal{D}(l_t) = D$. The former does not invalidate any of the invariants, while the latter is restricted by the assumption on $\succ\!\succ$.

# Match It or Die: Proving Integrity by Equality*

Matteo Centenaro and Riccardo Focardi

Università Ca' Foscari Venezia
{mcentena,focardi}@dsi.unive.it

**Abstract.** Cryptographic hash functions are commonly used as modification detection codes. The goal is to provide message integrity assurance by comparing the digest of the original message with the hash of what is thought to be the intended message. This paper generalizes this idea by applying it to general expressions instead of just digests: success of an equality test between a tainted data and a trusted one can be seen as a proof of high-integrity for the first item. Secure usage of hash functions is also studied with respect to the confidentiality of digests by extending secret-sensitive noninterference of Demange and Sands.

**Keywords:** Information Flow, Language-based Security, Security Type System, Hash Functions.

## 1 Introduction

A hash function takes as input an arbitrary message and 'summarizes' it into a *digest*. In cryptography, hash functions are commonly used as *modification detection codes* [9]: we are guaranteed of the integrity of a message $M$ whenever the hash of $M$ coincides with a previously computed digest of the original message. Moreover, hash functions are also commonly employed to protect data secrecy as done, e.g., in Unix password files. To provide both integrity and confidentiality, hash functions are required to respectively be *collision resistant* and *one-way* [9], meaning that it should be infeasible to exhibit two messages with the same digest and to find a message whose digest matches a given one.

A first example of everyday usage of hash functions is password-based authentication: a one-way hash of the user password is securely stored in the system and is compared with the hash of the password typed by the user at the login prompt, whenever the user wants to access her account. The following code is a simplified fragment of the Unix *su* utility used to let a system administrator perform privileged actions. The password file is modeled as an array `passwd[username]`.

```
trial = hash(t_pwd);
if (trial = passwd[root]) then
    << launch the administrator shell >>
```

* Work partially supported by Miur'07 Project SOFT: "*Security Oriented Formal Techniques*".

A. Armando and G. Lowe (Eds.): ARSPA-WITS 2010, LNCS 6186, pp. 130–145, 2010.

The typed password `t_pwd` is given as input to the program thus we regard it as untrusted. In fact, from the program perspective there could be an enemy 'out there' trying to impersonate the legitimate administrator. The same holds for `trial`, which is computed from an untrusted value. Existing type systems for noninterference would consequently consider the guard of the if branch as tainted, or low-integrity, since its value is computed from untrusted data and possibly under the control of the enemy. For this reason, the code in the if-then branch would be required to never modify high-integrity values. Clearly the administrator shell can make any change to the system including, e.g., modifying user passwords, and this program would be consequently rejected.

One of the motivations for hashing passwords is to protect confidentiality. In fact, if the hash function is one-way, it is infeasible for an opponent to find a password whose hash matches the one stored in the password file. In practice, brute force dictionary attacks suggest that the password file should be nevertheless kept inaccessible to non administrators, as it is done, e.g., in the *shadow password* mechanism of Unix. However, if password entropy is 'high enough' it might be safe to let every user access the hashed passwords. Formally, this would correspond to assigning the array `passwd[]` a low-confidentiality security level. Consider now the following update of Alice's password to the new, high-confidentiality value `alice_pwd`:

```
passwd[alice] := hash(alice_pwd);
```

This assignment would be rejected by usual type systems for noninterference, as it *downgrades* the confidentiality level of the password.

Hash functions are also often used for integrity checks. We consider a software producer who wants to distribute an application on the Internet, using different mirrors in order to speedup the downloads. A common way to assure users downloading a binary file `my_blob.bin` from mirrors of its integrity, is to provide them with a trusted digest `swdigest` of the original program. The browser would then run a code similar to the following:

```
if (hash(myblob.bin) = swdigest) then
    trusted_blob.bin := my_blob.bin;
    << install trusted_blob >>
```

The idea is that the user will install the given binary only if its digest matches the one of the original program provided by the software company. In fact, if the hash function is collision resistant, it would be infeasible for an attacker to modify the downloaded program while preserving the digest. Once the check succeeds, `my_blob.bin` can be safely 'promoted' to high-integrity and installed into the system. This is modelled by assigning `my_blob.bin` to the high-integrity variable `trusted_blob.bin`. This is usually regarded as a direct integrity flaw and rejected by usual type systems for noninterference. Moreover, installing the application can be thought as writing into a high-integrity area of the file system and, as for the root shell above, would be forbidden in a branch with a low-integrity guard.

**Our contribution.** We have discussed how typical examples of programs that use cryptographic hash functions break standard notions of noninterference, even if they are intuitively secure. In this work, we study how to extend noninterference notions so that such kinds of program can be type checked and proved secure. We model hash functions symbolically: the hash of a value $v$ is simply $\mathsf{h}(v)$. We do not assume any deconstructor allowing to recover $v$ from $\mathsf{h}(v)$ thus modelling the fact $\mathsf{h}$ is one-way, and we also assume $\mathsf{h}(v) = \mathsf{h}(v')$ if and only if $v = v'$, modelling collision resistance. As is customary in symbolic settings, what has negligible probability in the computational world becomes here impossible.

We focus on what we informally call 'match-it-or-die' programs which, like the above examples, always perform integrity checks at the outer level and fail whenever the check is not passed. For these programs, the attacker is not interested in causing a failure, as no code would be executed in such a case. This enables us to type check programs that assign to high-integrity variables even in a low-integrity if branch, as in the Unix *su* example. We then observe that assignments such as `trusted_blob.bin := my_blob.bin` are safe under the check `hash(myblob.bin) = swdigest`. In fact, since `swdigest` is high-integrity, when its value matches the one of `hash(myblob.bin)`, we are guaranteed that `myblob.bin` has not been tampered with. This allows us to type check programs like the application downloading example.

Moreover, we investigate the confidentiality requirements for using hash functions to preserve data secrecy. We first observe that if the entropy of the hashed value is low an attacker might try to compute, by brute force, the hash of all the possible values until he finds a match. We thus select, as our starting point, a recent noninterference variant called *secret-sensitive* noninterference [6] which distinguishes small and big secrets and allows us to treat their corresponding digests accordingly. If a secret is big, meaning that it is infeasible to guess its actual value, then the brute force attack above is also infeasible. We show that it is safe to downgrade the hash of a big secret, assuming some control over what secret is actually hashed. In fact, two hashes of the same big secret are always identical and the opponent might deduce some information by observing equality patterns of digests. This requires a nontrivial extension of the notion of memory equivalence so to suitably deal with such equality patterns.

Finally, we give a security type system to statically enforce that programs guarantee the proposed noninterference notions.

**Structure of the paper.** In Section 2 we give the background on secret-sensitive noninterference [6]; Section 3 extends the noninterference notions so to correctly deal with hash functions. Integrity check by equality is analyzed in Section 4. The security type system enforcing noninterference is given in Section 5 while Section 6 discusses related works. The paper closes with some final remarks and ideas for future work in Section 7.

## 2 Secret-Sensitive Noninterference

Secret-sensitive noninterference (SSNI) [6], by Demange and Sands, is a variant of noninterference which distinguishes small, guessable secrets from big, unguessable ones. As discussed in the introduction, this distinction will be useful to discipline the downgrading of digests of secret values, as we will see in Section 3.

**Size aware security lattice.** Secrets are partitioned into big ($\mathsf{H_b}$) and small ($\mathsf{H_s}$) ones. Preorder $\sqsubseteq_C$ among confidentiality levels is defined as $\mathsf{L} \sqsubseteq_C \mathsf{H_b} \sqsubseteq_C \mathsf{H_s}$, meaning that public, low data can be regarded as secret and, as discussed above, small secrets need to be treated more carefully than big ones. We extend this size aware confidentiality lattice by composing it with the basic two-level integrity lattice in which $\mathsf{H} \sqsubseteq_I \mathsf{L}$. Notice that integrity levels are contravariant: low-integrity, tainted values have to be used more carefully than high-integrity, untainted ones. The product of these two lattices is depicted in Figure 1. We will write $\ell = \ell_C \ell_I$ to range over the product lattice elements. The ordering between the new security levels $\ell$ is denoted by $\sqsubseteq$ and is defined as the componentwise application of $\sqsubseteq_C$ and $\sqsubseteq_I$.

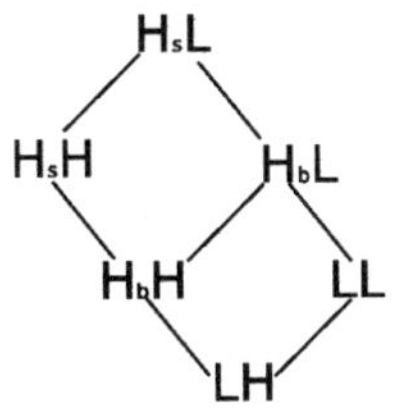

**Fig. 1.** Size aware Lattice

**Language.** Programs under analysis are written in a standard imperative while-language. We assume a set of variables *Var* ranged over by $x$, a set of values *Val* ranged over by $v$ and a set of arithmetic and boolean operations ranged over by $\mathsf{op}$ . The syntax for expressions $e$ and commands $\mathsf{c}$ follows.

$$e ::= x \mid e_1 \ \mathsf{op}\ e_2$$

$$\mathsf{c} ::= \mathsf{skip} \mid x := e \mid \mathsf{if}\ e\ \mathsf{then}\ \mathsf{c}_1\ \mathsf{else}\ \mathsf{c}_2 \mid \mathsf{while}\ e\ \mathsf{do}\ \mathsf{c} \mid \mathsf{c}_1; \mathsf{c}_2$$

Memories $\mathsf{M} : \mathit{Var} \rightarrow \mathit{Val}$ are finite maps from variables to values. We write $e \downarrow^{\mathsf{M}} v$ to note the atomic evaluation of expression $e$ to value $v$ in memory $\mathsf{M}$. Command semantics is given in terms of a small-step transition between configurations $\langle \mathsf{M}, \mathsf{c} \rangle$. Transitions are labeled with an *event* $\alpha \in \mathit{Var} \cup \{\tau\}$ indicating that an assignment to variable $\alpha$ (or no assignment if $\alpha$ is $\tau$) has happened. Command semantics rules are standard and are omitted here for lack of space; they can be found in the full version of the paper [4].

**Observable behaviour.** We assume to have a *security environment* $\Gamma$ mapping variables to their security levels. Users at level $\ell$ may only read variables whose level is lower or equal than $\ell$. Let $\mathsf{M}_{|\ell}$ be the projection of the memory $\mathsf{M}$ to level $\ell$, i.e., memory $\mathsf{M}$ restricted to variables visible at level $\ell$ or below.

**Definition 1 (Memories $\ell$-equivalence).** $\mathsf{M}$ *and* $\mathsf{M}'$ *are $\ell$-equivalent, written* $\mathsf{M} =_\ell \mathsf{M}'$, *if* $\mathsf{M}_{|\ell} = \mathsf{M}'_{|\ell}$.

Intuitively, users at level $\ell$ will never be able to distinguish two $\ell$-equivalent memories $\mathsf{M}$ and $\mathsf{M}'$.

Similarly, users may only observe transitions assigning to variables at or below their level. Transition $\xrightarrow{\alpha}_\ell$ is defined as the least relation among configurations such that:

$$\frac{\langle \mathsf{M}, \mathsf{c}\rangle \xrightarrow{x} \langle \mathsf{M}', \mathsf{c}'\rangle \quad \Gamma(x) \sqsubseteq \ell}{\langle \mathsf{M}, \mathsf{c}\rangle \xrightarrow{x}_\ell \langle \mathsf{M}', \mathsf{c}'\rangle}$$

$$\frac{\langle \mathsf{M}, \mathsf{c}\rangle \xrightarrow{\alpha} \langle \mathsf{M}', \mathsf{c}'\rangle \quad \alpha = \tau \text{ or } \alpha = x \text{ with } \Gamma(x) \not\sqsubseteq \ell}{\langle \mathsf{M}, \mathsf{c}\rangle \xrightarrow{\tau}_\ell \langle \mathsf{M}', \mathsf{c}'\rangle}$$

We write $\stackrel{\alpha}{\Rightarrow}_\ell$ to denote $\xrightarrow{\tau}_\ell^* \xrightarrow{\alpha}_\ell$, if $\alpha \neq \tau$, or $\xrightarrow{\tau}_\ell^*$ otherwise. Transitions $\stackrel{\tau}{\Rightarrow}_\ell$ are considered internal, silent reductions which are unobservable by anyone. Notice, instead, that for observable transitions $\stackrel{x}{\Rightarrow}_\ell$, the level of $x$ is always at or below $\ell$, i.e., $\Gamma(x) \sqsubseteq \ell$.

**Secure programs.** The main idea of SSNI [6] is that for unguessable secrets, brute force attacks will terminate only with negligible probability. Intuitively, this allows for adopting a termination insensitive equivalence notion when comparing program behaviour. Guessable secrets, instead, can be leaked by brute force using 'termination channels', and for those values it is necessary to distinguish between terminating and nonterminating executions.

A configuration $\langle \mathsf{M}, \mathsf{c}\rangle$ diverges for $\ell$, written $\langle \mathsf{M}, \mathsf{c}\rangle \Uparrow_\ell$, if it will never perform any $\ell$-observable transition $\xrightarrow{x}_\ell$. A termination insensitive $\ell$-bisimulation requires that observable transitions of the first program are simulated by the second one, unless the latter diverges on $\ell$ meaning that it cannot execute any observable action at or below $\ell$.

**Definition 1** (**Termination insensitive $\ell$-bisimulation**)
*A symmetric relation $\mathcal{R}$ on configurations is a* termination insensitive $\ell$-bisimulation ($\ell$-TIB) *if* $\langle \mathsf{M}_1, \mathsf{c}_1\rangle \mathcal{R} \langle \mathsf{M}_2, \mathsf{c}_2\rangle$ *implies* $\mathsf{M}_1 =_\ell \mathsf{M}_2$ *and whenever* $\langle \mathsf{M}_1, \mathsf{c}_1\rangle \xrightarrow{\alpha}_\ell \langle \mathsf{M}_1', \mathsf{c}_1'\rangle$ *then either*

- $\langle \mathsf{M}_2, \mathsf{c}_2\rangle \stackrel{\alpha}{\Rightarrow}_\ell \langle \mathsf{M}_2', \mathsf{c}_2'\rangle$ *and* $\langle \mathsf{M}_1', \mathsf{c}_1'\rangle \mathcal{R} \langle \mathsf{M}_2', \mathsf{c}_2'\rangle$ *or*
- $\langle \mathsf{M}_2, \mathsf{c}_2\rangle \Uparrow_\ell$

*Configurations* $\langle \mathsf{M}_1, \mathsf{c}_1\rangle$, $\langle \mathsf{M}_2, \mathsf{c}_2\rangle$ *are* termination insensitive $\ell$-bisimilar, *written* $\langle \mathsf{M}_1, \mathsf{c}_1\rangle \approx_\ell \langle \mathsf{M}_2, \mathsf{c}_2\rangle$, *if there exists a $\ell$-TIB relating them.*

Termination sensitive bisimulation, instead, always requires observable actions to be simulated.

**Definition 2** (**Termination sensitive $\ell$-bisimulation**)
*A symmetric relation $\mathcal{R}$ on configurations is a* termination sensitive $\ell$-bisimulation ($\ell$-TSB) *if* $\langle \mathsf{M}_1, \mathsf{c}_1\rangle \mathcal{R} \langle \mathsf{M}_2, \mathsf{c}_2\rangle$ *implies* $\mathsf{M}_1 =_\ell \mathsf{M}_2$ *and whenever* $\langle \mathsf{M}_1, \mathsf{c}_1\rangle \xrightarrow{\alpha}_\ell \langle \mathsf{M}_1', \mathsf{c}_1'\rangle$ *then* $\langle \mathsf{M}_2, \mathsf{c}_2\rangle \stackrel{\alpha}{\Rightarrow}_\ell \langle \mathsf{M}_2', \mathsf{c}_2'\rangle$, $\langle \mathsf{M}_1', \mathsf{c}_1'\rangle \mathcal{R} \langle \mathsf{M}_2', \mathsf{c}_2'\rangle$. *Configurations* $\langle \mathsf{M}_1, \mathsf{c}_1\rangle$ *and* $\langle \mathsf{M}_2, \mathsf{c}_2\rangle$ *are* termination sensitive $\ell$-bisimilar, *written* $\langle \mathsf{M}_1, \mathsf{c}_1\rangle \simeq_\ell \langle \mathsf{M}_2, \mathsf{c}_2\rangle$, *if there exists a $\ell$-TSB relating them.*

A secure program will preserve small secrets from being leaked via the termination channel while will be more liberal with respect to the big ones. This is achieved by requiring termination sensitive bisimilarity whenever the inspected memories are the same at level $\mathsf{H_bL}$, meaning they only differ on small secrets. Notice that, as usual, the attacker is assumed to be at level $\mathsf{LL}$.

**Definition 3 (Secret-sensitive NI)**
*A command* $\mathsf{c}$ *satisfies* secret-sensitive NI *if* $\forall\ \mathsf{M}_1 =_{\mathsf{LL}} \mathsf{M}_2$ *it holds*

1. $\langle \mathsf{M}_1, \mathsf{c}\rangle \approx_{\mathsf{LL}} \langle \mathsf{M}_2, \mathsf{c}\rangle$ *and*
2. $\mathsf{M}_1 =_{\mathsf{H_bL}} \mathsf{M}_2$ *implies* $\langle \mathsf{M}_1, \mathsf{c}\rangle \simeq_{\mathsf{H_bL}} \langle \mathsf{M}_2, \mathsf{c}\rangle$.

## 3 Hash Functions and Secrecy

This section extends secret-sensitive NI to programs that use hash functions. As already observed, hash functions could be subject to brute force attacks, unless the hashed messages are big enough to make exhaustive search infeasible. The idea is to take advantage of the two distinct secret levels $\mathsf{H_b}$ and $\mathsf{H_s}$ to protect digests of small secrets and treat more liberally the digests of big secrets.

**Hash expressions.** The language of the previous section is augmented with a new $\mathsf{hash}$ expression whose semantics is defined in terms of a special constructor $\mathsf{h}$. Formally, $\mathsf{hash}(e) \downarrow^{\mathsf{M}} \mathsf{h}(v)$ if $e \downarrow^{\mathsf{M}} v$ with $v \in \mathit{Val}$. We then partition $\mathit{Val}$ into the sets of small and big values $\mathit{Val}_s$, $\mathit{Val}_b$, ranged over by $v_s$ and $v_b$. We define the sets of small and big digests as $\mathit{Val}^d_\delta = \{\mathsf{h}(v) \mid v \in \mathit{Val}_\delta\}$, with $\delta \in \{s, b\}$. As discussed in the introduction, this simple modelling of hash functions is coherent with the assumption of being one-way (no deconstructor expressions) and collision resistant (digests of different values *never* collide).

**Memories $\ell$-equivalence.** Lifting the notion of memory equivalence when dealing with digests requires to carefully handle equality patterns. In fact, in our symbolic model, equal digests will correspond to equal hashed messages.

Consider the program $x := \mathsf{hash}(y)$, where $x$ is a public variable and $y$ is a secret one. It must be considered secure only if $y$ is a big secret variable, indeed leaking the digest of a small secret is equivalent to directly reveal the secret since an attacker could perform a brute force attack on the hash.

The equivalence notion between memories needs, however, to be relaxed in order to capture the fact that big secrets are, in practice, random unpredictable values. We illustrate considering again $x := \mathsf{hash}(y)$ and assuming $y$ to be a big secret variable. We let $\mathsf{M}_1(x) = 0 = \mathsf{M}_2(x)$, $\mathsf{M}_1(y) = v_b \neq v_b' = \mathsf{M}_2(y)$, then it holds $\mathsf{M}_1 =_{\mathsf{LL}} \mathsf{M}_2$. Executing the above code the resulting memories differ on the value stored in the public variable $x$: $\mathsf{M}_1'(x) = \mathsf{h}(v_b) \neq \mathsf{h}(v_b') = \mathsf{M}_2'(x)$. It follows that $\mathsf{M}_1' \neq_{\mathsf{LL}} \mathsf{M}_2'$ and the program does not respect noninterference so it would be rejected as insecure. However, $v_b$ and $v_b'$ are two big random numbers and we can never expect they are equal. Thus, the only opportunity for the attacker is to see if they correspond to other big values in the same memory. Requiring the equality of big secrets and digests across memories is, consequently, too strong.

This boils down to the idea of *patterns*, already employed in [5,7,8] for cryptographic primitives. We illustrate through an example. Consider program $z := \mathsf{hash}(x); w := \mathsf{hash}(y)$ where $z$ and $w$ are public variables and $x$ and $y$ are big secrets. Consider the following memories:

$$\begin{array}{l|l} \mathsf{M}_1 & \mathsf{M}_2 \\ \hline x : v_b & x : v_b \\ y : v_b' & y : v_b \\ z : 0 & z : 0 \\ w : 0 & w : 0 \end{array} \qquad (1)$$

executing the above code would make public two different digests in $\mathsf{M}_1$ and the very same digests in $\mathsf{M}_2$. The attacker is able to learn that the first memory stores two different secrets values while the second does not. In summary, we do not require the equality of big secrets and digests across memory but only that the equality patterns are the same.

As the last example shows, in order to safely downgrade digests of big secrets we need to control how big secrets are stored in the memories. We do this by projecting out from memories big secret values which are either stored in big secret variables or hashed and observable from $\ell$. This is done by the following function $\mathsf{r}$, taking as parameters the value $v$ and the level $\ell_v$ of a variable.

$$\mathsf{r}_\ell(v, \ell_v) = \begin{cases} v \text{ if } v \in Val_b \text{ and } \ell_v = \mathsf{H_b}\ell_I \\ v' \text{ if } v = \mathsf{h}(v'), v' \in Val_b \text{ and } \ell_v \sqsubseteq \ell \\ 0 \text{ otherwise} \end{cases}$$

A *big secret projection* $\mathsf{r}_\ell(\mathsf{M})$ is defined as $\mathsf{r}_\ell(\mathsf{M})(x) = \mathsf{r}_\ell(\mathsf{M}(x), \Gamma(x))$, for all $x \in Dom(\mathsf{M})$. Two memories will be *comparable* if their big secret projections can be matched by renaming big values , i.e., if two big values are the same in one projection then it will also be the case that they are equal in the other one.

**Definition 4 (Comparable memories)**
*Two memories* $\mathsf{M}_1$ *and* $\mathsf{M}_2$ *are* $\ell$-comparable, *noted* $\mathsf{M}_1 \bowtie_\ell \mathsf{M}_2$, *if there exists a bijection* $\mu : Val_b \to Val_b$ *such that* $\mathsf{r}_\ell(\mathsf{M}_1) = \mathsf{r}_\ell(\mathsf{M}_2)\mu$.

*Example 1.* The two above memories (1) are not comparable if observed at level $\mathsf{LL}$, i.e., $\mathsf{M}_1 \not\bowtie_{\mathsf{LL}} \mathsf{M}_2$. In fact, $\mathsf{r}_\ell(\mathsf{M}_1)(x) = v_b \neq v_b' = \mathsf{r}_\ell(\mathsf{M}_1)(y)$ while $\mathsf{r}_\ell(\mathsf{M}_2)(x) = v_b = v_b = \mathsf{r}_\ell(\mathsf{M}_2)(y)$. Thus there exists no bijection $\mu$ such that $\mathsf{r}_\ell(\mathsf{M}_1) = \mathsf{r}_\ell(\mathsf{M}_2)\mu$, since $\mu$ cannot map $v_b$ to both $v_b$ and $v_b'$.

Two memories are $\ell$-equivalent if they are $\ell$-comparable and their observable big digests expose the same equality patterns. A *digest substitution* $\rho$ is a bijection on digests of big values: $\rho : Val_b^d \to Val_b^d$.

**Definition 5 (Memory $\ell$-equivalence with hash functions)**
*Two memories,* $\mathsf{M}_1$ *and* $\mathsf{M}_2$*, are* $\ell$-equivalent, *written* $\mathsf{M}_1 =_\ell^h \mathsf{M}_2$, *if* $\mathsf{M}_1 \bowtie_\ell \mathsf{M}_2$ *and there exists a digest substitution* $\rho$ *such that* $\mathsf{M}_{1|\ell} = \mathsf{M}_{2|\ell}\, \rho$.

**Secure programs.** The bisimulation definitions given in the previous section are left unchanged except for the relation used to compare memories which is now $=_\ell^h$ in place of $=_\ell$. Secret-sensitive NI is thus rephrased as follows.

**Definition 6 (Secret-sensitive NI with hash functions)**
*A command* $\mathsf{c}$ *satisfies* secret-sensitive NI *if* $\forall\ \mathsf{M}_1 =^h_{\mathsf{LL}} \mathsf{M}_2$ *it holds*

1. $\langle \mathsf{M}_1, \mathsf{c}\rangle \approx_{\mathsf{LL}} \langle \mathsf{M}_2, \mathsf{c}\rangle$ *and*
2. $\mathsf{M}_1 =^h_{\mathsf{H_bL}} \mathsf{M}_2$ *implies* $\langle \mathsf{M}_1, \mathsf{c}\rangle \simeq_{\mathsf{H_bL}} \langle \mathsf{M}_2, \mathsf{c}\rangle$.

## 4 Proving Integrity by Equality

In a recent work [5], we prove integrity of low-integrity data using Message Authentication Codes (MACs). The secrecy of the MAC key ensures the integrity of the exchanged data: once the MAC is recomputed and checked, we are guaranteed that no one has manipulated the received data. This work generalizes the idea by applying it to the simpler case of an equality test with respect to a high-integrity value: if the test is successful we are guaranteed that the compared, low-integrity, value has not been tampered with.

Integrity can be checked via noninterference by placing the observer at level $\mathsf{H_sH}$. This amounts to quantifying over all the values in low-integrity variables and observing any interference they possibly cause on high-integrity variables.

**Definition 7 (Integrity NI)**
*A program* $\mathsf{c}$ *satisfies* integrity NI *if for all* $\mathsf{M}_1, \mathsf{M}_2$ *such that* $\mathsf{M}_1 =_{\mathsf{H_sH}} \mathsf{M}_2$ *it holds* $\langle \mathsf{M}_1, \mathsf{c}\rangle \approx_{\mathsf{H_sH}} \langle \mathsf{M}_2, \mathsf{c}\rangle$.

Consider the program `if (x = y) then` $\mathsf{c}_1$ `else` $\mathsf{c}_2$ where $x$ is a low-integrity variable and $y$ is a high-integrity one. If either $\mathsf{c}_1$ or $\mathsf{c}_2$ modifies high-integrity variables this program is rejected. If it were not, an opponent manipulating the low-integrity variable $x$ might force the program to execute one of the two branches and gain control on the fact high-integrity variables are updated via $\mathsf{c}_1$ or $\mathsf{c}_2$.

Consider now the case of the simplified *su* utility discussed in the introduction. Similarly to what we have seen above, an attacker might insert a wrong administrator password making the check fail. However, the program is in what we have called match-it-or-die form: the else branch is empty and nothing is executed after the if-then command. In the definition we have given, we obtain that the program diverges and the termination insensitive notion of Integrity NI would consider the program secure.

A special case of integrity test is the one which involves the comparison between the on-the-fly hash of a low-integrity message and a trusted variable. Upon success, integrity of the untrusted data will be proved and it will be possible to assign it to a high-integrity variable. Consider the following program where $y$ and $z$ are trusted variables while $x$ is a tainted one.

```
if (hash(x) = y) then
    z := x;
```

As in the software distribution example of the introduction the assignment is safe, since it will be executed only if the contents of the variable $x$ has been checked to be high-integrity by comparing its digest with the high-integrity digest $y$.

## 5 Security Type System

This section presents a security type system to statically analyze programs that use hash functions and derive data integrity by equality tests.

The proposed solution is based on the type system by Demange and Sands [6]. We only report typing rules for expressions and integrity check commands. All the remaining rules are as in [6].

We distinguish among four different types of values: small, big and their respective digests. Value types $VT$ are $\mathsf{S}$ (small), $\mathsf{B}$ (big), $\mathsf{S}^{\#}$ (hash of a small) and $\mathsf{B}^{\#}$ (hash of a big) and are ranged over by $vt$. These value types are populated by the respective values:

$$\text{(v-small)}\ \frac{v \in \mathit{Val}_s}{\vdash v : \mathsf{S}} \quad \text{(v-big)}\ \frac{v \in \mathit{Val}_b}{\vdash v : \mathsf{B}} \quad \text{(v-hashs)}\ \frac{v \in \mathit{Val}_{ds}}{\vdash v : \mathsf{S}^{\#}} \quad \text{(v-hashb)}\ \frac{v \in \mathit{Val}_{db}}{\vdash v : \mathsf{B}^{\#}}$$

Security types are of the form $\tau = \lambda\ell$, where $\lambda \in \{\mathsf{P}, \mathsf{D}\}$ distinguish between plain values and digests, while $\ell$ is the associated security level. A *security type environment* $\Delta$ is a mapping from variable to their security types. Given $\tau = \lambda\ell$ the two functions $\mathsf{T}$ and $\mathsf{L}$ give respectively its variable type and security level, i.e., $\mathsf{T}(\tau) = \lambda$ and $\mathsf{L}(\tau) = \ell$.

A subtype relation is defined over security types, it is meant to preserve $\lambda$, as we do not want to mix plain values with digests. Moreover plain big secrets do not appear in the relation meaning that they can only be picked from $\mathit{Val}_b$. Subtyping $\leq$ is the least relation such that $\tau_1 \leq \tau_2$ if $\mathsf{T}(\tau_1) = \mathsf{T}(\tau_2) = \mathsf{D}$ and $\mathsf{L}(\tau_1) \sqsubseteq \mathsf{L}(\tau_2)$ or $\mathsf{T}(\tau_1) = \mathsf{T}(\tau_2) = \mathsf{P}$, $\mathsf{L}(\tau_i) \neq \mathsf{H_b}\ell_I$ and $\mathsf{L}(\tau_1) \sqsubseteq \mathsf{L}(\tau_2)$.

To prove that the type system enforces the security properties stated above it must be that plain big secret variables really store big values. To guarantee that small values are never assigned to big variables a conservative approach will be taken: every expression which involves an operator and returns a plain value lifts the confidentiality level of its result to $\mathsf{H_s}$, whenever it would be $\mathsf{H_b}$. The following function on security levels performs this upgrade:

$$\ell^{\sqcup} = \begin{cases} \mathsf{H_s}\ell_I & \text{if } \ell = \mathsf{H_b}\ell_I \\ \ell & \text{otherwise} \end{cases}$$

A variable $x$ respects its security type $\tau = \lambda\ell$ with respect to a memory $\mathsf{M}$ if $\lambda = \mathsf{P}$ and $\vdash \mathsf{M}(x) : \mathsf{S}$ or $\vdash \mathsf{M}(x) : \mathsf{B}$ and similarly if $\lambda = \mathsf{D}$ then $\vdash \mathsf{M}(x) : \mathsf{S}^{\#}$ or $\vdash \mathsf{M}(x) : \mathsf{B}^{\#}$. A memory will be said to be well-formed if it respects the type of its variables, more precisely the expected properties are:

1. All variable respects their security types
2. Public variables do not store plain big values
3. Plain big secret variables only store big values.

**Table 1.** Security Type System - The Most Significant Rules

*Expressions*

$$\text{(var)}\ \frac{\Delta(x) = \tau}{\Delta \vdash x : \tau} \qquad \text{(sub)}\ \frac{\Delta \vdash e : \tau' \quad \tau' \leq \tau}{\Delta \vdash e : \tau}$$

$$\text{(eq)}\ \frac{\Delta \vdash e : \tau \quad \Delta \vdash e_2 : \tau \quad \mathsf{L}(\tau) = \ell}{\Delta \vdash e_1 = e_2 : \mathsf{P}\ell^{\sqcup}} \qquad \text{(op)}\ \frac{\Delta \vdash e_1 : \mathsf{P}\ell \quad \Delta \vdash e_2 : \mathsf{P}\ell}{\Delta \vdash e_1 \ \mathsf{op}\ e_2 : \mathsf{P}\ell^{\sqcup}}$$

$$\text{(hash-b)}\ \frac{\Delta \vdash x : \mathsf{PH_b}\ell_I}{\Delta \vdash \mathsf{hash}(x) : \mathsf{DL}\ell_I} \qquad \text{(hash-s)}\ \frac{\Delta \vdash x : \mathsf{P}\ell}{\Delta \vdash \mathsf{hash}(x) : \mathsf{D}\ell}$$

*Integrity Test Commands*

$$\text{(int-test)}\ \frac{\begin{array}{c}\Delta \vdash x : \tau \quad \Delta \vdash y : \tau' \quad \mathsf{T}(\tau) = \mathsf{T}(\tau') \\ \mathsf{L}(\tau) = \ell_C\mathsf{L} \quad \mathsf{L}(\tau') = \ell_C\mathsf{H} \qquad \ell_C \sqsubseteq_C \mathsf{H_b} \quad \Delta \vdash \mathsf{c} : (\ell_C\mathsf{H}, t, f)\end{array}}{\Delta \vdash \mathsf{if}\ x = y\ \mathsf{then\ c\ else\ FAIL} : (\ell_C\mathsf{H}, t \sqcup \ell_C\mathsf{L}, \uparrow)}$$

$$\text{(int-hash)}\ \frac{\begin{array}{c}\Delta \vdash x : \mathsf{P}\ell_C\mathsf{L} \quad \Delta \vdash y : \mathsf{D}\ell_C\mathsf{H} \\ \Delta(z) = \mathsf{P}\ell_C\mathsf{H} \qquad \ell_C \sqsubseteq_C \mathsf{H_b} \quad \Delta \vdash \mathsf{c} : (\ell_C\mathsf{H}, t, f)\end{array}}{\Delta \vdash \mathsf{if\ hash}(x) = y\ \mathsf{then}\ z := x; \mathsf{c\ else\ FAIL} : (\ell_C\mathsf{H}, t \sqcup \ell_C\mathsf{L}, \uparrow)}$$

From now on it will be supposed that all the memories are well-formed and indeed it can be proved that memory well-formedness is preserved by typed programs.

Expression typing rules are depicted in Table 1. Rules (var) and (sub) are standard. Rule (eq) types the equality test of two expressions requiring that they type the same $\tau$ and judging the (boolean) result as a plain small value. Rule (op) let any operator to be applied only to plain expressions, since in our symbolic model of the hash function no operation is defined on digests except for the equality test. These two rules use the $\ell^{\sqcup}$ function to promote the confidentiality level of their result to $\mathsf{H_s}$ whenever necessary, as already discussed above.

Hashes are typed either by (hash-b) or (hash-s). Rule (hash-b) performs a controlled declassification, the idea is that since the message is a plain big value its secrecy is not broken by releasing its digest. Indeed it can be proved that this does not break noninterference. The latter typing rule does nothing special and just preserve the security level of its argument.

The type system has to enforce a termination insensitive noninterference for big secrets and termination sensitive for small ones. This latter requirement can be achieved by some strong limitations on the while loops [13] or by accounting for the termination effect of a command [3,11]. Demange and Sands type system [6] is built upon the work of Boudol and Castellani [3]. For lack of space, we only illustrate the two new rules added to the SSNI original type system [6]. The remaining type system can be found in the full version of the paper [4].

A command type is a triple $(w, t, f)$ where $w$ and $t$ are security levels and $f$ is a termination flag ranging over $\downarrow$ and $\uparrow$ which respectively note that the command always terminates or that it could not terminate. A program is considered to be always terminating if it does not contain any while loop. The two flags are ordered as $\downarrow\sqsubseteq\uparrow$. A type judgement of the form $\Delta \vdash \mathsf{c} : (w, t, f)$ means that c does not assign to variables whose security level is lower than $w$ ($w$ is the writing effect of c), observing the termination of c gives information on variables at most at level $t$ ($t$ is the termination effect of c) and the termination behaviour is described by $f$.

Rules (int-test) and (int-hash) are new contributions of this work and implement the integrity verification tests discussed in Section 4. The former one let a trusted computation happens if the integrity of a tainted variable is proved by an equality test with an untainted one. The latter is pretty similar but is specific for the hash case and asserts that the intended original message, stored in the untrusted variable used to compute the on-the-fly digest, can be assigned to a trusted variable, whenever the check succeeds.

The else branch in both cases must be the special command FAIL. It is a silent diverging while loop of the form while true do skip. Requiring that each integrity test command executes such a program in case its guard condition is not satisfied assure that all the typed programs are in the 'match-it-or-die' form. In fact, upon failure no observable actions will be ever executed which is equivalent to say that, from an attacker point of view, no code would be run.

The confidentiality level of the variables involved in (int-test) and (int-hash) guard is constrained to be at most $\mathsf{H_b}$ to avoid brute force attacks to small secrets. The command in the if branch (c) is typed with a writing effect which has an high-integrity level, thus letting it to have write clearance to high-integrity variables, and the same confidentiality level as the two expressions compared in the guard. The termination effect of the overall command is constrained by the one of c and by $\ell_C\mathsf{L}$ since the test contains variables which are at most at that security level. Note that the two integrity tests would be potentially non terminating due to the FAIL branch.

**Results.** The proposed type system enforces the security properties given in Section 3 and Section 4: If a program type checks then it is both secret-sensitive and integrity noninterferent.

**Theorem 1 (SSNI by typing)**
*If* $\Delta \vdash \mathsf{c} : (w, t, f)$ *then* c *satisfies Secret-sensitive NI.*

**Theorem 2 (Integrity NI by typing)**
*If* $\Delta \vdash \mathsf{c} : (w, t, f)$ *then* c *satisfies integrity NI.*

Proofs are omitted here for lack of space but can be found in the full version of the paper [4]. In the Appendix the simplified *su* utility and the software distribution examples given in the introduction, are shown to type check. A program which let a user update its password is also presented and typed.

## 6 Related Works

This section discusses related work in the literature.

**Hash functions.** A secure usage of hash function in the setting of information flow security has been already explored by Volpano in [12]. There are, however, many difference with respect to our work. First, Volpano does not account for data integrity and, consequently, integrity checks, which is one of the major contributions of our work. On the other side, we limit our study to a symbolic treatment of hash functions, distinguishing between two different kind of secrets, while Volpano aims at a computational result.

**Secrecy.** The use of patterns to define a memory equivalence notion suitable to be used to compare digests, originates from the work of Abadi and Rogaway [2] and Abadi and Jürjens [1] whose aim was to establish a link between the formal and computational treatment of encryption. The same idea has recently been applied in the information flow security [7,8] to prove that randomized cyphertexts could be leaked without breaking noninterference. Deterministic encryption has been modeled in a symbolic setting for information flow by Centenaro, Focardi, Luccio and Steel [5] extending the idea of pattern. That work anyway does not account for hash functions. The distinction between big and small secrets and the two different bisimilarity notions which have to be applied to protect them is completely inspired by Demange and Sands [6].

**Integrity checks.** A recent work on the type checking of PIN processing security APIs [5] already implements an integrity test by means of Message Authentication Codes (MACs). It might appear that this was possible thanks to the usage of a secret key in the computation of the MAC. Instead, this work shed new light on the fundamental reasoning underlying such integrity checks, which are generalized to a less restrictive context and also applied to the special case of the hash function.

## 7 Conclusions

We have studied the security of programs that use hash functions in the setting of information flow security. We have shown how to prove data integrity via equality tests between a low and a high-integrity variable.

We have extended secret-sensitive noninterference to guarantee that leaks via the hash operator could not occur: the intuition is that the digest of a big enough secret $s$ would not be subject to a brute force attack and so releasing it to the public will not break the confidentiality of $s$.

A classical noninterference property has been instead used to check that secure programs do not taint high-integrity data. Equality tests to enforce data integrity have been introduced: this idea is a generalization of the integrity proof performed using Message Authentication Codes (MACs) in [5]. The equality of a tainted variable with a trusted one is regarded as an evidence of the fact that the value stored in the untrusted variable is indeed untainted. This kind of integrity proof is widely adopted in real applications and this work gives the tools to reason about its security.

**Future Work.** Hash functions could be used in commitment protocols. Suppose Anna challenges Bruno to solve a problem and claims she has solved it. To prove her statement Anna takes the answer and appends it to a random secret *nonce*, she then sends the hash of such message to Bruno. When the challenge finishes or when Bruno gives up, Anna has to reveal him the secret nonce thus he can check that the correct answer was sent in the first step of the process.

Formally studying this scenario in an information flow setting would be challenging. Some form of declassification would be allowed since at certain point in time the secret nonce has to be released. When the random will be downgraded then the digest could not be thought to protect Anna's answer anymore. Analyzing the security of this problem will require an interaction of a declassification mechanism, suitable to reason about the *when* dimension of downgrading [10], with the solution presented here for the secure usage of hash functions.

To guarantee that small values are never assigned to big variables we have taken the very conservative approach of forbidding expressions to return a big secret. In practice, this might be relaxed by adding some data flow analysis in order to track values derived from big secrets. For example, the xor of two different big secrets might be considered a big secret, but the xor of two equal big secrets is 0. We intend to investigate this issue more in detail in the next future.

One of the anonymous reviewer has let us notice a strong similarity between our notion of memory equivalence, based on patterns, and the notion of *static equivalence* in process calculi. Big secrets resemble the notion of bound names which can be $\alpha$-converted preserving equality patterns. We leave as a future work the intriguing comparison between the two formal notions.

***Acknowledgements.*** We would like to thank the anonymous reviewers for their very helpful comments and suggestions.

## References

1. Abadi, M., Jürjens, J.: Formal eavesdropping and its computational interpretation. In: Kobayashi, N., Pierce, B.C. (eds.) TACS 2001. LNCS, vol. 2215, pp. 82–94. Springer, Heidelberg (2001)
2. Abadi, M., Rogaway, P.: Reconciling two views of cryptography (the computational soundness of formal encryption). JCRYPTOL: Journal of Cryptology 15(2), 103–127 (2002)
3. Boudol, G., Castellani, I.: Noninterference for concurrent programs. In: Orejas, F., Spirakis, P.G., van Leeuwen, J. (eds.) ICALP 2001. LNCS, vol. 2076, pp. 382–395. Springer, Heidelberg (2001)
4. Centenaro, M., Focardi, R.: Match it or die: Proving integrity by equality (2009), `http://www.dsi.unive.it/~mcentena/cf-hash-full.pdf`
5. Centenaro, M., Focardi, R., Luccio, F.L., Steel, G.: Type-based analysis of pin processing apis. In: Backes, M., Ning, P. (eds.) ESORICS 2009. LNCS, vol. 5789, pp. 53–68. Springer, Heidelberg (2009)
6. Demange, D., Sands, D.: All secrets great and small. In: Castagna, G. (ed.) ESOP 2009. LNCS, vol. 5502, pp. 207–221. Springer, Heidelberg (2009)

7. Focardi, R., Centenaro, M.: Information flow security of multi-threaded distributed programs. In: Proceedings of the 3rd ACM SIGPLAN Workshop on Programming Languages and Analysis for Security (PLAS), Tucson, AZ, USA, June 8, pp. 113–124. ACM Press, New York (2008)
8. Laud, P.: On the computational soundness of cryptographically masked flows. In: Necula, G.C., Wadler, P. (eds.) 35th Annual ACM SIGPLAN-SIGACT Symposium on Principles of Programming Languages (POPL), San Francisco, Ca, USA, January 10-12, pp. 337–348. ACM Press, New York (2008)
9. Menezes, A.J., van Oorschot, P.C., Vanstone, S.A.: Handbook of Applied Cryptography. CRC Press, Boca Raton (1997)
10. Sabelfeld, A., Sands, D.: Declassification: Dimensions and principles. Journal of Computer Security 17(5), 517–548 (2009)
11. Smith, G.: A new type system for secure information flow. In: Proceedings of the 14th IEEE Computer Security Foundations Workshop (CSFW), Cape Breton, Nova Scotia, June 11-13, pp. 115–125. IEEE, Los Alamitos (2001)
12. Volpano, D.: Secure introduction of one-way functions. In: Proceedings of the 13th IEEE Computer Security Foundations Workshop (CSFW), Cambridge, England, July 3-5, pp. 246–254. IEEE, Los Alamitos (2000)
13. Volpano, D., Smith, G.: Eliminating covert flows with minimum typings. In: Proceedings of the 10th Computer Security Foundations Workshop (CSFW), Rockport, Massachusetts, USA, June 10-12, pp. 156–169. IEEE Computer Society, Los Alamitos (1997)


# Appendix

## A Case Studies

In this section the case studies presented in the introduction are shown to type check and a new example will be introduced. Note that some syntactic sugars which were given introducing the examples has been removed here in order to show fully typed codes.

**A simplified *su* command.** The first example is a simplified version of the *su* Unix utility. Let `root_shell` be a command which requires an high-integrity level to be computed, i.e., $\Delta \vdash \texttt{root\_shell} : (\ell_C\mathsf{H}, t, f)$. The user entered password `t_pwd` will be deemed to be secret and low-integrity, i.e., $\Delta(\texttt{t\_pwd}) = \mathsf{PH_bL}$. `root_passwd`, instead, stores the digest of the administrator password and it will be a high-integrity data since it is supposed to be stored in a write-protected file, let $\Delta(\texttt{root\_passwd}) = \mathsf{D}\ell_C\mathsf{H}$. Note that the array notation have been replaced by a single variable, this does not affect the aim of the example which is proving the security of the Unix implementation of the password-based authentication mechanism.

```
trial := hash(t_pwd);
if (trial = root_passwd) then
    root_shell;
else
    FAIL;
```

The password is supposed to be strong thus it has been typed as a big secret. If such an assumption is removed, the code does not type, indeed the above program could be used to mount a brute-force attack on the password. The type system prevents such fact by requiring that the confidentiality level of the guard is at most a big secret in rule (int-test).

The confidentiality level of `root_passwd` could be either setted to $\mathsf{L}$ or $\mathsf{H_b}$. This models the fact that having strong passwords, they could be safely stored in a public location.

Let $\Delta(\mathtt{trial}) = \mathsf{DH_bL}$, the expression $\mathsf{hash}(\mathtt{pwd})$ is typed $\mathsf{DH_bL}$ by rule (hash-b) and the first assignment is then typed $(\mathsf{H_bL}, \mathsf{LH}, \downarrow)$ by (assign). The if branch is typed $(\mathsf{H_bH}, \mathsf{H_bL} \sqcup t, \uparrow)$ by (int-test): if $\ell_C = \mathsf{L}$ by sub-typing `root_passwd` will be typed $\mathsf{DH_bH}$ while if $\ell_C = \mathsf{H_b}$ nothing special is needed. The sequential composition of the two commands is then typed by (seq-1), indeed $\mathsf{LH} \sqsubseteq \mathsf{H_bL}$.

**Software Distribution.** A software company distributes an application using different mirrors on the Internet. Having downloaded the program from one of the mirrors, a user will install the given binary only if its digest matches the one of the original application provided by the software company.

```
if (hash(my_blob.bin) = swdigest) then
    trusted_blob.bin := my_blob.bin;
    install := 1;
else
    FAIL;
```

Let `my_blob.bin` be the variable storing the downloaded binary, it is a low-integrity public variable, i.e., $\Delta(\mathtt{my\_blob.bin}) = \mathsf{PLL}$. The trusted digest given by the software company is stored in the `swdigest` variable which is a high-integrity one ($\Delta(\mathtt{swdigest}) = \mathsf{DLH}$). The installation of the application is simulated by first saving the low-integrity binary in the trusted location `trusted_blob.bin` ($\Delta(\mathtt{trusted\_blob.bin}) = \mathsf{PLH}$) and then by assigning 1 to the high-integrity variable `install` ($\Delta(\mathtt{install}) = \mathsf{PLH}$).

The if branch types $(\mathsf{LH}, \mathsf{LL}, \uparrow)$ by (int-hash), indeed all the requirements on variables are satisfied by letting $\ell_C = \mathsf{L}$ in the typing rule and, the assignment to `install` types $(\mathsf{LH}, \mathsf{LH}, \downarrow)$.

A new case study is now introduced, it shows a program which let a system administrator to manage the password file.

**A simplified *passwd*.** This example presents a password update utility. It is a simplified version of the *passwd* Unix command where we require that only the administrator can perform such a task. This is due to the fact that the integrity of the password file must be preserved.

Three parameters are expected: the administrator password and the user old and new passwords.

```
root_trial := hash(t_root);
```

```
user_trial := hash(old);
if (root_trial = root_passwd) then
    if(user_trial = user_passwd) then
        user_passwd := hash(new);
    else
        FAIL;
else
    FAIL;
```

Variable `root_passwd` stores the digest of the root password while `user_passwd` the hash of the user one. These model, as in the first example, the needed portions of the password file ($\Delta$(`root_passwd`) $= \mathsf{DH_bH}$ and $\Delta$(`user_passwd`) $= \mathsf{DH_bH}$). The typed root password `t_root` is low-integrity, i.e., $\Delta$(`t_root`) $= \mathsf{PH_bL}$ as well as the `root_trial` variable used to store its digest ($\Delta$(`root_trial`) $= \mathsf{DH_bL}$). Similarly, $\Delta$(`old`) $= \mathsf{PH_bL}$ and $\Delta$(`user_trial`) $= \mathsf{DH_bL}$. The `new` variable which stores the new user password must be regarded as high-integrity ($\Delta$(`new`) $= \mathsf{PH_bH}$). This time the user input will be considered trusted since the intended user will be authenticated and only in that case the new password will be used. This is the only way to make the hash operator to type at a high-integrity level when storing the digest of the new password to `user_passwd`. In fact, there is no way to prove the integrity of a fresh new password by equality test.

The first two assignments type $(\mathsf{H_bL}, \mathsf{LH}, \downarrow)$ by (assign). The innermost if branch types $(\mathsf{H_bH}, \mathsf{H_bL}, \uparrow)$ by (int-test): variable `user_passwd` types $\mathsf{DH_bH}$ and `user_trial` $\mathsf{DH_bL}$, the assignment to `user_passwd` types $(\mathsf{H_bH}, \mathsf{LH}, \downarrow)$ by (assign) and the hash expression is typed by $\mathsf{DLH}$ by (hash-b) and promoted by subtyping to $\mathsf{DH_bH}$. In a similar way the main if branch is again typed by (int-test) obtaining $(\mathsf{H_bH}, \mathsf{H_bL}, \uparrow)$.

The whole program is thus typed $(\mathsf{H_bH}, \mathsf{H_bL}, \uparrow)$ by (seq-1).

# Towards Automatic Analysis of Election Verifiability Properties⋆,⋆⋆

Ben Smyth[1,2], Mark Ryan[1], Steve Kremer[3], and Mounira Kourjieh[1,4]

[1] School of Computer Science, University of Birmingham, UK
[2] École Normale Supérieure & CNRS & INRIA, France
[3] LSV, ENS Cachan & CNRS & INRIA, France
[4] Université de Toulouse, France
research@bensmyth.com, M.D.Ryan@cs.bham.ac.uk,
kremer@lsv.ens-cachan.fr, kourjieh@irit.fr

**Abstract.** We present a symbolic definition that captures some cases of election verifiability for electronic voting protocols. Our definition is given in terms of reachability assertions in the applied pi calculus and is amenable to automated reasoning using the software tool ProVerif. The definition distinguishes three aspects of verifiability, which we call individual, universal, and eligibility verifiability. We demonstrate the applicability of our formalism by analysing the protocols due to Fujioka, Okamoto & Ohta and a variant of the one by Juels, Catalano & Jakobsson (implemented as Civitas by Clarkson, Chong & Myers).

**Keywords:** Electronic voting protocols, election verifiability, applied pi calculus, ProVerif, automated reasoning.

## 1 Introduction

Electronic voting systems are being introduced, or trialled, in several countries to provide more efficient voting procedures with an increased level of security. However, current deployment has shown that the security benefits are very hard to realise [10,21,9,25]. Those systems rely on the trustworthiness of the hardware and software that is used to collect, tally, and count the votes, and on the individuals that manage those systems. In practice, it is very hard to establish the required level of trust.

The concept of *election verifiability* that has emerged in the academic literature [16,19,23] aims to address this problem. It significantly reduces the necessity to trust electronic systems, by allowing voters and election observers to verify independently that votes have been recorded, tallied and counted correctly. To

⋆ A preliminary version of this work was presented at the WISSec'09 workshop.

⋆⋆ This work has been partly supported by the EPSRC projects *UbiVal* (EP/D076625/2), *Trustworthy Voting Systems* (EP/G02684X/1) and *Verifying Interoperability Requirements in Pervasive Systems* (EP/F033540/1); the *ANR SeSur AVOTÉ* project; the *Direction Générale pour l'Armement* (DGA); and the University of Birmingham's *Blue BEAR* cluster.

A. Armando and G. Lowe (Eds.): ARSPA-WITS 2010, LNCS 6186, pp. 146–163, 2010.

emphasise a voter's ability to verify the results of the entire election process, it is sometimes called *end-to-end* verifiability [22].

We present a preliminary definition of election verifiability in a formal and general setting, and we analyse voting protocols from the literature. We work in the applied pi calculus [2], and we use the ProVerif software tool [8] to automate verification. (The calculus and the tool have already been successful in analysing other properties of electronic voting systems [14,4].) Our approach puts significant emphasis on the automatic analysis of the verifiability property, using ProVerif. To that end, we introduce a number of encodings that make ProVerif work more efficiently, which are of independent interest.

Election verifiability allows voters and observers to verify that the election outcome corresponds to the votes legitimately cast. We distinguish three aspects of verifiability:

***Individual verifiability:*** a voter can check that her own ballot is included in the bulletin board.

***Universal verifiability:*** anyone can check that the election outcome corresponds to the ballots.

***Eligibility verifiability:*** anyone can check that each vote in the election outcome was cast by a registered voter and there is at most one vote per voter.

(Note that some authors use the term "universal verifiability" to refer to the conjunction of what we call "universal verifiability" and "eligibility verifiability." This distinction is made for compatibility with protocols which do not offer eligibility verifiability.) These three aspects of verifiability are related to the following *correctness properties* [4], defined with respect to honest protocol executions:

***Inalterability:*** no one can change a voter's vote.

***Declared result:*** the election outcome is the correct sum of the votes cast.

***Eligibility:*** only registered voters can vote and at most once.

Election verifiability properties are different from correctness properties, since they assert that voters and observers can check that the correctness properties hold, even when administrators deviate from the protocol (that is, do not perform an honest execution).

We define election verifiability as a family of three tests, corresponding to the three aspects identified above. The individual verifiability test is performed by each voter. The other two tests can be conducted by any observer.

### 1.1 Contribution

We present a definition of election verifiability which captures the three desired aspects: individual verifiability, universal verifiability and eligibility verifiability. The definition is a sufficient condition for election verifiability, but it is not be necessary; that is, there are some protocols which offer verifiability but are not captured by our definition.

We formalise our definition as reachability assertions in the applied pi calculus. This makes the definition amenable to automated reasoning. In order to make ProVerif work better with our definitions, we introduce a number of encodings and optimisations.

We demonstrate the applicability of our definition by analysing three protocols. The first protocol is a simple illustrative protocol which is trivially verifiable because voters digitally sign their ballot. (Note that this protocol does not achieve other properties such as privacy). We then analyse the protocol by Fujioka *et al.* [16], and a variant of the one by Juels *et al.* [19]; the latter has been implemented as Civitas [13,12].

### 1.2 Related Work

Juels, Catalano & Jakobson [18,19] present the first definition of universal verifiability in the provable security model. Their definition assumes voting protocols produce signature proofs of knowledge demonstrating the correctness of tallying. Automated analysis is not discussed.

Universal verifiability was also studied by Chevallier-Mames et al. [11] with the aim of showing an incompatibility result: protocols cannot satisfy verifiability and vote privacy in an unconditional way (without relying on computational assumptions). To see this, note that they require functions $f$ and $f'$ such that for any bulletin board $BB$ and list of eligible voters $L$ the function $f(BB, L)$ returns the list of actual voters and $f'(BB, L)$ returns the election outcome (see Definition 1 of [11]). From these functions one could consider any single bulletin board entry $b$ and compute $f(\{b\}, L)$, $f'(\{b\}, L)$ to reveal a voter and her vote. As witnessed by [18,19], weaker versions of verifiability and vote privacy properties can hold simultaneously. Our definitions do not reflect such an incompatibility with vote-privacy and permit a large class of electronic voting protocols claiming to provide verifiability to be considered.

Baskar, Ramanujan & Suresh [7] and subsequently Talbi et al. [24] have formalised individual and universal verifiability with respect to the FOO [16] electronic voting protocol. Their definitions are tightly coupled to that particular protocol and cannot easily be generalised. Moreover, their definitions characterise individual executions as verifiable or not; whereas such properties should be considered with respect to every execution (that is, the entire protocol).

During the period between the ARSPA-WITS workshop and the post proceedings we have taken the opportunity to revise the definitions presented here to cater for a larger class of electronic voting protocols. A preliminary version of this new work appears in [20].

### 1.3 Outline

Section 2 recalls the applied pi calculus. In Section 3 we introduce a generic definition of verifiability which is independent of any particular formal framework. In Section 4 our definition is formalised as reachability assertions in the context of the applied pi calculus. The three case studies are analysed in Section 5. Finally, we conclude and give directions for future work (Section 6).

## 2 Applied Pi Calculus

The applied pi calculus [2] is a language for modelling concurrent systems and their interactions. It is an extension of the pi calculus which was explicitly designed for modelling cryptographic protocols. For this purpose, the applied pi calculus allows terms to be constructed over a signature rather than just names. This term algebra can be used to model cryptographic primitives.

### 2.1 Syntax

The calculus assumes an infinite set of names $a, b, c, k, m, n, s, t, r, \ldots$, an infinite set of variables $v, x, y, z, \ldots$ and a finite signature $\Sigma$, that is, a finite set of function symbols each with an associated arity. A function symbol of arity 0 is a constant. We use metavariables $u, w$ to range over both names and variables. Terms $F, L, M, N, T, U, V$ are built by applying function symbols to names, variables and other terms. Tuples $u_1, \ldots, u_l$ and $M_1, \ldots, M_l$ are occasionally abbreviated $\tilde{u}$ and $\tilde{M}$. We write $\{^{M_1}/_{x_1}, \ldots, ^{M_l}/_{x_l}\}$ for substitutions that replace $x_1, \ldots, x_l$ with $M_1, \ldots, M_l$. The applied pi calculus relies on a simple type system. Terms can be of sort Channel for channel names or Base for the payload sent out on these channels. Function symbols can only be applied to, and return, terms of sort Base. A term is ground when it does not contain variables. The grammar for processes is shown in Figure 1 where $u$ is either a name or variable of channel sort. Plain processes are standard. As usual we abbreviate conditionals as if $M = N$ then $P$, when $Q$ is the null process; and similarly we may omit the process $P$ in message input and output when $P$ is 0. Extended processes introduce *active substitutions* which generalise the classical let construct: the process $\nu\, x.(\{^M/_x\} \mid P)$ corresponds exactly to the process let $x = M$ in $P$. As usual names and variables have scopes which are delimited by restrictions and by inputs. All substitutions are assumed to be cycle-free.

The sets of free and bound names, respectively variables, in process $A$ are denoted by fn($A$), bn($A$), fv($A$), bv($A$). We also write fn($M$), fv($M$) for the names, respectively variables, in term $M$. An extended process $A$ is *closed* if it has no free variables. A *context* $C[\_]$ is an extended process with a hole. We obtain $C[A]$ as the result of filling $C[\_]$'s hole with $A$. An *evaluation context*

| $P, Q, R$ ::= | processes | $A, B, C$ ::= | extended processes |
|---|---|---|---|
| $0$ | null process | $P$ | plain process |
| $P \mid Q$ | parallel | $A \mid B$ | parallel composition |
| $!P$ | replication | $\nu\, n.A$ | name restriction |
| $\nu\, n.P$ | name restriction | $\nu\, x.A$ | variable restriction |
| $u(x).P$ | message input | $\{^M/_x\}$ | active substitution |
| $\overline{u}\langle M\rangle.P$ | message output | | |
| if $M = N$ then $P$ else $Q$ | conditional | | |

**Fig. 1.** Applied pi calculus grammar

is a context whose hole is not under a replication, a conditional, an input, or an output.

The signature $\Sigma$ is equipped with an equational theory $E$, that is a finite set of equations of the form $M = N$. We define $=_E$ as the smallest equivalence relation on terms, that contains $E$ and is closed under application of function symbols, substitution of terms for variables and bijective renaming of names.

We introduce *linear* processes as a subset of plain processes generated by the grammar

$$\begin{aligned} P ::= & \ 0 \mid \nu n.P \mid c(x).P \mid \overline{c}\langle M\rangle.P \\ & \mid \text{if } M = N \text{ then } P \text{ else } 0 \quad (P \neq 0) \\ & \mid \text{if } M = N \text{ then } 0 \text{ else } P \quad (P \neq 0) \end{aligned}$$

Linear processes can be sequentially composed in a natural way. Let $P$ be a linear processes and $Q$ a plain process. We define the plain process $P \circ Q$ to be $Q$ if $P = 0$ and otherwise by replacing the unique occurrence of ".0" in $P$ by ".$Q$". (Note that ".0" does not occur in "else 0". ) Moreover, we note that if $P$ and $Q$ are both linear processes then $P \circ Q$ is also a linear process.

## 2.2 Semantics

We now define the operational semantics of the applied pi calculus by the means of two relations: structural equivalence and internal reductions. *Structural equivalence* ($\equiv$) is the smallest equivalence relation closed under $\alpha$-conversion of both bound names and variables and application of evaluation contexts such that:

| | | | |
|---|---|---|---|
| PAR-0 | $A \mid 0 \equiv A$ | REPL | $!P \equiv P \mid !P$ |
| PAR-A | $A \mid (B \mid C) \equiv (A \mid B) \mid C$ | REWRITE | $\{^M/_x\} \equiv \{^N/_x\}$ |
| PAR-C | $A \mid B \equiv B \mid A$ | | if $M =_E N$ |
| NEW-0 | $\nu n.0 \equiv 0$ | ALIAS | $\nu x.\{^M/_x\} \equiv 0$ |
| NEW-C | $\nu u.\nu w.A \equiv \nu w.\nu u.A$ | SUBST | $\{^M/_x\} \mid A \equiv \{^M/_x\} \mid A\{^M/_x\}$ |

$$\text{NEW-PAR} \quad A \mid \nu u.B \ \equiv \ \nu u.(A \mid B) \quad \text{if } u \notin \text{fn}(A) \cup \text{fv}(A)$$

*Internal reduction* ($\rightarrow$) is the smallest relation closed under structural equivalence, application of evaluation contexts and such that

| | | |
|---|---|---|
| COMM | $\overline{c}\langle x\rangle.P \mid c(x).Q \rightarrow P \mid Q$ | |
| THEN | if $M = M$ then $P$ else $Q \rightarrow P$ | |
| ELSE | if $M = N$ then $P$ else $Q \rightarrow Q$ | if $M, N$ ground and $M \neq_E N$ |

## 2.3 Notational Conventions

By convention we assume a signature contains: the binary function $\mathsf{pair}$; the unary functions $\mathsf{fst}$, $\mathsf{snd}$; and the constant $\varepsilon$. Moreover, the associated equational theory includes the equations $\mathsf{fst}(\mathsf{pair}(x, y)) = x$ and $\mathsf{snd}(\mathsf{pair}(x, y)) = y$. Arbitrary length tuples can be constructed as $\mathsf{pair}(x_1, \mathsf{pair}(x_2, \ldots, \mathsf{pair}(x_n, \varepsilon)))$; which, for convenience, we abbreviate $(x_1, \ldots, x_n)$. We also write $M_j$ for

$\mathsf{fst}(\mathsf{snd}(\mathsf{snd}(\ldots\mathsf{snd}(M))))$ where $j \geq 1$ and there are $j-1$ occurrences of $\mathsf{snd}$. We also write sometimes $c(x_1,\ldots,x_n)$ (or $c(\tilde{x})$) for the sequence of inputs $c(x_1).\ \ldots\ .c(x_n)$.

To aid readability, we also allow boolean combinations of $M = N$ in conditionals in the "if-then-else" process, and in the output of terms. If $\phi$ is such a combination, then the output $\overline{c}\langle\phi\rangle.P$ is an abbreviation for "if $\phi$ then $\overline{c}\langle\mathsf{true}\rangle.P$". Boolean combinations of conditionals in "if" statements are handled as follows. First, the boolean combination is written using only the boolean connectives $\wedge$ and $\neg$. Then $\wedge$ is encoded using nested "if" processes; and negation ($\neg$) is encoded by swapping "then" and "else" branches.

### 2.4 Events and Reachability Assertions

For the purpose of protocol analysis processes are annotated with *events* which mark important actions performed by the protocol which do not otherwise affect behaviour. We adopt the formalism presented by Abadi, Blanchet & Fournet [1] to capture events. Events are modelled as outputs $\overline{\mathtt{f}}\langle M\rangle$ where $\mathtt{f} \in \mathcal{F}$ is an *"event channel"*: a name in a particular set $\mathcal{F}$ disjoint from the set of ordinary channels $a, b, c$. Message input on event channels must use *"event variables"* $e, e'$.

We assume that protocols should be executed in the presence of a so-called Dolev-Yao adversary [15]. The adversary is permitted to input $\mathtt{f}(e)$ on event channels but is forbidden from using the bound event variable $e$ in any other manner. The former condition prevents processes blocking, whereas the latter ensures the adversary's knowledge cannot be extended by the occurrence of events.

**Definition 1 (Adversary).** *An* adversary *is a closed process such that, any event channel* $\mathtt{f} \in \mathcal{F}$ *and event variable* $e$*, only occur in inputs of the form* $\mathtt{f}(e)$.

A reachability assertion is specified as an event $\overline{\mathtt{f}}\langle\tilde{X}\rangle$ where $\tilde{X}$ is a tuple of variables and constants. A process satisfies reachability if there exists an adversary who is able to expose the event (Definition 2). When such an adversary does not exist, we say the process satisfies the unreachability assertion $\overline{\mathtt{f}}\langle\tilde{X}\rangle$.

**Definition 2 (Reachability).** *The closed process* $P$ *satisfies the* reachability *assertion* $\overline{\mathtt{f}}\langle\tilde{X}\rangle$ *where* $\tilde{X}$ *is a tuple of variables and constants if there exists an adversary* $Q$ *such that* $P \mid Q \rightarrow^* C[\overline{\mathtt{f}}\langle\tilde{X}\rangle.P']$ *for some evaluation context* $C$ *and process* $P'$.

## 3 Election Verifiability

Election verifiability can be formalised with respect to tests $\Phi^{IV}$, $\Phi^{UV}$, $\Phi^{EV}$ corresponding to the three aspects of our formalisation. A protocol is said to be election-verifiable if three such tests exist that satisfy some conditions that we detail below. Each of the tests $\Phi^{IV}$, $\Phi^{UV}$, $\Phi^{EV}$ is a predicate which after substitutions from the bulletin board and elsewhere evaluates to true or false. The designers of electronic voting protocols need not explicitly specify these cryptographic tests since our definition assumes the existence of tests (perhaps devised after design) which satisfy our conditions. This extends the applicability of our methodology whilst also permitting the scrutiny of tests specified by protocol designers.

### 3.1 Overview

*Individual verifiability.* The test $\Phi^{IV}$ takes parameters $v$ (a vote), $\tilde{x}$ (a voter's knowledge), $y$ (a voter's public credential) and $z$ (a bulletin board entry). For $\Phi^{IV}$ to be a suitable test it must allow a voter to identify her bulletin board entry. Formally we require for all votes $s$, if the voter with public credential $D$ votes for candidate $s$, then there exists an execution of the protocol which produces $\tilde{M}$ such that some bulletin board entry $B$ satisfies:

$$\Phi^{IV}\{^s/_v, ^{\tilde{M}}/_{\tilde{x}}, ^D/_y, ^B/_z\} \tag{1}$$

Moreover, the bulletin board entry should determine the vote; that is, for all bulletin board entries $B$, public credentials $D, D'$ votes $s, s'$ and tuples $\tilde{M}, \tilde{M}'$ we have:

$$\Phi^{IV}\{^s/_v, ^{\tilde{M}}/_{\tilde{x}}, ^D/_y, ^B/_z\} \wedge \Phi^{IV}\{^{s'}/_v, ^{\tilde{M}'}/_{\tilde{x}}, ^{D'}/_y, ^B/_z\} \Rightarrow (s = s') \tag{2}$$

This ensures the test will hold for at most one vote. Additionally, individual verifiability requires voters to accept distinct bulletin board entries:

$$\textit{Bulletin board entries are distinct} \tag{3}$$

This condition requires protocol executions to introduce some freshness (e.g. randomness).

*Universal verifiability.* This property is encapsulated by the test $\Phi^{UV}$ which takes parameters $v$ (a vote) and $z$ (a bulletin board entry). Given $\Phi^{IV}$, the test $\Phi^{UV}$ is suitable if every bulletin board entry which is accepted by a voter is also accepted by an observer; and the entry is counted by the observer in the correct way. The property requires that for all executions of the protocol producing $\tilde{M}$ with respect to the voter's vote $s$, if there exists a bulletin board entry $B$ and public credential $D$ such that the voter accepts the bulletin board entry as hers, then the observer also accepts the entry:

$$\Phi^{IV}\{^s/_v, ^{\tilde{M}}/_{\tilde{x}}, ^D/_y, ^B/_z\} \Rightarrow \Phi^{UV}\{^s/_v, ^B/_z\} \tag{4}$$

Moreover, the observer counts the vote correctly. That is, for all bulletin board entries $B$ and votes $s, s'$ if the test succeeds for $s$ and $s'$ then they must be votes for the same candidate:

$$\Phi^{UV}\{^s/_v, ^B/_z\} \wedge \Phi^{UV}\{^{s'}/_v, ^B/_z\} \Rightarrow (s = s') \tag{5}$$

This ensures that an observer may only count a vote in one way.

We remark that the implication in property (4) is only one way because the adversary is able to construct ballots which would be accepted by an observer; however, such a ballot should not be accepted by a voter. This malicious behaviour can be detected by eligibility verifiability. We also note that this formalisation is stronger than what is actually required: here a voter needs to be able to identify the bulletin board entry corresponding to her vote. This is not the case in all protocols, for example in the protocol by Juels *et al.* (described in Section 5) the connection between the set of bulletin board entries and the election outcome is lost by the mix. However, this formalisation has the advantage of being amenable to automated verification.

*Eligibility verifiability.* The property is encoded by the test $\Phi^{EV}$ which takes parameters $y$ (a voter's public credential) and $z$ (a bulletin board entry). Given $\Phi^{IV}$, the test $\Phi^{EV}$ is considered suitable if it ensures: 1) an observer can attribute a bulletin board entry to a public credential if and only if the corresponding voter would accept that entry as hers; and 2) a bulletin board entry can be attributed to at most one voter. Formally the property requires for all bulletin board entries $B$ and executions of the protocol producing $\tilde{M}$, with respect to the voter's vote $s$ and public voter credential $D$, the voter accepts $B$ as hers iff the bulletin board entry can be attributed to her public credential:

$$\Phi^{IV}\{^{s}/_{v}, ^{\tilde{M}}/_{\tilde{x}}, ^{D}/_{y}, ^{B}/_{z}\} \Leftrightarrow \Phi^{EV}\{^{D}/_{y}, ^{B}/_{z}\} \qquad (6)$$

This ensures that if $\Phi^{IV}$ succeeds for a voter then she is assured that her vote is considered eligible by an observer; and if $\Phi^{EV}$ succeeds for a public credential then the corresponding voter must have constructed that bulletin board entry. The condition relies upon a relationship between the voter's knowledge $\tilde{M}$ and the voter's public credential $D$ . As for universal verifiability this condition may be too strong as some verifiable protocols do not allow a voter to link a bulletin board entry to her credentials.

The second condition requires that the test must uniquely determine who cast a bulletin board entry (hence we can ensure that at most one ballot per registered credential may appear on the bulletin board); that is, for all bulletin board entries $B$ and public voter credentials $D, D'$ if the test succeeds for $D$ and $D'$ then the credentials are equivalent:

$$\Phi^{EV}\{^{D}/_{y}, ^{B}/_{z}\} \wedge \Phi^{EV}\{^{D'}/_{y}, ^{B}/_{z}\} \Rightarrow (D = D') \qquad (7)$$

This property enables re-vote elimination. The concept of re-voting is particularly useful since it is used by some protocols to provide coercion resistance. In such protocols re-vote elimination is performed with respect to a publicly defined policy to ensure voters vote at most once. Finally, eligibility verifiability also requires that voters must have unique public credentials:

*Public voter credentials are distinct* (8)

### 3.2 Verifying an Election

Voters and observers check the outcome of the election by performing the tests $\Phi^{IV}$, $\Phi^{UV}$ and $\Phi^{EV}$ on the bulletin board and data derived from elsewhere (for example, learnt by the voter during an execution of the protocol). For individual verifiability, each voter should be in possession of her vote $s$, public credential $D$ and $\tilde{M}$ representing the knowledge learnt during an execution of the protocol, such that there exists $j \in [1, |\tilde{B}|]$ satisfying the test $\Phi^{IV}\{^{s}/_{v}, ^{\tilde{M}}/_{\tilde{x}}, ^{D}/_{y}, ^{B_j}/_{z}\}$. For universal verifiability, the bulletin board must be such that the observer can map the ballots to the votes appearing in the election outcome. That is, there exists a bijective function $f : \{1, \ldots, |\tilde{B}|\} \to \{1, \ldots, |\tilde{B}|\}$, such that for all $j \in [1, |\tilde{B}|]$, the test $\Phi^{UV}\{^{s_j}/_{v}, ^{B_{f(j)}}/_{z}\}$ holds. Similarly, for eligibility verifiability to hold an observer must be able to map each public credential to a bulletin board entry. That is, there exists a bijective function $g : \{1, \ldots, |\tilde{B}|\} \to \{1, \ldots, |\tilde{B}|\}$ such that for all $j \in [1, |\tilde{B}|]$ the test $\Phi^{EV}\{^{D_j}/_{y}, ^{B_{g(j)}}/_{z}\}$ holds.

*Compatibility with privacy.* Some electronic voting protocols utilise mixnets to obtain privacy. For simplicity we omit formalising the security of mixnets and hence omit modelling the mix. This clearly violates privacy properties. However, since mixnets are verifiable, privacy and election verifiability properties may coexist in practice.

## 4 Election Verifiability in the Applied Pi Calculus

A voting protocol is captured by a voter process $V$ and a process $K$ modelling administrators whom are required to be honest for the purpose of election verifiability. Dishonest administrators need not be explicitly modelled since they are part of the adversarial environment. The process $K$ is assumed to publish public voter credentials; and is commonly responsible for the distribution of voter keys. Channels $\tilde{a}$ are assumed to be private and appear in both $V, K$. In addition, we consider a context $A$ which performs setup duties; for example, the instantiation of keys for honest administrators. Dishonest administrator keys are modelled as free names. Definition 3 formalises a voting process specification accordingly. The definition allows us to analyse election verifiability with respect to an unbounded number of voters and arbitrarily many candidates.

**Definition 3 (Voting process specification).** *A voting process specification is a tuple $\langle A, V, K[\overline{c}\langle D\rangle], \tilde{a}\rangle$ where $V$ is a linear process, $A$ and $K$ are contexts such that $V, A, K$ do not contain any occurrence of event channels and event variables. The term $D$ models public voter credentials. The variable $v \in fv(V)$ refers to the value of the vote, $v \notin (bv(A) \cup bv(V))$, $c \notin (\tilde{a} \cup bn(A[V \mid K]))$ and $(fv(V)\backslash\{v\} \cup fv(K)) \subseteq bv(A)$.*

We also suppose that the votes are generated by a special vote generation process $G$ which "chooses" the vote for a given voter and sends it to the voter on a channel name $b$. A typical vote generation process would be

$$G \mathrel{\hat{=}} !\nu\, s.((!\overline{b}\langle s\rangle) \mid \overline{c}\langle s\rangle)$$

This process models the generation of all possible votes. Intuitively, the channel $b$ allows the voter to select her vote $v$ and the nested replication allows several voters to choose the same vote $s$, while other voters may vote differently. Each vote $s$ is also made available to the environment by publishing it on the channel $c$. Unless specified differently we suppose in the remaining that $G$ is defined as above. Given a voting process specification $\langle A, V, K[\overline{c}\langle D\rangle], \tilde{a}\rangle$ and a vote generation process $G$ we can build the process modelling the voting protocol VP as follows:

$$\mathsf{VP} \mathrel{\widehat{=}} \nu\, b.(A[!\nu\, \tilde{a}.((b(v).V) \mid K[\overline{c}\langle D\rangle])] \mid G)$$

where $b \notin (\tilde{a} \cup \text{fn}(A[V \mid K]) \cup \text{bn}(A))$. Observe that since the key generation process is under replication it is possible to construct unique credentials for each voter.

The formalisation of election verifiability (Definition 5) can naturally be expressed as reachability assertions [26,8] associated with the properties 1-8 of §3.1 which relate to tests $\Phi^{IV}, \Phi^{UV}, \Phi^{EV}$. First the tests must be incorporated into an augmented voting process (Definition 4).

**Definition 4 (Augmented voting process).** *Given a voting process specification* $\langle A, V, K[\overline{c}\langle D\rangle], \tilde{a}\rangle$*, a vote generation process* $G$ *and tests* $\Phi^{IV}, \Phi^{UV}, \Phi^{EV}$ *the* augmented voting process *is defined as* $\mathsf{VP}^{+} = \nu\, b.(A[!\nu\, \tilde{a}, b'.(\widehat{V} \mid \widehat{K})] \mid G \mid P) \mid Q \mid R$ *where*

$$\begin{aligned}
\widehat{V} &= b(v).V \circ c(z).b'(y).(\overline{\mathtt{pass}}\langle(\Phi^{IV}, z)\rangle \mid \overline{\mathtt{fail}}\langle\psi\rangle)\\
\widehat{K} &= K[\overline{b'}\langle D\rangle \mid \overline{\mathtt{cred}}\langle D\rangle \mid \overline{c}\langle D\rangle]\\
P &= b(v').b(v'').c(\tilde{x}').c(\tilde{x}'').c(y').c(y'').c(z').\overline{\mathtt{fail}}\langle\phi' \vee \phi'' \vee \phi'''\rangle\\
Q &= \mathtt{pass}(e).\mathtt{pass}(e').\overline{\mathtt{fail}}\langle e_1 \wedge e_1' \wedge (e_2 = e_2')\rangle\\
R &= \mathtt{cred}(e).\mathtt{cred}(e').\overline{\mathtt{fail}}\langle e = e'\rangle
\end{aligned}$$

$$\begin{aligned}
\psi &= (\Phi^{IV} \wedge \neg\Phi^{UV}) \vee (\Phi^{IV} \wedge \neg\Phi^{EV}) \vee (\neg\Phi^{IV} \wedge \Phi^{EV})\\
\phi' &= \Phi^{IV}\{^{v'}/_{v}, ^{\tilde{x}'}/_{\tilde{x}}, ^{y'}/_{y}, ^{z'}/_{z}\} \wedge \Phi^{IV}\{^{v''}/_{v}, ^{\tilde{x}''}/_{\tilde{x}}, ^{y''}/_{y}, ^{z'}/_{z}\} \wedge \neg(v' = v'')\\
\phi'' &= \Phi^{UV}\{^{v'}/_{v}, ^{z'}/_{z}\} \wedge \Phi^{UV}\{^{v''}/_{v}, ^{z'}/_{z}\} \wedge \neg(v' = v'')\\
\phi''' &= \Phi^{EV}\{^{y'}/_{y}, ^{z'}/_{z}\} \wedge \Phi^{EV}\{^{y''}/_{y}, ^{z'}/_{z}\} \wedge \neg(y' =_E y'')
\end{aligned}$$

*such that* fail, pass, cred *are event channels,* $\tilde{x} = (bv(V) \cap (fv(Riv) \backslash \{z\}))$*, and* $b, b'$ *are fresh, that is,* $b, b' \notin (\tilde{a} \cup fn(A[V \mid K]) \cup bn(A[V \mid K]))$.

The augmented voting process extends $V$ to bind the voter's intended vote $v$, assigns the voter's public credential to $y$ and introduces a claimed bulletin board entry $z$. As in the non-augmented process, the process $!\nu\, s.((!\overline{b}\langle s\rangle) \mid \overline{c}\langle s\rangle)$ produces candidates for whom the voters are allowed to vote. The number of candidates and for whom each voter casts her vote is controlled by the adversarial environment. The events capture the desired reachability assertions. That is, reachability of $\overline{\mathtt{pass}}\langle(\Phi^{IV}, z)\rangle$ captures propositional property 1 of §3.1; unreachability of $\overline{\mathtt{fail}}\langle\psi\rangle$ models propositional properties 4 and 6 of §3.1; and unreachability of $\overline{\mathtt{fail}}\langle\phi' \vee \phi'' \vee \phi'''\rangle$ denotes properties 2, 5 and 7 of §3.1. The universal quantifiers of the propositional properties 2,4-7 are captured by allowing the adversary to input the required parameters. Process $Q$ exploits communication on event channel pass to detect the scenario in which two voters accept the same bulletin board entry, hence capturing property 3 of §3.1, by the unreachability of the event $\overline{\texttt{fail}}\langle e_1 \wedge e_1' \wedge (e_2 = e_2')\rangle$ where $e_1$ and $e_1'$ capture whether two distinct voters accept the bulletin boards $e_2$ and $e_2'$. Similarly, communication on the event channel `cred` is used to detect the situation in which two voters are assigned the same public credential, thus modelling property 8 of §3.1 by the unreachability of $\overline{\texttt{fail}}\langle e = e'\rangle$.

**Definition 5 (Election verifiability).** *A voting process specification* $\langle A, V, K[\overline{c}\langle D\rangle], \tilde{a}\rangle$ *satisfies* election verifiability *if there exists tests* $\Phi^{IV}, \Phi^{UV}, \Phi^{EV}$ *such that the augmented voting process* $\mathsf{VP}^+$ *and tests satisfy the following conditions:*

1. $\mathsf{VP}^+$ *satisfies the unreachability assertion:* $\overline{\texttt{fail}}\langle \mathsf{true}\rangle$.
2. $\mathsf{VP}^+$ *satisfies the reachability assertion:* $\overline{\texttt{pass}}\langle(\mathsf{true}, x)\rangle$.
3. *The tests* $\Phi^{IV}, \Phi^{UV}, \Phi^{EV}$ *satisfy the following constraints:*
   - $fv(\Phi^{IV}) \subseteq bv(V) \cup \{v, y, z\}$
   - $fv(\Phi^{UV}) \subseteq \{v, z\}$
   - $fv(\Phi^{EV}) \subseteq \{y, z\}$
   - $(fn(\Phi^{IV}) \cup fn(\Phi^{UV}) \cup fn(\Phi^{EV})) \cap bn(\mathsf{VP}^+) = \emptyset$

We remark that the restriction $\mathrm{fn}(\Phi^{IV}) \cap \mathrm{bn}(\mathsf{VP}^+) = \emptyset$ does not lose generality, since restricted names "$\nu\, n$" can be referenced by variables as follows: "$\nu\, n.\mathrm{let}\ x\_n = n$ in".

Many protocols in literature do not provide eligibility verifiability. We therefore define a *weakly augmented voting process* and *weak election verifiability* to capture only individual and universal verifiability. A *weakly augmented voting process* is defined as an augmented voting process but with $R = 0$, $\psi = (\Phi^{IV} \wedge \neg\Phi^{UV})$ and replacing $\overline{\texttt{fail}}\langle\phi' \vee \phi'' \vee \phi'''\rangle$ with $\overline{\texttt{fail}}\langle\phi' \vee \phi''\rangle$. The definition of *weak election verifiability* is obtained by omitting conditions on $\Phi^{EV}$ from Definition 5.

## 5 Case Studies

We demonstrate the applicability of our methodology by analysing electronic voting protocols from literature. The ProVerif tool [8] has been used for automation and our input scripts are available online[1]. ProVerif's ability to reason with reachability assertions is sound (when no trace is found the protocol is guaranteed to satisfy the unreachability assertion) but not complete (false reachability traces may be found). As a consequence reachability traces output by ProVerif for Condition 2 of Definition 5 must be checked by hand. In this paper all such traces correspond to valid reachable states.

### 5.1 Postal Ballot Protocol

*Description.* Consider an electronic variant of a *"postal ballot"* (or *"mail-in ballot"*) protocol whereby a voter receives her private signing key $sk_V$ from

[1] `http://www.bensmyth.com/publications/10arspa/`

a keying authority, constructs her signed ballot and sends it to the bulletin board. The keying authority is also responsible for publishing the voter's public verification key $\mathsf{pk}(sk_V)$ which will serve as her public credential. The protocol does not satisfy all of the desirable electronic voting properties; but it should certainly provide election verifiability.

*Formalisation in applied pi.* The corresponding voting process specification is given by $\langle A, V, K[\overline{c}\langle D\rangle], (a)\rangle$ where

$$A \mathrel{\widehat{=}} \_ \qquad\qquad K[\overline{c}\langle D\rangle] \mathrel{\widehat{=}} \nu\, sk_V.(\overline{a}\langle sk_V\rangle \mid \overline{c}\langle D\rangle)$$
$$V \mathrel{\widehat{=}} a(x).\overline{c}\langle(v, \mathsf{sign}(v,x))\rangle \qquad\qquad D \mathrel{\widehat{=}} \mathsf{pk}(sk_V)$$

We model digital signatures (without message recovery) by the equation

$$\mathsf{checksign}(\mathsf{sign}(x,y), x, \mathsf{pk}(y)) = \mathsf{true}$$

The resulting (non-augmented) voting process is then defined as

$$\begin{aligned} \mathsf{VP}_{\mathsf{postal}} \mathrel{\widehat{=}} \nu b.(\ & !\nu a.\ (b(v).a(x).\overline{c}\langle(v, \mathsf{sign}(v,x))\rangle \\ & \qquad\qquad \mid \nu\, sk_V.(\overline{a}\langle sk_V\rangle \mid \overline{c}\langle \mathsf{pk}(sk_V)\rangle))) \\ & \mid !\nu s.(!\overline{b}\langle s\rangle \mid \overline{c}\langle s\rangle)) \end{aligned}$$

*Analysis.* The augmented voting process $\mathsf{VP}^+$ can be derived with respect to tests:

$$\begin{aligned} \Phi^{IV} &\mathrel{\widehat{=}} z =_E (sign(v,x), v, pk(x)) \\ \Phi^{UV} &\mathrel{\widehat{=}} \mathsf{checksign}(z_1, z_2, z_3) =_E \mathsf{true} \wedge v =_E z_2 \\ \Phi^{EV} &\mathrel{\widehat{=}} \mathsf{checksign}(z_1, z_2, z_3) =_E \mathsf{true} \wedge y =_E z_3 \end{aligned}$$

ProVerif is able to automatically verify the protocol satisfies election verifiability.

### 5.2 Protocol Due to Fujioka, Okamoto and Ohta

*Description.* The FOO protocol [16] involves voters, a registrar and a tallier. The protocol relies on a commitment scheme and blind signatures which we model by the following equational theory.

$$\begin{aligned} \mathsf{checksign}(\mathsf{sign}(x,y), x, \mathsf{pk}(y)) &= \mathsf{true} \\ \mathsf{unblind}(\mathsf{sign}(\mathsf{blind}(x,y), z), y) &= \mathsf{sign}(x,z) \\ \mathsf{unblind}(\mathsf{blind}(x,y), y) &= x \\ \mathsf{open}(\mathsf{commit}(x,y), y) &= x \end{aligned}$$

The voter first computes her ballot as a commitment to her vote $m' = \mathsf{commit}(v,r)$ and sends the signed blinded ballot $\mathsf{sign}(\mathsf{blind}(m',r'), sk_V)$ to the registrar. The registrar checks the signature belongs to an eligible voter and returns $\mathsf{sign}(\mathsf{blind}(m',r'), sk_R)$ the blind signed ballot. The voter verifies that this input (variable $bsb$ in the process $V$ below) corresponds to the registrar's signature and unblinds the message to recover her ballot signed by the registrar $m = \mathsf{sign}(m', sk_R)$. The voter then posts her signed ballot to the bulletin board.

Once all votes have been cast the tallier verifies all the entries and appends an identifier $l$ to each valid record[2]. The voter then checks the bulletin board for her entry, the triple $(l, m', m)$, (modelled in $V$ below by the input in variable $bbe$) and appends the commitment factor $r$. Finally, using $r$ the tallier opens all of the ballots and announces the declared outcome. The protocol claims to provide individual and universal verifiability but does not consider eligibility verifiability.

*Formalisation in applied pi.* The voting process specification is $\langle \_, V, K[\overline{c}\langle \mathsf{pk}(x)\rangle], (a)\rangle$ where $K = c(x).(\overline{a}\langle x\rangle \mid \_)$ and $V$ is defined as follows:

$$
\begin{aligned}
V = \ & \nu\, r.\text{let } x\_r = r \text{ in} \\
& \nu\, r'.\text{let } x\_r' = r' \text{ in} \\
& a(x). \\
& \text{let } m' = \mathsf{commit}(v, r) \text{ in} \\
& \overline{c}\langle(\mathsf{pk}(x), \mathsf{blind}(m', r'), \mathsf{sign}(\mathsf{blind}(m', r'), x))\rangle. \\
& c(bsb). \\
& \text{if } \mathsf{checksign}(bsb, \mathsf{blind}(m', r'), \mathsf{pk}(sk_R)) = \mathsf{true} \text{ then} \\
& \text{let } m = \mathsf{unblind}(bsb, r') \text{ in} \\
& \overline{c}\langle(m', m)\rangle. \\
& c(bbe). \\
& \text{if } m' = bbe_2 \wedge m = bbe_3 \text{ then} \\
& \overline{c}\langle(bbe_1, r)\rangle
\end{aligned}
$$

*Analysis.* Let tests $\Phi^{IV}, \Phi^{UV}$ be defined as follows:

$$
\begin{aligned}
\Phi^{IV} \ \widehat{=}\ & z =_E \langle bbe_1, \mathsf{commit}(v, x\_r), \mathsf{unblind}(bsb, x\_r'), x\_r, v\rangle \\
& \wedge\ \mathsf{checksign}(z_3, z_2, \mathsf{pk}(sk_R)) =_E \mathsf{true} \\
\Phi^{UV} \ \widehat{=}\ & z_2 =_E \mathsf{commit}(z_5, z_4) \wedge \mathsf{checksign}(z_3, z_2, \mathsf{pk}(sk_R)) =_E \mathsf{true} \wedge z_5 =_E v
\end{aligned}
$$

ProVerif enables automatic verification of election verifiability with respect to weak election verifiability.

## 5.3 Protocol Due to Juels, Catalano and Jakobsson and Clarkson, Chong and Myers

*Description.* The protocol due to Juels, Catalano & Jakobsson [19], which has been implemented by Clarkson, Chong & Myers as Civitas [13,12], involves voters, registrars and talliers.

The registrars announce the candidate list $\tilde{s} = (s_1, \ldots, s_l)$ and provide an *anonymous credential* $k$ to each legitimate voter. For each such credential an encrypted version $\mathsf{penc}(k, r'', \mathsf{pk}(sk_T))$ is published on the bulletin board.

Each voter selects her vote $s \in \tilde{s}$ and computes the ciphertexts $M = \mathsf{penc}(s, r, \mathsf{pk}(sk_T))$ and $M' = \mathsf{penc}(k, r', \mathsf{pk}(sk_T))$. The first ciphertext contains her vote and the second contains her credential. In addition, the voter constructs a signature proof of knowledge, that is, a non-interactive zero-knowledge proof of

[2] The value $l$ is used for practical purposes only; it does not affect security.

knowledge, demonstrating the correct construction of her ciphertexts and that she has chosen a valid candidate; that is, $s \in \tilde{s}$. The voter posts her ciphertexts and signature proof of knowledge to the bulletin board.

After some predefined deadline the outcome is computed as follows. First, the talliers discard any entries for which signature proofs of knowledge do not hold and eliminate re-votes by performing pairwise plaintext equivalence tests[3] on all the ciphertexts containing voting credentials posted by the voter. Re-vote elimination is performed in a verifiable manner with respect to some publicly defined policy, e.g. keeping the last vote. Then, the talliers perform a verifiable re-encryption mix on the votes and credentials, keeping the link between each such pair. The aim of this mix is that the voter herself cannot trace her vote anymore which allows the protocol to achieve coercion-resistance. After the mix all invalid credentials are discarded using plaintext equivalence tests between the entries posted to the bulletin board by the mix and those published by the registrar. Finally, the talliers perform a verifiable decryption and publish the result.

*Formalisation in applied pi.* We model a simplified version of the protocol described above which omits the mix. The resulting protocol is not coercion-resistant, but still provides anonymity. This change is made because our definition is too strong to hold on the complete protocol. We discuss future work regarding a more general definition in our conclusion.

The formalisation of signature proofs of knowledge in the applied pi calculus that we adopt is due to Backes *et al.* [5,6]. A signature proof of knowledge is a term $\mathsf{spk}_{i,j}(\tilde{U}, \tilde{V}, F)$ where $\tilde{U} = (U_1, \ldots, U_i)$ denotes the witness (or private component), $\tilde{V} = (V_1, \ldots, V_j)$ defines the public parameters and $F$ is a formula over those terms. More precisely $F$ is a term without names or variables, but includes distinguished constants $\alpha_k, \beta_l$ where $k, l \in \mathbb{N}$. The constants $\alpha_k, \beta_l$ in $F$ denote placeholders for the terms $U_k \in \tilde{U}$, $V_l \in \tilde{V}$ used within a signature of knowledge $\mathsf{spk}_{i,j}(\tilde{U}, \tilde{V}, F)$. For example, the signature proof of knowledge used by voters in the Juels, Catalano & Jakobsson voting protocol [19] demonstrates possession of a vote $s$, credential $k$ and randomisation factors $r, r'$ such that $M = \mathsf{penc}(s, r, \mathsf{pk}(sk_T))$, $M' = \mathsf{penc}(k, r', \mathsf{pk}(sk_T))$ and $s \in \tilde{s}$; that is, the proof shows the ciphertexts are correctly formed and $s$ is a valid candidate. This can be captured by $\mathsf{spk}_{4,3+l}((s, r, k, r'), (M, M', \mathsf{pk}(sk_T), s_1, \ldots, s_l), \mathcal{F})$ where $\mathcal{F}$ is defined as $\beta_1 = \mathsf{penc}(\alpha_1, \alpha_2, \beta_3) \wedge \beta_2 = \mathsf{penc}(\alpha_3, \alpha_4, \beta_3) \wedge (\alpha_1 = \beta_4 \vee \ldots \vee \alpha_1 = \beta_{4+l})$. A term $\mathsf{spk}_{i,j}(\tilde{U}, \tilde{V}, F)$ represents a valid signature if the term obtained by substituting $U_k, V_l$ for the corresponding $\alpha_k, \beta_l$ evaluates to $\mathsf{true}$. Verification of such a statement is modelled by the function $\mathsf{ver}_{i,j}$. The equational theory includes the following equations over all $i, j \in \mathbb{N}$, tuples $\tilde{x} = (x_1, \ldots, x_i)$, $\tilde{y} = (y_1, \ldots, y_j)$ and formula $F$ which is a ground term over $\Sigma \cup \{\alpha_k, \beta_l \mid k \leq i,\, l \leq j\}$ without any names:

[3] A *plaintext equivalence test* [17] is a cryptographic predicate which allows the comparison of two ciphertexts. The test returns true if the ciphertexts contain the same plaintext.

$$\mathsf{public_p}(\mathsf{spk}_{i,j}(\tilde{x}, \tilde{y}, F)) = y_p \text{ where } p \in [1, j]$$
$$\mathsf{formula}(\mathsf{spk}_{i,j}(\tilde{x}, \tilde{y}, F)) = F$$

In addition, we define equations such that $\mathsf{ver}_{i,j}(F, \mathsf{spk}_{i,j}(\tilde{U}, \tilde{V}, F')) =_E \mathsf{true}$ if $F =_E F'$ and $F\{^{U_1}/_{\alpha_1}, \ldots, ^{U_i}/_{\alpha_i}, ^{V_1}/_{\beta_1}, \ldots, ^{V_j}/_{\beta_j}\}$ holds where $i = |\tilde{U}|, j = |\tilde{V}|$ and $F, F'$ are ground terms over $\Sigma \cup \{\alpha_k, \beta_l \mid k \leq i, l \leq j\}$ without names. We omit the details of these equations which are similar to [5,6].

The protocol uses a variant of the ElGamal encryption scheme [19]. In addition to the standard equation $\mathsf{dec}(\mathsf{penc}(x, y, \mathsf{pk}(z)), z) = x$, this scheme allows the construction of a dedicated decryption key for a particular ciphertext which is modelled by the equation:

$$\mathsf{dec}(\mathsf{penc}(x, y, \mathsf{pk}(z)), \mathsf{commit}(\mathsf{penc}(x, y, \mathsf{pk}(z)), z)) = x$$

Verifiable decryption can then be achieved using the signature proof of knowledge $\mathsf{spk}_{1,3}((\alpha_1), (\beta_1, \beta_2), \mathcal{F}')$ where $\mathcal{F}'$ is given by $\beta_1 = \mathsf{commit}(\beta_2, \alpha_1)$. The proof shows that if $\beta_2 = \mathsf{penc}(M, N, \mathsf{pk}\alpha_1)$ for some terms $M, N$, then $\beta_1$ is a decryption key for $\beta_2$. Finally, plaintext equivalence tests are modelled by the equation

$$\begin{aligned}&\mathsf{pet}(\mathsf{penc}(x, y, pk(z)), \mathsf{penc}(x, y', \mathsf{pk}(z)),\\ &\qquad \mathsf{petkey}(\mathsf{penc}(x, y, \mathsf{pk}(z)), \mathsf{penc}(x, y', \mathsf{pk}(z)), z)) = \mathsf{true}\end{aligned}$$

The voting process specification can now be defined as $\langle A, V, K[\overline{c}\langle D\rangle], (a)\rangle$ where public credential $D = \mathsf{penc}(k, r'', \mathsf{pk}(sk_T))$ and $A, V, K$ are specified as follows:

$$\begin{aligned}
A &= \nu\, sk_T.(\overline{c}\langle \mathsf{pk}(sk_T)\rangle \mid (!A') \mid _)\\
V &= \nu\, r.\text{let } x_r = r \text{ in } \nu\, r'.\text{let } x_r' = r' \text{ in } a(x_k).\\
&\quad \text{let } x_s_1 = s_1 \text{ in } \ldots \text{ let } x_s_l = s_l \text{ in}\\
&\quad \text{let } x_pkT = \mathsf{pk}(sk_T) \text{ in}\\
&\quad \text{let } M = \mathsf{penc}(v, r, \mathsf{pk}(sk_T)) \text{ in}\\
&\quad \text{let } M' = \mathsf{penc}(x_k, r', \mathsf{pk}(sk_T)) \text{ in}\\
&\quad \text{let } N = \mathsf{spk}_{4,3+l}((v, r, x_k, r'), (M, M', \mathsf{pk}(sk_T), s_1, \ldots, s_l), \mathcal{F}) \text{ in}\\
&\quad \overline{c}\langle (M, M', N)\rangle\\
K &= \nu\, k.\nu\, r''.(\overline{a}\langle k\rangle \mid _)\\
A' &= c(y).\text{if } \mathsf{ver}_{4,3+l}(\mathcal{F}, y) = \mathsf{true} \text{ then}\\
&\quad c(z).\text{if } \mathsf{pet}(z, \mathsf{public}_2(y), \mathsf{petkey}(z, \mathsf{public}_2(y), sk_T)) = \mathsf{true} \text{ then}\\
&\quad \overline{c}\langle \mathsf{spk}_{1,2}((sk_T), (\mathsf{commit}(\mathsf{public}_1(y), sk_T), \mathsf{public}_1(y)), \mathcal{F}')\rangle).\\
&\quad \overline{c}\langle \mathsf{petkey}(z, \mathsf{public}_2(y), sk_T)\rangle
\end{aligned}$$

For simplicity we consider a single registrar $K$ and tallier $A'$ who are assumed to be honest. Moreover, we assume the existence of a secure mix protocol and hence do not model or verify the shuffle. The registrar process is standard and is responsible for publishing the public voter credentials. Process $A'$ captures the tallier's responsibility to provide suitable keys for plaintext equivalence tests used for eligibility checking and performing verifiable decryption of honestly constructed ballots.

*Analysis.* The protocol is dependent on the candidate list and therefore cannot be verified with respect to an arbitrary number of candidates. We must therefore restrict the adversarial environment to consider a fixed number of candidates. We therefore define the vote generation process as $G \mathrel{\hat{=}} (!\bar{b}\langle s_1\rangle) \mid \ldots \mid (!\bar{b}\langle s_l\rangle)$ where $s_1, \ldots, s_l$ are free names representing the candidates for whom voters may cast their votes. Let the tests $\Phi^{IV}, \Phi^{UV}, \Phi^{EV}$ be defined as follows:

$$\begin{aligned}
\Phi^{IV} &\mathrel{\hat{=}} \phi' \wedge z_1 =_E \mathsf{spk}_{4,3+l}((v, x_r, x_k, x_r'), (M, M', x_pkT, x_s_1, \ldots, x_s_l), \mathcal{F}) \\
\Phi^{UV} &\mathrel{\hat{=}} \phi\ \wedge \mathsf{dec}(\mathsf{public}_2(z_2), \mathsf{public}_1(z_2)) =_E v \\
\Phi^{EV} &\mathrel{\hat{=}} \phi' \wedge \mathsf{ver}_{4,3+l}(\mathcal{F}, z_1) =_E \mathsf{true}
\end{aligned}$$

$$\begin{aligned}
\phi &\mathrel{\hat{=}} \mathsf{ver}_{1,2}(\mathcal{F}', z_2) =_E \mathsf{true} \wedge \mathsf{public}_1(z_1) =_E \mathsf{public}_2(z_2) \\
\phi' &\mathrel{\hat{=}} \phi \wedge \mathsf{pet}(y, \mathsf{public}_2(z_1), z_3) =_E \mathsf{true}
\end{aligned}$$

where $M = \mathsf{penc}(v, x\_r, x\_pkT)$ and $M' = \mathsf{penc}(x\_k, x\_r', x\_pkT)$. The augmented voting process can now be derived with respect to the size of the candidate list $l$. Using ProVerif in association with a PHP script that generates ProVerif scripts for different values of $l$, the protocol can be successfully verified to satisfy election verifiability with respect to $l \in [1, 100]$.

## 6 Conclusion

This paper presents a preliminary formal definition of election verifiability for electronic voting protocols. The idea of tests for individual, universal and eligibility verifiability (and the associated acceptability conditions) is independent of any particular formalism. We instantiate this idea in terms of reachability assertions in the context of the applied pi calculus. The definition is suitable for automated reasoning using the ProVerif software tool, which we demonstrate by providing the code used for our analysis of the protocol by Fujioka, Okamoto & Ohta [16] and a variant of the one by Juels, Catalano & Jakobsson [19] and Clarkson, Chong & Myers [13,12].

The definition is work in progress, because it is currently insufficiently general to take account of protocols that use homomorphic encryption (such as Helios 2.0 [3]). Moreover, it is likely that the 'pointwise' nature of the tests $\Phi^{UV}$ and $\Phi^{EV}$ is too strong for some protocols; more likely, the observer performs a test on the whole bulletin board at once, rather than a separate test on each of its entries. In future work, we intend to generalise our definitions of universal verifiability and eligibility verifiability to work with a greater variety of voting systems. We also intend to study more carefully the relation between verifiability and coercion resistance. Finally, we aim to formalise the security of re-vote elimination policies, present in many realistic systems, which we omitted from our case studies.

## Acknowledgements

We are particularly grateful to Michael Clarkson for careful reading of an earlier draft, and for his perceptive questions and comments. In addition, we would like to thank the anonymous WISSec'09 reviewers for helpful remarks.

## References

1. Abadi, M., Blanchet, B., Fournet, C.: Just fast keying in the pi calculus. ACM Transactions on Information and System Security (TISSEC) 10(3), 1–59 (2007)
2. Abadi, M., Fournet, C.: Mobile values, new names, and secure communication. In: POPL 2001: Proceedings of the 28th ACM Symposium on Principles of Programming Languages, pp. 104–115. ACM, New York (2001)
3. Adida, B., de Marneffe, O., Pereira, O., Quisquater, J.-J.: Electing a university president using open-audit voting: Analysis of real-world use of Helios. In: Electronic Voting Technology/Workshop on Trustworthy Elections, EVT/WOTE (2009)
4. Backes, M., Hritcu, C., Maffei, M.: Automated verification of remote electronic voting protocols in the applied pi-calculus. In: CSF 2008: Proceedings of the 21st IEEE Computer Security Foundations Symposium, Washington, USA, pp. 195–209. IEEE, Los Alamitos (2008)
5. Backes, M., Maffei, M., Unruh, D.: Zero-Knowledge in the Applied Pi-calculus and Automated Verification of the Direct Anonymous Attestation Protocol. Cryptology ePrint Archive: Report 2007/289 (July 2007)
6. Backes, M., Maffei, M., Unruh, D.: Zero-Knowledge in the Applied Pi-calculus and Automated Verification of the Direct Anonymous Attestation Protocol. In: S&P 2008: Proceedings of the 2008 IEEE Symposium on Security and Privacy, Washington, DC, USA, pp. 202–215. IEEE Computer Society, Los Alamitos (2008)
7. Baskar, A., Ramanujam, R., Suresh, S.P.: Knowledge-based modelling of voting protocols. In: TARK 2007: Proceedings of the 11th International Conference on Theoretical Aspects of Rationality and Knowledge, pp. 62–71. ACM, New York (2007)
8. Blanchet, B.: Automatic verification of correspondences for security protocols. Journal of Computer Security 17(4), 363–434 (2009)
9. Bowen, D.: Secretary of State Debra Bowen Moves to Strengthen Voter Confidence in Election Security Following Top-to-Bottom Review of Voting Systems. California Secretary of State (August 2007), press release DB07:042, `http://www.sos.ca.gov/elections/voting_systems/ttbr/db07_042_ttbr_system_decisions_release.pdf`
10. Bundesverfassungsgericht (Germany's Federal Constitutional Court). Use of voting computers in 2005 Bundestag election unconstitutional (March 2009), Press release 19/2009, `http://www.bundesverfassungsgericht.de/en/press/bvg09-019en.html`
11. Chevallier-Mames, B., Fouque, P.-A., Pointcheval, D., Stern, J., Traore, J.: On Some Incompatible Properties of Voting Schemes. In: WOTE 2006: Proceedings of the International Association for Voting Systems Sciences Workshop on Trustworthy Elections (2006)

12. Clarkson, M.R., Chong, S., Myers, A.C.: Civitas: Toward a secure voting system. Technical Report 2007-2081, Cornell University (May 2007), http://hdl.handle.net/1813/7875 (Revised, March 2008)
13. Clarkson, M.R., Chong, S., Myers, A.C.: Civitas: Toward a secure voting system. In: S&P 2008: Proceedings of the 2008 IEEE Symposium on Security and Privacy, pp. 354–368. IEEE Computer Society, Los Alamitos (2008)
14. Delaune, S., Kremer, S., Ryan, M.D.: Verifying privacy-type properties of electronic voting protocols. Journal of Computer Security 17(4), 435–487 (2009)
15. Dolev, D., Yao, A.C.: On the security of public key protocols. Information Theory 29, 198–208 (1983)
16. Fujioka, A., Okamoto, T., Ohta, K.: A Practical Secret Voting Scheme for Large Scale Elections. In: ASIACRYPT 1992: Proceedings of the Workshop on the Theory and Application of Cryptographic Techniques, London, pp. 244–251. Springer, Heidelberg (1992)
17. Jakobsson, M., Juels, A.: Mix and match: Secure function evaluation via ciphertexts. In: Okamoto, T. (ed.) ASIACRYPT 2000. LNCS, vol. 1976, pp. 162–177. Springer, Heidelberg (2000)
18. Juels, A., Catalano, D., Jakobsson, M.: Coercion-Resistant Electronic Elections. Cryptology ePrint Archive, Report 2002/165 (2002)
19. Juels, A., Catalano, D., Jakobsson, M.: Coercion-resistant electronic elections. In: WPES 2005: Proceedings of the 2005 ACM workshop on Privacy in the electronic society, pp. 61–70. ACM, New York (2005), http://www.rsa.com/rsalabs/node.asp?id=2860
20. Kremer, S., Ryan, M., Smyth, B.: Election verifiability in electronic voting protocols. Technical Report CSR-10-06, University of Birmingham (2010)
21. Ministerie van Binnenlandse Zaken en Koninkrijksrelaties (Netherland's Ministry of the Interior and Kingdom Relations). Stemmen met potlood en papier (Voting with pencil and paper) (May 2008), Press release, http://www.minbzk.nl/onderwerpen/grondwet-en/verkiezingen/nieuws-en/112441/stemmen-met-potlood
22. Participants of the Dagstuhl Conference on Frontiers of E-Voting. Dagstuhl accord. (2007), http://www.dagstuhlaccord.org/
23. Sako, K., Kilian, J.: Secure voting using partially compatible homomorphisms. In: Desmedt, Y.G. (ed.) CRYPTO 1994. LNCS, vol. 839, pp. 411–424. Springer, Heidelberg (1994)
24. Talbi, M., Morin, B., Tong, V.V.T., Bouhoula, A., Mejri, M.: Specification of Electronic Voting Protocol Properties Using ADM Logic: FOO Case Study. In: Chen, L., Ryan, M.D., Wang, G. (eds.) ICICS 2008. LNCS, vol. 5308, pp. 403–418. Springer, Heidelberg (2008)
25. UK Electoral Commission. Key issues and conclusions: May 2007, electoral pilot schemes (2007) http://www.electoralcommission.org.uk/elections/pilots/May2007
26. Woo, T.Y.C., Lam, S.S.: A semantic model for authentication protocols. In: S&P 1993: Proceedings of the 1993 IEEE Symposium on Security and Privacy, Washington, DC, USA, pp. 178–194. IEEE Computer Society, Los Alamitos (1993)

# AnBx - Security Protocols Design and Verification*

Michele Bugliesi and Paolo Modesti

Università Ca' Foscari Venezia
Dipartimento di Informatica
{bugliesi,modesti}@dsi.unive.it

**Abstract.** Designing distributed protocols is challenging, as it requires actions at very different levels: from the choice of network-level mechanisms to protect the exchange of sensitive data, to the definition of structured interaction patterns to convey application-specific guarantees. Current security infrastructures provide very limited support for the specification of such guarantees. As a consequence, the high-level security properties of a protocol typically must often be hard-coded explicitly, in terms of low-level cryptographic notions and devices which clutter the design and undermine its scalability and robustness.

To counter these problems, we propose an extended *Alice & Bob* notation for protocol narrations (`AnBx`) to be employed for a purely declarative modelling of distributed protocols. These abstractions provide a compact specification of the high-level security guarantees they convey, and help shield the design from the details of the underlying cryptographic infrastructure. We discuss an implementation of the abstractions based on a translation from the `AnBx` notation to the AnB language supported by the OFMC [1,2] verification tool. We show the practical effectiveness of our approach by revisiting the $iKP$ e-payment protocols, and showing that the security goals achieved by our declarative specification outperform those offered by the original protocols.

## 1 Introduction

On-line transactions represent an important share of the overall world trade and security constitutes a major concern in these kind of applications, as agreeing, on the terms of a transaction in a distributed and open environment like the internet, requires protection against threats from intruders and/or from the potential misbehavior of other participants. Establishing the desired safeguards is challenging as it involves actions at different levels: from the choice of core, network-level mechanisms to protect the exchange of sensitive data, to the definition of structured, application-specific measures to enforce the high-level behavioral invariants of the participants. Current security infrastructures offer effective abstractions only for the core mechanisms, based on tools such as TLS/SSL [3]

* Work partially supported by MIUR Projects SOFT "*Security Oriented Formal Techniques*" and IPODS "*Interacting Processes in Open-ended Distributed Systems*".

A. Armando and G. Lowe (Eds.): ARSPA-WITS 2010, LNCS 6186, pp. 164–184, 2010.

to provide tunneling support for communication. On the other hand, little to no support is provided for the specification of more structured interaction patterns, so that high-level security invariants must typically be expressed, and hard-coded explicitly, in terms of low-level cryptographic notions such as salting, nonces, keyed-hashing, encryptions, signature schemes, and compositions thereof. As a result, the application code and data structures get intertwined with low-level code that not only gets in the way of a clear understanding of the applications' business logic, but also undermines its scalability and robustness.

To counter these problems, various papers in the recent literature (see, e.g., [4,5,6]) have advocated a programming discipline based on (*i*) high-level security abstractions and mechanisms for composing them to support structured interaction patterns [7,8], and (*ii*) automatic techniques to build defensive implementations on top of well-established cryptographic infrastructures and tools.

Following this line of research, in the present paper we isolate a core set of channel and data abstractions to be employed for a purely declarative modelling of distributed protocols. Our abstractions are part of `AnBx`, a dialect of the well-known *Alice & Bob* (AnB) notation for protocol narrations, which supports various mechanisms for securing remote communications based on abstract security *modes*, without any reference to explicit cryptography. The `AnBx` abstractions are readily translated into corresponding public-key cryptographic protocols described by standard AnB narrations. This provides an abstract, yet effective implementation of the `AnBx` specification language, to be employed as the basis for the development of fully-fledged implementation.

**Main contributions and results.** We developed a compiler for the automatic translation from `AnBx` to the AnB notation used in the symbolic model-checker OFMC (Open-source Fixed-point Model Checker [1,2]), and verified the soundness of our implementation with OFMC itself. The translation allows the verification of `AnBx` protocols with any OFMC-interoperable verification tool [9]. To experiment and validate the practical effectiveness of the `AnBx` approach to protocol design, we revisited the *iKP* e-payment protocol family (Internet Keyed Payment Protocol [10,11]) as a case study, and contrasted the security goals achieved by our version with those offered by the original protocol.

Interestingly, our `AnBx` versions of the iKP protocols outperform the original protocols (for all *i*'s), i.e. they satisfy stronger security goals and properties. This is largely a consequence of the declarative nature of the specification style supported by `AnBx`: being defined as channel-level abstractions, the `AnBx` primitives convey protection on *all* message components, not just on some components as in the original iKP specification, yielding stronger encapsulation mechanisms, and consequently, stronger and more scalable security guarantees. As a byproduct of our comparative analysis, we also found a (to the best of our knowledge) new flaw in the original specification of {2,3}KP, and proposed an amended version that rectifies the problem.

**Plan of the paper.** In Section 2 we introduce the `AnBx` specification language together with our high-level security abstractions; in Section 3 we outline a

**Table 1.** AnBx communication modes

| $\eta$ | *mode* | *semantics* |
|---|---|---|
| $(-,-)$ | plain | conveys no security guarantee |
| $(A,-)$ | from $A$ | a public, but *authentic* exchange which provides the receiver with a guarantee on the origin of the message |
| $(@A,-)$ | fresh from $A$ | $(A,-)$ with the additional guarantee that the message is fresh, and may not be replayed |
| $(-,B)$ | secret for $B$ | a *secret* transmission, providing guarantees that only the intended receiver $B$ will be exposed to the message payload: an intruder may become aware of the existence of an output, but not of the message contents |
| $(A,B)$ | from $A$, secret for $B$ | combines the guarantees of modes $(A,-)$ and $(-,B)$ |
| $(@A,B)$ | fresh from $A$, secret for $B$ | combines the guarantees of modes $(@A,-)$ and $(-,B)$ |
| $\uparrow \eta_0$ | forward | conveys some of the guarantees given by $\eta_0$ and signals that the message did not originate at the sender's; $\eta_0$ can not be a forward mode itself |

translation of the abstractions into a low-level, cryptographic language. In Section 4 we present the AnBx compiler that implements that translation using the AnB• cryptographic language supported by OFMC as a target, and discuss the soundness of the translation. In Section 5 we show the abstractions at work on the specification of the iKP protocols, and discuss their properties. Section 6 concludes the presentation.

## 2 AnBx: Declarative Protocol Narrations

Looking at the existing protocols for electronic transactions, such as e-payment, e-cash and e-voting, one notices that they are characterized by very specific interaction patterns, expressed by few messaging primitives and data structures. In this section, we isolate a core set of these primitives, and encode them in terms of (*i*) different *modes* for remote communication, and of (*ii*) a hiding transformer on data. We inject these modes and the data transformer into an extended version of the familiar AnB specifications for security protocols, whose syntax may be defined as follows:

| | |
|---|---|
| $A : \alpha$ | local action performed by $A$ |
| $i.\ A \rightarrow B, \eta : m$ | $A$ sends a message $m$ to $B$ in mode $\eta$ (symmetrically $\leftarrow$receives from) |

The action statements $A : \alpha$ may be employed to specify operations performed by a principal, such as the generation of a new key or a test evaluation, as well

**Table 2.** AnBx forward modes

| $A \to B, \eta_0 : m$ | $B \to C, \eta_1 : m$ | *mode* | *semantics* |
| --- | --- | --- | --- |
| $(-, C)$ | $\uparrow (-, C)$ | blind | - Secrecy for $C$ is preserved<br>- $B$ is not exposed to $m$ |
| $(A, C)$ | $\uparrow (A, C)$ | blind | - Authenticity from $A$ is preserved<br>- Secrecy for $C$ is preserved<br>- $B$ is not exposed to $m$ |
| $(A, -)$<br>$(A, B)$<br>$(@A, -)$<br>$(@A, B)$ | $\uparrow (A, -)$ | sighted | - Authenticity from $A$ is preserved<br>- Freshness (if present) is lost<br>- $B$ is exposed to $m$ |
| $(A, -)$<br>$(A, B)$<br>$(@A, -)$<br>$(@A, B)$ | $\uparrow (A, C)$ | sighted secret | - Authenticity from $A$ is preserved<br>- Freshness (if present) is lost<br>- Secrecy for $C$ is added to $m$, but C can not make any assumption on secrecy at origin $A$<br>- $B$ is exposed to $m$ |

as to declare the initial knowledge that we assume is available to the principal. In the exchange statements $i.\ A \to B, \eta :\ m$, $i$ is an index labelling a protocol step: the mode $\eta$ and the format of the message $m$ are discussed below.

**Message formats.** An important aspect of our abstractions is the choice of the message formats. A message may either be a tuple of names ($\tilde{n}$), or a reference to a message exchanged at a previous protocol step ($\uparrow i$), or a message digest $[\tilde{m}]$. Notice that no explicit cryptographic operator is available for message formation, and the only operation on data is the creation of *digests* (or footprints) needed in most e-commerce and e-voting protocols: being able to form $[m]$ proves the knowledge of $m$ without leaking it. We assume digests to be resistant to chosen-plaintext attacks, hence presuppose an implementation based on a hashing scheme that packages $m$ together with a randomized quantity known to the principals that possess $m$ (the designated verifier of $[m]$), and is never leaked to any principals that do not have knowledge of $m$. To ease the implementation, we allow digests to be tagged with an annotation that specifies the intended verifier, as in $[\tilde{m} : B]$.

**Communication modes.** Following [12,13], our abstractions encompass two fundamental mechanisms for security, based on secrecy and authentication, and include the communication modes that result from their possible combinations. The mode $\eta$ is encoded by a pair (*source*, *destination*) that qualifies the security guarantees conveyed at the two end-points of the remote communication. The structure and the informal reading of the communication modes are described in Table 1.

**Forward modes.** They can be used to model some three party exchanges, in $n$-party protocols where $n > 2$. The statement $B \to C, \eta_1 : m$ with $\eta_1 = \uparrow\eta$

expresses the intention of $B$ to forward a message $m$ to $C$. The statement is legal just in case $B$ has been the target of a previous exchange $A \to B, \eta_0 : m$, where $m$ is the same in both statements (or else $m = \uparrow i$ where $i$ is the label identifying the $A \to B$ exchange).

When this is the case, the mode $\eta$ used in the forward statement will preserve, and possibly extend, the security properties specified by $\eta_0$. There are additional coherence constraints that must be satisfied when specifying the mode of an exchange, to rule out unwanted effects of impersonation, and other inconsistencies that would result into unexecutable or broken protocols:

- the legal combination of $\eta_0$ and $\eta_1$ only are those in Table 2 and they specify possible forward modes;
- in $A \to B, \eta : m$, $\eta$ may not specify a source other than $A$, unless $\eta$ is a forward mode;
- if $\eta$ specifies a destination other than $B$, then $m$ can be forwarded only blindly.

## 3 A Cryptographic Translation for AnBx

We outline a translation of the abstract specification language we just introduced into an intermediate representation based on few, well defined building blocks: keys, cryptographic operations and primitives for remote communication. The intermediate notation, displayed in Table 3, is derived from the well known AnB security protocol notation, and represents the low-level counterpart of the AnBx abstract notation discussed in Section 2. The core resulting from the translation can then be further compiled against a specific and concrete target (operating system, programming language, cryptographic libraries, network protocols, etc) to produce the running code.

This translation is based on public key cryptography, and presupposes the existence of a Public Key Infrastructure (PKI) supporting a robust distribution (and use) of public keys and certificates (including their verification). We also assume that the underling PKI supports dual key pairs, for encryption and digital signatures [14]. Each AnBx principal may thus possess up to two pairs of certified encryption keys: if it does posses both key pairs, we say that the principal is *certified.*

We also use symmetric encryption schemes, which are notoriously computationally more efficient than the asymmetric counterpart. Ideally perfect encryption is assumed and the hashing functions are expected to be collision-free and non-invertible. Practically, the *secrecy* notion we expect is the standard computational secrecy, i.e. all polynomial time adversaries have negligible success probabilities. This allows us to use real cryptographic protocols for a concrete implementation.

**Communication Modes Translation.** Table 4 summarizes the translation of the different AnBx communication modes into a sequence of AnB statements and shows which principals must be certified. In a real implementation we could

**Table 3.** AnB-like Intermediate Syntax Notation

| *syntax* | *description* |
|---|---|
| $(PK_A, PK_A^{-1})$ | long term (pub, priv) key pair used by principal $A$ for encryption |
| $(SK_A, SK_A^{-1})$ | long term (pub, priv) key pair used by $A$ for signature |
| $\{m\}_{PK_A}$ | message $m$ encrypted with the public key $P_{KA}$ of principal $A$ |
| $\{m\}_{PK_A^{-1}}$ | message $m$ decrypted with the private key $PK_A^{-1}$ by principal $A$ |
| $\{m\}_K \quad \{m\}_{K^{-1}}$ | message $m$ encrypted (decrypted) with a symmetric key $K$ |
| $\{H(m)\}_{SK_A^{-1}} \equiv sig_A(m)$ | digital signature of the message $m$, signed by principal $A$, where $H$ is the hash function specified by the digital signature scheme |
| $(m, sig_A(m)) \equiv S_A(m)$ | message $m$ digitally signed by principal $A$ |
| $n_A$ | nonce generated by principal $A$ |
| $new\ K$ | fresh symmetric key, randomly generated |
| $g^x \mod p$<br>$g^y \mod p$ | fresh half keys generated during a discrete logarithm based agreement protocol (e.g. Diffie-Hellman), where $p$ is prime and $g$ is primitive root $mod\, p$ |
| $g^{xy}$ | fresh symmetric key, computed using a discrete logarithm based agreement protocol ($mod\, p$ is omitted in the notation) |
| $Hmac_K(m)$ | HMAC of message $m$, computed with the key $K$ |
| $A : \alpha$ | action $\alpha$ performed by principal $A$ |
| $A \rightarrow B : m$ | $A$ sends a message $m$ to principal $B$ (symmetrically $\leftarrow$) |

include, for robustness, also some additional information (tags) such as protocol name, version, step number, process identifier, origin, destination, but at this level of abstraction we can skip these details.

The *authenticity* property enforced by the "*fresh from*" mode corresponds to Lowe's injective agreement [15] while the property enforced by the "*from*" mode corresponds to Lowe's non-injective agreement. In the former case we say that $B$ authenticates $A$ on $m$, while in the latter the authentication is only *weak*. We use mostly standard techniques, hence here we will underline only few additional points.

- in *authentic* exchanges the identity of the intended recipient $B$ is included to comply with the definition of the Lowe's non-injective agreement, (injective for *fresh* exchanges) [15];
- in *secret* exchanges we use a hybrid construction, with the fresh symmetric key $K$ acting as a confounder. If both, key and data encapsulation schemes, are secure against adaptive chosen ciphertext attacks, then the hybrid scheme inherits that property as well [16];
- combining authenticity and secrecy, we first sign and then encrypt [17];

**Table 4.** Exchange Modes Translation of $A \to B, \eta : m$

| $\eta$ | *mode* | *translation* | *certified* |
|---|---|---|---|
| $(-,-)$ | plain | $A \to B:\ m$ | - |
| $(A,-)$ | from $A$ | $A \to B:\ S_A(B,m)$ | $A$ |
| $(-,B)$ | secret for $B$ | $A:\ new\ K$<br>$A \to B:\ \{K\}_{PK_B}, \{m\}_K$ | $B$ |
| $(A,B)$ | from $A$,<br>secret for $B$ | $A:\ new\ K$<br>$A \to B:\ \{K\}_{PK_B}, \{S_A(B,m)\}_K$ | $A,B$ |
| $(@A,-)$ | fresh from $A$ | $A \to B:\ A$<br>$A \leftarrow B:\ \{n_B, B\}_{PK_A}$<br>$A \to B:\ \{n_B, sig_A(B,m)\}_{PK_B}, S_A(B,m)$ | $A,B$ |
| $(@A,-)$ | fresh from $A$<br>with DH* | $A \to B:\ g^x$<br>$A \leftarrow B:\ \{g^y, n_B, B\}_{PK_A}$<br>$A \to B:\ \{n_B, sig_A(B,m)\}_{g^{xy}}, S_A(B,m)$ | $A$ |
| $(@A,B)$ | fresh from $A$,<br>secret for $B$ | $A \to B:\ A$<br>$A \leftarrow B:\ \{n_B, B\}_{PK_A}$<br>$A:\ new\ K$<br>$A \to B:\ \{n_B, K\}_{PK_B}, \{S_A(B,m)\}_K$ | $A,B$ |

* this translation is used only when the intended recipient $B$ is not certified, and therefore the standard *fresh from A* can not be applied

**Table 5.** Forward modes translation

| $\eta_0$ | $\eta_1$ | *mode* | $m_1$ | *certified* | *notes* |
|---|---|---|---|---|---|
| $(-,C)$ | $\uparrow(-,C)$ | blind | $\{K\}_{PK_C}, \{m\}_K$ | $C$ | $m_0 = m_1$ |
| $(A,C)$ | $\uparrow(A,C)$ | blind | $\{K\}_{PK_C}, \{S_A(C,m)\}_K$ | $A,C$ | $m_0 = m_1$ |
| $(A,-)$<br>$(@A,-)$ | $\uparrow(A,-)$ | sighted | $S_A(C,B,msg)$ | $A$ | $m_1 \subseteq m_0$<br>$m = C, msg$ |
| $(A,B)$<br>$(@A,B)$ | $\uparrow(A,-)$ | sighted | $S_A(C,B,msg)$ | $A,B$ | $m_1 \subseteq m_0$<br>$m = C, msg$ |
| $(A,-)$<br>$(@A,-)$ | $\uparrow(A,C)$ | sighted secret | $\{K\}_{PK_C}, \{S_A(C,B,msg)\}_K$ | $A,C$ | $S_A(C,B,msg) \subseteq m_0$<br>$m = C, msg$ |
| $(A,B)$<br>$(@A,B)$ | $\uparrow(A,C)$ | sighted secret | $\{K\}_{PK_C}, \{S_A(C,B,msg)\}_K$ | $A,B,C$ | $S_A(C,B,msg) \subseteq m_0$<br>$m = C, msg$ |

AnBx specification: $A \to B, \eta_0 : m;\ B \to C, \eta_1 : m$

$m_1 \subseteq m_0$ : message $m_1$ is a component of message $m_0$

**Table 6.** Message Formats Translation (digest formed by principal $A$)

| *digest* | *translation* | *certified* | *notes* |
|---|---|---|---|
| $[m : B]$ | $A : new\ K$<br>$A \rightarrow B : Hmac_K(m), \{K\}_{PK_B}$ | $B$ | *Obfuscated verifiable digest*<br>Can be verified only by B,<br>if B knows $m$<br>(besides the digest's creator A) |
| $[m : -]$ | $A : new\ K$<br>$A \rightarrow B : Hmac_K(m)$ | - | *Obfuscated unverifiable digest*<br>Cannot be verified by anyone<br>(except the digest's creator A) |
| $[m]$ | $\mathscr{H}(m)$ | - | *Plain digest*<br>Can be verified by everyone knowing $m$<br>$\mathscr{H}$ cryptographic hash function |
| $[m : C]$ | $p : new\ K$<br>$p \rightarrow C : \{\mathscr{H}(m_p)\}, \{K_p\}_{PK_C}$ | $C$ | *Digest verifiable by proxy*<br>$p \in \{A, B\}$<br>C can notify to any principal if<br>$\mathscr{H}(m_A) = \mathscr{H}(m_B)$ or not |

- in *fresh* exchanges we use a challenge-response technique based on nonces. We do not use timestamps, because they require synchronization (time servers), and this introduces more complexity (attacks, failures, etc);
- in *fresh from* exchanges, when the intended recipient is not certified, we use a combination of challenge-response and Diffie-Hellman key agreement protocol;

**Forward Modes Translation.** Table 5 outlines the translation of the forward modes. Each clause gives the translation of the statement $B \rightarrow C, \eta_1, m$ with reference to the statement $A \rightarrow B, \eta_0, m$ that originated $m$: we only give the translation for the legal combinations of $\eta_0, \eta_1$: in all other cases the translation is undefined.

Given that the forward modes in $\eta_1$ will never include the freshness tag @, the translation of $B \rightarrow C, \eta_1, m$ amounts to just one AnB step, $B \rightarrow C, m_1$ with $m_1$ as defined in Table 5.

Notice that $m_1$ is always defined in terms of $m_0$, which is the closing *AnB* message resulting from the translation of the reference `AnBx` statement $A \rightarrow B, \eta_0, m$. In the *sighted* modes, the presence of the identities $B$ and $C$ is necessary because both principals have to authenticate A on $msg$, which represents the real high level payload of the three-party exchange.

**Message Format Translation.** (Table 6). As we observed, an implementation of a message digest $[m]$ should guarantee that the only principals entitled to verify that $[m]$ matches $m$ are those who already know $m$, either as initial information, or provided explicitly by a legitimate source. In addition, a robust implementation should protect the digest against chosen-plaintext attacks, and additionally guarantee that even in case $m$ is disclosed to a non-legitimate principal any time in the future, that principal should not be able to use $m$ to match $[m]$.

These guarantees can be made by interpreting (and translating) the digest formation in terms of a hashing scheme that packages $m$ together with a randomized quantity known to the principals that possess $m$, and never leaked to any principals that do not have knowledge of $m$. A hashing scheme with these properties is supported by what is known as keyed-Hash Message Authentication Code (HMAC).

The subtlety in our translation is in the way the secret keys are made available to the legitimate principals, as the structure of the digest $[m]$ does not inform on who is intended to act as the digest's verifier. In certain cases, that information may be recovered by an analysis of the initial knowledge of the participants. However, in general, it requires the designer's intervention to tag each digest occurrence $[m]$ with an annotation $[m : B]$ that signals that $B$ is the designated verifier of $[m]$ (a digest can also be always verified by its creator). Table 6 illustrates the translation scheme for digests based on these additional annotations also proposing alternatives when the digest cannot directly be verified, due to the lack of certification of some participant. When and how to use these alternatives should be carefully evaluated since it could allow an intruder to perform downgrade attacks.

## 4 Implementing the Translation: The `AnBx` Compiler

We have implemented the `AnBx` translation previously outlined using a subset of the AnB cryptographic language supported by the OFMC model checker as a target. In this section, we briefly outline the implementation and discuss its soundness.

**An overview of OFMC.** OFMC [1,2]) supports two protocol specification languages, the Intermediate Format (IF) and a dialect of the AnB style of protocol narrations, that we will refer to as OFMC-AnB. Details about of OFMC-AnB can be found in [18] and in documentation included in the OFMC software package, so we will give a very short description. A protocol specification comprises various sections:

- `Types`: describes the entities (agents/principals) involved in the protocol, as well as protocol data and data operators (constants, cryptographic functions, ... etc.)
- `Knowledge`: specifies the initial knowledge of each principal
- `Actions`: specifies the sequence of statements that constitute the ideal, unattacked run of the protocol;
- `Goals`: specifies the goals that the protocol is meant to convey.

A sample specification is reported in Table 7, where we give the AnB narration of the low-level translation for the "fresh-from" `AnBx` messaging primitive.

`Msg` is the message being authenticated, using `N1` to complete the nonce-exchange; `pk` and `sk`, generate the public keys for encryption and signing. Each

**Table 7.** AnB OFMC specification of "*fresh from*" mode

```
Protocol: Fresh_From_A
Types:
    Agent A,B;
    Number Msg,N1;
    Function pk,sk,hash
Knowledge:
    A: A,B,pk,sk,inv(pk(A)),inv(sk(A));
    B: A,B,pk,sk,inv(pk(B)),inv(sk(B))
Actions:
    A -> B: A
    B -> A: {N1,B}pk(A)
    A -> B: {N1,hash({B,Msg}inv(sk(A)))}pk(B),{B,Msg}inv(sk(A))
Goals:
    B authenticates A on Msg
```

principal is assumed to know its own and its partner's identities, the public key of all known principals and its own private keys. The specification is completed with the authentication goal for the transmitted message `Msg`. This goal already implies the freshness of the message, since in OFMC authenticity goals correspond to the requirements of Lowe's injective agreement.

**`AnBx` and its compiler.** `AnBx` is defined as a variant of OFMC-AnB that supports the messaging modes discussed in §2 as well as few additional features in the preamble sections. A sample `AnBx` specification is reported in Table 8, where we give the `AnBx` specification of the "fresh from" messaging primitive. Notice that while in the action section we use `AnBx` syntax to specify the transmission modes, the protocol goals are expressed by means of OFMC-AnB goal statements.

Given an `AnBx` specification, the compiler generates a corresponding OFMC-AnB protocol specification that results from composing the translations of each `AnBx` statement into a corresponding OFMC-AnB protocol, as outlined in §3. Thus, while `AnBx` supports abstract messaging primitives for secrecy and authentication, the code generated by the compiler only involves standard, "plain"

**Table 8.** `AnBx` specification of "*fresh from*" mode

```
Protocol: Fresh_From_A Types:
    Agent A,B;
    Certified A,B;
    Number M1,M2;
    Function id
Definitions
    Msg: M1,M2
Knowledge:
    A: A,B;
    B: A,B
Actions:
    A -> B,(@A,-): Msg
Goals:
    B authenticates A on Msg
```

message exchanges, and relies of the cryptographic constructions of §3 to achieve the desired security guarantees. In addition to generating the AnB protocol steps, the compiler creates the entries in the preamble sections (`Types` and `Knowledge`) required to make a consistent OFMC-AnB specification. To illustrate, the AnB protocol in table 7 is, in fact, the result of compiling the `AnBx` in Table 8.

One may wonder why we did not take advantage of the bulleted OFMC-AnB channels in our translation. The fact is that the combination of the three OFMC basic channel types (authentic, confidential, secure) does not allow one to express communication patterns as those defined by the forward modes.

This can be easily seen if we try to build the following *sighted forward* exchange: $A \rightarrow B, (@A, -) : m$, $B \rightarrow C, \uparrow (A, -) : m$ . If we attempt to use a bulleted channel to translate the first instruction, as in `A*->B:B,m`, there is no bulleted equivalent to express the second one. On the other hand, if we provide a translation over a plain channel for the second instruction as the following, `B->C:{B,C,Msg}inv(sk(A))`, OFMC will deem the protocol non-runnable. In fact OFMC works at the symbolic level, and the term `{B,C,Msg}inv(sk(A))` can be used in the second instruction only if it is has appeared earlier in the network, because only principal $A$ could have created such a term, being the only one knowing `inv(sk(A))`. Therefore OFMC rejects a protocol where the term `{B,C,Msg}inv(sk(A))` appears for the first time in an exchange originating from $B$. In other words, there is no way to bind the bulleted and the unbulleted channels in order to satisfy the expected goals for the forward modes. Hence in order to provide a coherent translation of all `AnBx` modes we need the plain channel as target in all cases.

**Soundness.** To verify the soundness of the implementation, we coded in OFMC-AnB all the `AnBx` primitives listed in §3, defining the expected security goals. The full list is given in Appendix (Table 13). Then we ran OFMC to verify the safety of each protocol. We tested, successfully, all the resulting protocols with OFMC, in one and two sessions (both typed and untyped) with the classical mode. Most protocols were also verified in classical typed mode up to four sessions. We also checked the new fixpoint module for unbounded number of sessions, but limited to secrecy and weak authenticity goals, which are the only goals currently supported by OFMC 2009c.

**A note on compositionality.** Having validated the implementation of each `AnBx` primitive against its expected goals does not in itself provide any validation guarantee on the implementation of a structured `AnBx` specification. In fact, composing the implementation protocols resulting from the translation of each `AnBx` step may, in principle, break the security guarantees provided by each of the component protocols: this is an instance of the well-known compositionality problems in security. While we do not yet have a formal compositionality proof for our translations, we are confident that such result can be proved: in fact, the implementation protocols satisfy all the static conditions, such as the use of encryption keys from disjoint key-spaces that constitute the standard sufficient conditions for compositionality.

In addition, although compositionality is certainly an interesting and useful property, it does not represent a primary concern for our present endeavour. Our main interest is in making `AnBx` interoperable with existing verification tools like OFMC rather than in defining a new tool. Thus, as long as the security goals of a given `AnBx` protocol narration provide an adequate specification of the security properties we expect of the protocol, we may safely content ourselves with validating the AnB protocol resulting from our translation, rather than the `AnBx` specification itself.

A similar approach is gaining popularity in the literature on typed process calculi targeted at the specification of distributed protocols and systems (see, e.g., [19,20]). In these papers, the typed calculi provide for idealized specifications which are implemented by translations into low-level, but still typed, cryptographic languages. Rather than showing the translations sound, the process calculi specifications are shown secure by directly proving that *the result of the translations* are secure, just as we propose here: the difference is that in a typed calculus, security is by (well) typing, while in `AnBx` we prove security by model-checking.

## 5 A Case Study: e-Payment Systems

We show `AnBx` at work on the specification of systems for e-payment. We start by outlining a general e-payment scheme which captures the essential ingredients of most of the existing e-payment protocols, among which IBM's iKP [10,11], SET [21] and 3-D Secure [22] adopted by VISA.

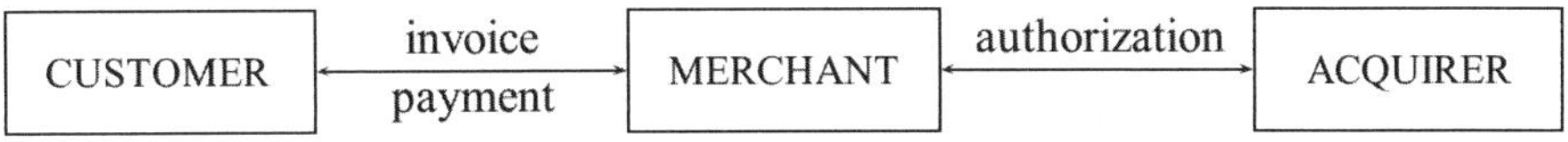


Each principal has an initial knowledge shared with other participants. In particular, since most e-commerce protocols describe only the payment transaction, we assume that customer and merchant have agreed on a *contract*, that includes an *order description* (*desc*) and a *price*. We also assume that payments are based on existing credit-card systems operated by an acquirer who shares with the customer the *customer's account number (can)* comprising the credit card number and the associated PIN. In summary, the initial knowledge of the parties is the following:

- Customer $C$: *price, desc, can*
- Merchant $M$: *price, desc*
- Acquirer $A$: *can*

To make each transaction univocally identified, the merchant generates a unique transaction ID (*tid*) and associates the transaction also with a *date* (or any appropriate time information). Both pieces of information must be communicated to the other parties. Summarizing, the transaction is characterized by the the tuple *(price, tid, date, can, desc)* which also constitutes the payment order information: if customer and merchant reach an agreement on this tuple, and they can prove their agreement to the acquirer, then the transaction can be completed successfully.

However, two security concerns arise here: on the one hand, customers typically wish to avoid leaking credit-card information to the merchant; on the other hand, customers and the merchant would not let the acquirer know the details of the order or the services involved in the transaction. Both these requirements can be enforced by protecting the exchange of *can* and *desc* with the digests we introduced in Section 2 and implemented as described in Table 6. The tuple that represent the *contract* among the three parties may thus be represented as $(price, tid, date, [can][desc])$, while *auth* is the transaction authorization result returned by the acquirer.

**Revisiting iKP.** The *i*KP protocol family {i=1,2,3} was developed at IBM Research [10,11,23] to support credit card-based transactions between customers and merchants (under the assumption that payment clearing and authorization may be handled securely off-line). All protocols in the family are based on public-key cryptography, and vary in the number of parties that own individual public key-pairs to generate digital signatures: this is reflected by the name of the different protocols – 1KP, 2KP, 3KP – which offer increasing levels of security. The structure of all the protocols can be specified by means of the `AnBx` messaging primitives as follows:

1. $C \rightarrow M, \eta_1 : [can : A], [desc : M]$
2. $C \leftarrow M, \eta_2 : price, tid, date, [contract]$
3. $C \rightarrow M, \eta_3 : price, tid, can, [can : A], [contract]$
4. $M \rightarrow A$
   (a) $M \rightarrow A, \eta_{4a} : price, tid, can, [can : A], [contract]$
   (b) $M \rightarrow A, \eta_{4b} : price, tid, date, [desc : M], [contract]$
5. $M \leftarrow A, \eta_5 : auth, tid, [contract]$
6. $C \leftarrow M, \eta_6 : auth, tid, [contract]$

The digests $[can]$ and $[desc]$ are annotated with their intended verifiers, $A$ and $M$ respectively (in 1KP $[desc]$ deserves some more care, as we will discuss shortly). Correspondingly, *contract* is the tuple $price, tid, date, [can : A], [desc : M]$ and its digests can be left as $[contract]$ as all the sensitive data is already protected against chosen plaintext attacks by the nested digests.

By instantiating the exchange modes $\eta_i$ one may generate different versions of the protocol, achieving different security guarantees. In Table 9 we report the protocols resulting from the choice of the exchange modes $\eta_i$ that offer the strongest level of security for a given number $(i)$ of participants having public key-pairs at their disposal. The resulting protocols constitute the `AnBx` counterpart of the *i*Kp protocol family.

**Security Verification.** We verified the `AnBx` specifications of {1,2,3}KP by compiling them into OFMC-AnB and running OFMC on the generated protocols against the strongest possible goals, for each of the protocols.

**Table 9.** Exchange modes for the revisited iKP e-commerce protocol

| *mode/step* | $\rightarrow$ | 1KP | 2KP | 3KP |
|---|---|---|---|---|
| $\eta_1$ | $C \rightarrow M$ | $(-,-)$ | $(-,M)$ | $(@C,M)$ |
| $\eta_2$ | $C \leftarrow M$ | $(-,-)$ | $(@M,-)$ | $(@M,C)$ |
| $\eta_3$ | $C \rightarrow M$ | $(-,A)$ | $(-,A)$ | $(C,A)$ |
| $\eta_{4a}$ | $M \rightarrow A$ | $\uparrow(-,A)$ | $\uparrow(-,A)$ | $\uparrow(C,A)$ |
| $\eta_{4b}$ | $M \rightarrow A$ | $(-,A)$ | $(@M,A)$ | $(@M,A)$ |
| $\eta_5$ | $M \leftarrow A$ | $(@A,-)$ | $(@A,M)$ | $(@A,M)$ |
| $\eta_6$ | $C \leftarrow M$ | $\uparrow(A,-)$ | $\uparrow(A,-)$ | $\uparrow(A,C)$ |
| *certified* | | $A$ | $M,A$ | $C,M,A$ |

**Table 10.** Security goals satisfied by Original and Revised iKP

| | 1KP | | 2KP | | 3KP | |
|---|---|---|---|---|---|---|
| Goal | O | R | O | R | O | R |
| *can* secret between $C$,$A$ | - | - | - | - | + | + |
| $C \rightarrow *a$ : *can* | + | + | + | + | + | + |
| $A$ authenticates $C$ on *can* | - | - | - | - | - | + |
| *desc* secret between $C$,$M$ | + | + | + | + | + | + |
| *Auth* secret between $C$,$M$,$A$ | - | - | - | - | - | + |
| $M$ authenticates $A$ on *Auth* | - | + | +* | + | +* | + |
| $C$ authenticates $A$ on *Auth* | - | + | +* | + | +* | + |
| *tid* secret between $C$,$M$,$A$ | - | - | - | - | - | + |
| *price* secret between $C$,$M$,$A$ | - | - | - | - | - | + |
| [*contract*] secret between $C$,$M$,$A$ | - | - | - | - | - | + |
| a authenticates C on [*contract*] | - | - | - | + | + | + |
| a authenticates M on [*contract*] | - | - | - | + | + | + |

* goal satisfied only fixing the definition of $Sig_A$

We also carried out a corresponding analysis of the original specifications, as reported in [11] and later amended in [24]. Below, we refer to this amended version as the "original" iKP, to be contrasted with the "revised", `AnBx` version discussed above. In both versions, we run our tests assuming that the acquirer is trusted (technically, modelled as a constant in the OFMC specification). This appears reasonable in an e-commerce application, since the acquirer is always certified. Furthermore, to compare the results of the analysis we treated the messages *common* and *contract*, in the original and in the revised version, respectively, as equivalent (indeed, they do provide the same abstraction conceptually).

On each protocol, we ran OFMC in classic mode with 1 and 2 sessions (typed and untyped): with 2 sessions we were sometimes unable to complete the test due to search space explosion. We also ran intensive tests limiting the depth of the search space to remain within the available memory space (2Gb). Below, we report on the results of such tests. For 3KP, the `AnBx` code for the revised and the original versions is shown in the Appendix (Tables 11 and 12).

**Main results.** In general, our implementation of the iKP protocols outperforms the original version, i.e. it satisfies more and stronger security goals, for all $i$'s. This is largely due to the declarative nature of `AnBx` messaging primitives, which being defined as channel abstractions provide strong encapsulation mechanisms on the messages they exchange. One of the design goals of iKP was scalability, to support increasing security with the increase of the number of certified principals. In the original version, scalability is achieved by including extra components (e.g. signatures) in the messages exchanged in the different instances of the protocols. Conversely, the `AnBx` versions are naturally scalable, as the different instances of the protocol are simply encoded by tuning the exchange modes employed at the different steps (9). The only price to pay with respect to the original iKP is that we need to split step 4 in two substeps, plus one additional step to return the initiative to the merchant after step 4a. (Obviously the compiled AnB code involves more additional steps in order to achieve the freshness when required).

As we mentioned earlier, the `AnBx` specification are not just more scalable: they provide stronger security guarantees (cf. Table 13). During the analysis of the original 2KP and 3KP we found what, to the best of our knowledge, is a new flaw. It is related with the authenticity of the Authorization response (*auth*) that is generated by the acquirer and then sent to the other principals at step 5 and 6. The authenticity of the response is very important for the correct termination of the transaction because otherwise, in case of controversy customer and merchant could not rely on a robust proof of payment. The starred goals in Table 13 are met only after fixing this flaw that is in relation with how injective agreement is defined (and to its notion of authenticity). The change we propose is to add the identities of merchant and customer in $Sig_A$, adding the identities of merchant and customer (in 2KP this can be done with an ephemeral identity derived from the credit card number). Therefore in the original specification [11]: $Sig_A : \{hash(Auth, hash(Common))\}_{SK_A^{-1}}$ should be replaced by $Sig_A : \{hash(C, M, Auth, hash(Common))\}_{SK_A^{-1}}$.

Our revisited 2KP performs almost as good the original 3KP. The only goal not satisfied is *can* secret between *C,A*. This does not mean that the credit card is leaked but only that is not strongly authenticated by the acquirer. In 3KP the credit card number can be signed by C, whereas this is not possible in 2KP and 1KP (neither in the original, nor in the revised versions). In this case, the acquirer weakly authenticates the customer by means of the credit card number, which is a shared secret among the two parties.

We mentioned earlier that some care must be taken in the revisited version of 1KP to compute the digest [*desc:M*]. In fact $M$ is not certified, so we cannot calculate the digest verifiable by $M$ (Table 6). Therefore we must adopt one of the possible alternatives and this requires a slight modification of the protocol. If we decide to use the unverifiable digest, as done by the original iKP, it is advisable to have $M$ generate the digest rather than $C$, because *[can:A]* is already

**Table 11.** AnBx specification of revised 3KP

```
Protocol: Revised_3KP
Types:
  Agent C,Me,a;
  Certified C,Me,a;
  Number TID,Auth,Desc,Price;
  Function can
Definitions:
  Contract: Price,TID,dig(can(C),a),dig(Desc,Me)
Knowledge:
  C: C,Me,a,can(C);
  Me: C,Me,a;
  a: C,Me,a
Actions:
  # 0. Setup/Initial Knowledge
  C *->*Me: Price,Desc
  Me -> C: empty
  C -> Me,(@C,Me): dig(can(C),a),dig(Desc,Me)
  Me -> C,(@Me,C): TID,dig(Contract)
  C -> Me,(C,a): Price,TID,can(C),dig(can(C),a),dig(Contract)
  Me -> a,^(C,a): Price,TID,can(C),dig(can(C),a),dig(Contract)
  a -> Me: empty
  Me -> a,(@Me,a): Price,TID,dig(Desc,Me),dig(Contract)
  a  -> Me,(@a,Me): C,Auth,TID,dig(Contract)
  Me -> C,^(a,C): C,Auth,TID,dig(Contract)
Goals:
  can(C) secret between C,a
  a authenticates C on can(C)
  Desc secret between C,Me
  Auth secret between C,Me,a
  Me authenticates a on Auth
  C authenticates a on Auth
  TID secret between C,Me,a
  Price secret between C,Me,a
  dig(Contract) secret between C,Me,a
```

**Table 12.** Portion of the AnBx specification of original 3KP

```
Protocol: Original_3KP
Types:
  Agent C,Me,A;
  Certified C,Me,A;
  Number TID,Auth,empty,Desc,Price,ID,SALTC,SALTMe,V,VC,NONCE,RC;
  Function pk,sk,hash,hmac,can
Definitions:
  IDC: hmac(RC,can(C));
  Common: Price,ID,TID,NONCE,hmac(RC,can(C)),hmac(SALTC,Desc),hash(V),hash(VC);
  Clear: ID,TID,NONCE,hash(Common),hash(V),hash(VC);
  Slip: Price,hash(Common),can(C),RC,SALTMe;
  EncSlip: {Slip}pk(A);
  SigMe: {hash(Common),EncSlip}inv(sk(Me));
  SigC: {hash(EncSlip,hash(Common))}inv(pk(C));
  SigA: {C,Me,hash(Auth,hash(Common))}inv(sk(A))
Knowledge: [...]
Actions:
  C *->* Me: Price,Desc
  Me -> C: empty
  C -> Me: SALTC,IDC
  Me -> C: Clear,SigMe
  C -> Me: EncSlip,SigC
  Me -> A: Clear,hmac(SALTC,Desc),EncSlip,SigMe,SigC
  A -> Me: Auth, SigA
  Me -> C: Auth,SigA,V,VC
Goals: [...]
```

**Table 13.** Map of AnBx communication and forward modes

| *exchange* | *mode* | *OFMC goals* |
|---|---|---|
| **Communication Modes** - Tables 1,4 | | |
| $A \rightarrow B, (-,-) : Msg$ | plain | - |
| $A \rightarrow B, (A,-) : Msg$ | from $A$ | `B weakly authenticates A on Msg` |
| $A \rightarrow B, (@A,-) : Msg$ | fresh from $A$ | `B authenticates A on Msg` |
| $A \rightarrow B, (-,B) : Msg$ | secret for $B$ | `A->*B: Msg` |
| $A \rightarrow B, (A,B) : Msg$ | from $A$,<br>secret for $B$ | `B weakly authenticates A on Msg`<br>`Msg secret between A,B` |
| $A \rightarrow B, (@A,B) : Msg$ | fresh from $A$,<br>secret for $B$ | `B authenticates A on Msg`<br>`Msg secret between A,B` |
| **Forward Modes** - Tables 2,5 | | |
| $A \rightarrow B, (-,C) : Msg$<br>$B \rightarrow C, \uparrow (-,C) : Msg$ | blind | `A->*C: Msg` |
| $A \rightarrow B, (A,C) : Msg$<br>$B \rightarrow C, \uparrow (A,C) : Msg$ | blind | `Msg secret between A,C`<br>`C weakly authenticates A on Msg` |
| $A \rightarrow B, (A,-) : C, Msg$<br>$B \rightarrow C, \uparrow (A,-) : C, Msg$ | sighted | `B weakly authenticates A on Msg`<br>`C weakly authenticates A on Msg` |
| $A \rightarrow B, (A,B) : C, Msg$<br>$B \rightarrow C, \uparrow (A,-) : C, Msg$ | sighted | `B weakly authenticates A on Msg`<br>`C weakly authenticates A on Msg`<br>`A->*B: Msg` |
| $A \rightarrow B, (@A,-) : C, Msg$<br>$B \rightarrow C, \uparrow (A,-) : C, Msg$ | sighted | `B authenticates A on Msg`<br>`C weakly authenticates A on Msg` |
| $A \rightarrow B, (@A,B) : C, Msg$<br>$B \rightarrow C, \uparrow (A,-) : C, Msg$ | sighted | `B authenticates A on Msg`<br>`C weakly authenticates A on Msg`<br>`A->*B: Msg` |
| $A \rightarrow B, (A,-) : C, Msg$<br>$B \rightarrow C, \uparrow (A,C) : C, Msg$ | sighted<br>secret | `B weakly authenticates A on Msg`<br>`C weakly authenticates A on Msg` |
| $A \rightarrow B, (@A,-) : C, Msg$<br>$B \rightarrow C, \uparrow (A,C) : C, Msg$ | sighted<br>secret | `B authenticates A on Msg`<br>`C weakly authenticates A on Msg` |
| $A \rightarrow B, (A,B) : C, Msg$<br>$B \rightarrow C, \uparrow (A,C) : C, Msg$ | sighted<br>secret | `B weakly authenticates A on Msg`<br>`C weakly authenticates A on Msg`<br>`Msg secret between A,B,C` |
| $A \rightarrow B, (@A,B) : C, Msg$<br>$B \rightarrow C, \uparrow (A,C) : C, Msg$ | sighted<br>secret | `B authenticates A on Msg`<br>`C weakly authenticates A on Msg`<br>`Msg secret between A,B,C` |

generated by C, and since the digest generation implies the usage of fresh keys as confounders, it is appropriate that those two values are generated by two different principals. In 2KP and 3KP, [*desc*:$M$] is verifiable by $M$ and this concern is not present. Finally, we notice that in 1KP the only information really protected is the credit card number (Goal $C \rightarrow * a : can$). Since this is one of the main concerns of all e-commerce users, it is indeed good news.

## 6 Related Work and Conclusion

The benefits of a programming discipline based on high-level abstractions for security are increasingly being recognized as important in the design of distributed systems. We believe that the experience with `AnBx` we have reported in this paper provides further evidence of the advantages of the approach: as we have illustrated, using adequate abstractions results not only in simpler design, but also in a more robust code and stronger security. In fact, being defined as channel-level abstractions, the `AnBx` primitives convey protection on *all* message components, yielding stronger encapsulation mechanisms, and consequently, stronger and more scalable security guarantees.

Our approach shares motivations and ideas with various papers on design and implementation of high-level process calculi for distributed protocols and systems [4,25,26,6,27]. While related in their initial motivations, these approaches differ significantly from our present endeavour in their technical development. In addition, the abstractions we discuss here capture more expressive security mechanisms such as those needed in the design of structured e-commerce protocols. Some research more closely related to ours has been carried out in [28,29,2]. Guttman [28] has proposed a protocol design process centered on the authentication tests, a method for protocol verification based on the strand space theory. Guttman, Herzog, Ramsdell, and Sniffe [29] attached trust management assertions to protocol actions, constraining the behavior of a principal to be compatible with its own trust policy, and proposed the CPPL language for design and verification. However their language still makes use of cryptographic primitives while we avoid any reference to explicit cryptography.

Mödersheim and Viganò [2] described security protocols with three basic kinds of channels (authentic, confidential, secure). An Ideal and a Cryptographic Channel Model, describe the ideal functionality of the channels and the concrete cryptographic messages on insecure channels. The meaning of channels is defined as goals proving that, under certain restrictions, composing individually secure protocols results in a secure protocol. We used their OFMC tool [1,2] to verify the `AnBx` compiled protocols. Our set of channel modes has a wider extension with respect to the OFMC bulleted channels and in §4 we showed that our forward modes (and their associated goals) cannot be specified only by means of the bulleted channels.

Future plans include work along several directions. Specifically, we are interested in developing a typed version of our primitives to provide static support for security, according to the design principles that are often referred to as *language-based security.* The resulting typed abstractions could then be integrated into a programming language. Meanwhile we are coding a Java library to be used to experiment with real applications. Also, it would be interesting to investigate the effectiveness of our approach in expressing other properties, such as anonymity and privacy, and work with the corresponding application domains such as e-cash and e-voting.

## References

1. Basin, D., Mödersheim, S., Viganò, L.: OFMC: A symbolic model checker for security protocols. International Journal of Information Security 4(3), 181–208 (2005)
2. Mödersheim, S., Viganò, L.: The open-source fixed-point model checker for symbolic analysis of security protocols. In: Foundations of Security Analysis and Design V, p. 194. Springer, Heidelberg (2009)
3. Dierks, T., Allen, C.: Rfc2246: The TLS protocol version 1.0. Internet RFCs (1999)
4. Abadi, M., Fournet, C., Gonthier, G.: Authentication primitives and their compilation. In: Proceedings of the 27th ACM SIGPLAN-SIGACT symposium on Principles of programming languages, pp. 302–315. ACM, New York (2000)
5. Bugliesi, M., Focardi, R.: Language Based Secure Communication. In: IEEE 21st Computer Security Foundations Symposium, CSF 2008, pp. 3–16 (2008)
6. Adao, P., Fournet, C.: Cryptographically Sound Implementations for Communicating Processes. In: Bugliesi, M., Preneel, B., Sassone, V., Wegener, I. (eds.) ICALP 2006. LNCS, vol. 4052, pp. 83–94. Springer, Heidelberg (2006)
7. Corin, R., Dénielou, P.M., Fournet, C., Bhargavan, K., Leifer, J.J.: Secure implementations of typed session abstractions. In: CSF 2007, pp. 170–186. IEEE, Los Alamitos (2007)
8. Bhargavan, K., Corin, R., Dénielou, P.M., Fournet, C., Leifer, J.J.: Cryptographic protocol synthesis and verification for multiparty sessions. In: CSF 2009 (2009)
9. Armando, A., Basin, D., Boichut, Y., Chevalier, Y., Compagna, L., Cuellar, J., Drielsma, P., Héam, P., Kouchnarenko, O., Mantovani, J., et al.: The AVISPA tool for the automated validation of internet security protocols and applications. In: Etessami, K., Rajamani, S.K. (eds.) CAV 2005. LNCS, vol. 3576, pp. 281–285. Springer, Heidelberg (2005)
10. Bellare, M., Garay, J., Hauser, R., Herzberg, A., Krawczyk, H., Steiner, M., Tsudik, G., Waidner, M.: iKP A Family of Secure Electronic Payment Protocols. In: Proceedings of the 1st USENIX Workshop on Electronic Commerce (1995)
11. Bellare, M., Garay, J., Hauser, R., Herzberg, A., Krawczyk, H., Steiner, M., Tsudik, G., Van Herreweghen, E., Waidner, M.: Design, implementation, and deployment of the iKP secure electronic payment system. IEEE Journal on selected areas in communications 18(4), 611–627 (2000)
12. Maurer, U., Schmid, P.: A calculus for secure channel establishment in open networks. In: Gollmann, D. (ed.) ESORICS 1994. LNCS, vol. 875, p. 175. Springer, Heidelberg (1994)
13. van Doorn, L., Abadi, M., Burrows, M., Wobber, E.: Secure network objects. In: Secure Internet Programming, pp. 395–412 (1999)
14. Kelsey, J., Schneier, B., Wagner, D.: Protocol interactions and the chosen protocol attack. LNCS, pp. 91–104. Springer, Heidelberg (1998)
15. Lowe, G.: A hierarchy of authentication specifications, pp. 31–43. IEEE Computer Society Press, Los Alamitos (1997)

16. Cramer, R., Shoup, V.: Design and analysis of practical public-key encryption schemes secure against adaptive chosen ciphertext attack. SIAM Journal on Computing(Print) 33(1), 167–226 (2004)
17. Abadi, M., Needham, R.: Prudent engineering practice for cryptographic protocols. In: Proceedings of 1994 IEEE Computer Society Symposium on Research in Security and Privacy, pp. 122–136 (1994)
18. Mödersheim, S.: Algebraic properties in alice and bob notation. In: International Conference on Availability, Reliability and Security, pp. 433–440 (2009)
19. Backes, M., Hritcu, C., Maffei, M.: Type-checking zero-knowledge. In: Ning, P., Syverson, P.F., Jha, S. (eds.) ACM Conference on Computer and Communications Security, pp. 357–370. ACM, New York (2008)
20. Corin, R., Deniélou, P.M., Fournet, C., Bhargavan, K., Leifer, J.J.: A secure compiler for session abstractions. Journal of Computer Security 16(5), 573–636 (2008)
21. Bella, G., Massacci, F., Paulson, L.: An overview of the verification of SET. International Journal of Information Security 4(1), 17–28 (2005)
22. Visa: Visa 3-D Secure Specifications. Technical report (2002)
23. O'Mahony, D., Peirce, M., Tewari, H.: Electronic payment systems for e-commerce. Artech House Publishers (2001)
24. Ogata, K., Futatsugi, K.: Formal analysis of the iKP electronic payment protocols. LNCS, pp. 441–460. Springer, Heidelberg (2003)
25. Abadi, M., Fournet, C., Gonthier, G.: Secure implementation of channel abstractions. Information and computation(Print) 174(1), 37–83 (2002)
26. Abadi, M., Fournet, C.: Private authentication. Theor. Comput. Sci. 322(3), 427–476 (2004)
27. Bugliesi, M., Giunti, M.: Secure implementations of typed channel abstractions. In: Hofmann, M., Felleisen, M. (eds.) POPL, pp. 251–262. ACM, New York (2007)
28. Guttman, J.: Security protocol design via authentication tests. In: Proceedings of 15th IEEE Computer Security Foundations Workshop. IEEE Computer, Los Alamitos (2002)
29. Guttman, J., Herzog, J., Ramsdell, J., Sniffen, B.: Programming cryptographic protocols. In: De Nicola, R., Sangiorgi, D. (eds.) TGC 2005. LNCS, vol. 3705, pp. 116–145. Springer, Heidelberg (2005)

# Appendix

## Revised iKP Narration

The ideal narration of the revised iKP protocol given in Section 5 is, basically, the following:

- Step 1 and 2: customer and merchant exchange data that let them build independently the *contract*. They must tell their "own version of the story" to the acquirer $A$. Customer $C$ declares $[can : C]$, the credit card will be used in *contract*, sending the protected digest of *can* to the merchant $M$. The customer also informs (and agrees with) the merchant on the digest of *desc* they will use to define the *contract*. The merchant $M$ generates a (fresh) transaction ID (*tid*) and the *date* of transaction ($C$ and $M$ already had agreed on *price* and *desc*, being part of their initial knowledge). $C$ can verify the integrity of $[desc : M]$, form the *contract*, and then compute its digest. The tuple $(price, tid, date, [contract])$ is sent to $C$ which, upon receiving it, can compute $[contract]$ and verify that it matches the digest provided by $M$. If the match succeeds, the protocol execution continues, otherwise it stops.
- Step 3: the customer prepares a secret message for the acquirer containing the information necessary to complete the transaction: *contract*, credit card number (*can*), amount of the transaction (*price*) and transaction ID *(tid)*. However this message is sent to the merchant and not to the acquirer, because this protocol does not allow direct interaction between customers and acquirer, but only through merchant mediation. We assume that the merchant $M$ is cooperating in delivering messages. Hence $M$ receives an opaque message, and all it can do is to blindly forward it to the acquirer A (step 4a).
- Step 4: the merchant M sends the tuple $price, tid, date, [desc : M], [contract]$ to the acquirer (step 4b). This information is necessary to complete the payment. In particular *date* and $[desc : M]$ are required by the acquirer to compute independently the digest of *contract*. Upon reception of the two versions of $[contract]$ originating from the two other principals, the acquirer can also compute the same value autonomously. If all three match, the transaction can be authorized, since this is the proof of the complete agreement between the customer and the merchant.
- Step 5: the acquirer $A$ sends the authorization response to the merchant, within a fresh authentic message, containing also *tid* and $[contract]$. This is done in order to bind all the information, and produce a proof that the payment has been authorized for that specific transaction and that specific contract.
- Step 6: the merchant $M$ forwards the message received from the acquirer $A$ to the customer $C$. This is a notification of the result of the transaction. In this way $C$ receives, via the merchant, a proof of payment from the acquirer. Since the message is signed by the acquirer, the merchant cannot alter the message without being discovered.

# Author Index

Printing: Mercedes-Druck, Berlin
Binding: Stein + Lehmann, Berlin